THE BIRTH OF
SYDNEY

THE BIRTH OF
SYDNEY

EDITED AND WITH AN INTRODUCTION BY

TIM FLANNERY

GROVE PRESS
New York

Acknowledgments

This book has benefited from the inspiration and dedication of many. Michael Heyward of Text Publishing conceived the idea, edited the material and polished my contributions. Melanie Ostell, Emma Gordon Williams and Stuart Kells performed critical interventions during the arduous production, chasing down errant authors, correcting various defects and sourcing details of contributions, times and places. I cannot thank them enough. Always by my side has been Alexandra Szalay, who helped collect materials, organised vast piles of paper and read proofs on two continents and in three cities as this book gestated. Without her help all would have been chaos. George Thomas also proofread the manuscript, bringing uniformity and correctness to an unruly collection.

The production of a work such as this is simply not possible without the co-operation, indeed enthusiasm, of the custodians of archival records and rare books in institutions across the continent. Carol Cantrell of Information Services at the Australian Museum, Jennifer Broomhead of the Mitchell Library and Des Cowley and Gerard Hayes of the State Library of Victoria all played vital roles in providing access to material.

Originally published in 1999 by The Text Publishing Company, Melbourne, Victoria, Australia

Published simultaneously in Canada
Printed in the United States of America

FIRST AMERICAN EDITION

Library of Congress Cataloging-in-Publication Data
The birth of Sydney / edited and introduced by Tim Flannery.
    p.   cm.
    Originally published: Melbourne : Text Pub., 1999.
    Includes bibliographical references.
    ISBN 0-8021-3699-0
    1. Sydney (N.S.W.)—History. I. Flannery, Tim F. (Tim Fridtjof), 1956–

DU178 .B54 2000
994.4'1—dc21

        00-022769

Designed by Chong Wengho
Map drawn by Norman Robinson

Grove Press
841 Broadway
New York, NY 10003

00 01 02 03   10 9 8 7 6 5 4 3 2 1

To the Cadigaleans—
with the deepest regret that our shared
history is not different, and with a promise to
cherish Cadi and all its creatures.

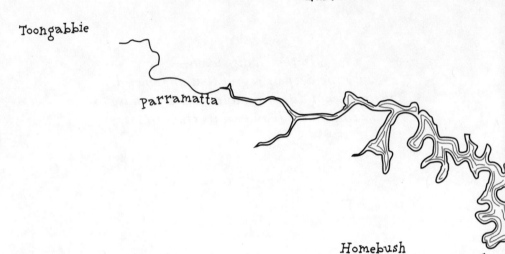

Eastwood

Toongabbie

Parramatta

Homebush

Five Dock

Port Jackson

Millers Point

Dawes Point

Bennelong Point

Pinchgut Island

Mrs Macquaries Point

The Rocks

Sydney Cove

Government House

Farm Cove

Royal Botanic Gardens

Macquarie Pl

O'Connell St

Kent St

George St

Hunter St

York St

Pitt St

Castlereagh St

The Domain

Market St

Kent St

Liverpool St

Hyde Park

Brickfield Hill

Oyster Bay

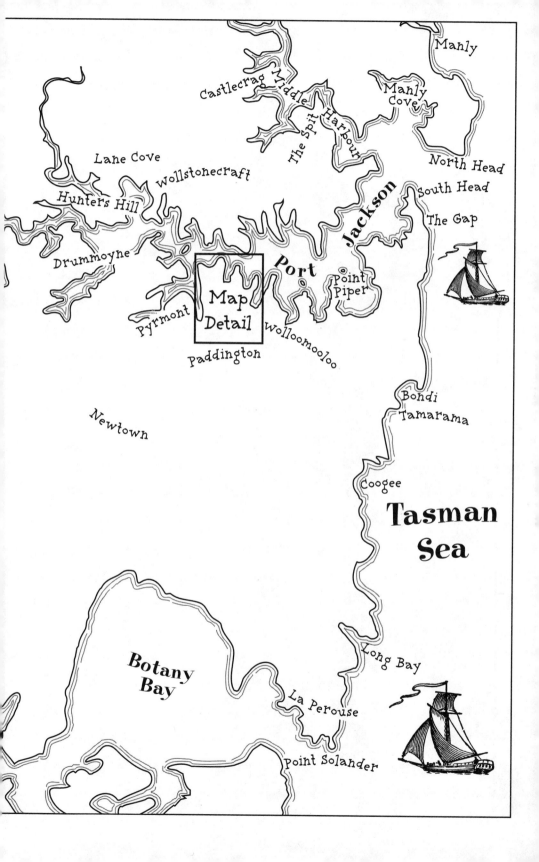

Contents

The Sandstone City by Tim Flannery 1

James Cook 43

Philip Gidley King 44

Watkin Tench 47

John White 48

Ralph Clark 50

John White 52

William Bradley 53

Ralph Clark 58

Arthur Bowes Smyth 59

Ralph Clark 64

Arthur Bowes Smyth 65

Ralph Clark 67

John White 70

Daniel Southwell 75

Anonymous 79

Robert Ross 81

Arthur Phillip 83

Watkin Tench 87

David Collins 92

Ralph Clark 95

Anonymous   97

Richard Johnson   99

Daniel Southwell   103

Watkin Tench   104

Elizabeth Macarthur   109

William Dawes   111

Arthur Phillip   115

Francis Grose   117

Francisco Xavier de Viana   118

Alexandro Malaspina   121

Thomas Watling   128

Richard Johnson   132

Thomas Palmer   134

David Collins   135

Elizabeth Macarthur   136

David Collins   140

John Hunter   144

Bennelong   146

David Collins   147

John Hunter   149

David Collins   150

John Hunter   152

David Collins   154

Stephen Hutchinson   163

John Hunter — 164

Richard Johnson — 165

Joseph Holt — 171

John Turnbull — 173

François Péron — 175

Robert Hobart — 182

Sydney Gazette — 182

John Harris — 187

George Caley — 191

George Suttor — 194

George Johnston — 197

Sydney Gazette — 199

George Caley — 202

Sydney Gazette — 203

Lachlan Macquarie — 211

Sydney Gazette — 216

Aleksey Rossiysky — 217

Jacques Arago — 221

Rose de Freycinet — 226

James O'Connell — 229

Hyacinthe de Bougainville — 235

Peter Cunningham — 239

Roger Therry — 244

Charles von Hügel — 247

Charles Darwin   252

James Mudie   257

Louisa Ann Meredith   261

Joseph Smith   265

J. C. Byrne   267

George Bennett   268

Godfrey Charles Mundy   273

Sydney Morning Herald   279

Ebenezer Beriah Kelly   280

Sydney Morning Herald   282

William Jevons   288

Blanche Mitchell   291

Frank Fowler   293

Sydney Morning Herald   297

Anthony Trollope   301

Obed West   306

Edmond Marin la Meslée   316

Mark Twain   319

Nat Gould   329

Notes on Sources   337

Notes on Illustrations   348

TIM FLANNERY

The Sandstone City

O n 6 February 1788, Sydney was ten days old. The men of
the First Fleet, both soldiers and prisoners, had already
been ashore at Port Jackson for much of that time, preparing the
ground and setting up camp. Now the women convicts were set
ashore. There were more than 700 convicts but fewer than 200 of
them were female, and the sexes had been kept apart in hulks,
prisons or transports for at least a year.

The women had enjoyed solid ground beneath their feet for
only an hour when the sweltering summer evening was lit up by a
prodigious thunderstorm. Lightning knocked a sentry to the
ground and temporarily blinded him; a pig and at least five of
the colony's precious sheep were electrocuted. The storm was a
manifestation of austral nature at its grandest, and it terrified
many of the newly arrived Europeans, who cringed in their cabins
or prayed by their bunks.

With authority blinded or cowering under cover, the lower

orders seized the moment. The sailors of the *Lady Penrhyn* obtained a double ration of rum to celebrate the offloading of the women convicts, and fortified with the ardent spirit they soon found amusement singing, fighting and fucking.

A few days later the prudish Lieutenant Ralph Clark lamented at what he had seen, presumably intermittently as lightning struck the various unfortunates: 'Good God what a Seen of Whordome is going on there in the women's camp…I would call it by the name Sodom for there is more sin committed in it, than in any other part of the world.' Clark's comparison with Sodom soon proved more accurate than he imagined.

The tempests continued for several days, but the mornings were tranquil, steamy and sodden, as is so often the case after the passing of a summer storm in Sydney. The record of what happened on one such morning is incomplete, but from the evidence I can imagine the scene that unfolded. In the dawn light a party of marines is trudging through the mud towards the women's camp. They search tent after tent, evicting scrawny, rag-clad convicts and poxy sailors nursing hangovers. Sometimes one, perhaps two or three emerge from a tent, holding their heads as a convict moll screams at the soldiers, 'You can kiss my c…' Grim-faced the marines continue with their task until out of one tent is dragged a ship's carpenter. 'You're for it, mate,' whispers a marine through clenched teeth to the malefactor, whose transgression is all the worse because he is supposed to be one of the few figures of respectability in the settlement. The carpenter's paramour follows, but then to everyone's surprise a third figure emerges. It's the cabin boy from the *Prince of Wales* transport.

An exasperated Arthur Phillip, governor of the colony, seems to have been as uncertain of the appropriate punishment as he was of the nature of the crime, so he ordered the cabin boy and the carpenter paraded out of camp to that sprightly, sardonic tune 'The Rogue's March'. The fife-players probably gave a fine rendition, for they were doubtless well practised; the ceremonial salute in reverse was heard more often than any tune in the early days of the colony, except perhaps 'God Save the King'.

The scene that followed was a sort of prototype for Sydney's Gay and Lesbian Mardi Gras. The hungover convicts, scurvy-plagued sailors and red-coated marines were assembled into files, through which the curious procession of miscreants marched. First came the fifes, playing the mocking air with all the vigour they could muster. Close behind came the disgraced carpenter, his hands bound behind him, while bringing up the rear was the cabin boy, arraigned in petticoats and heartily jeered by the crowd. When the motley procession reached the camp boundary there must have been a moment of hesitation, for beyond the rough clearing there was nothing—no European settlement for thousands of kilometres. Their punishment over, the cabin boy and the carpenter straggled back into camp. There was simply nowhere else to go.

After that first night of debauchery, Governor Phillip desperately needed to restore law and order. He held a formal parade, adding to the agony of the revellers' hangovers with a reading of his 'letters patent' establishing his own authority and the various courts. He further assured them 'that if they attempted to get into the women's tents of a night there were positive orders for firing upon them'. The order did little good, for the party continued.

And so passed Sydney's first weeks, its first crimes and its official founding. It was a salty, saucy and insolent affair full of irony, colour and sex. It was as if the constraints of old Europe had been irrevocably left behind in this vast island prison, and the unbuttoned nature of the town, which remains characteristic, was stamped indelibly on it from the first.

It's hard for us to imagine the excitement and furore created when the destination of the First Fleet was announced, for the enterprise was breathtaking in its audacity. Eleven ships carrying about 1500 souls (roughly half of whom were convicts) would be launched on an eight-month journey halfway around the globe. Once at Botany Bay they would establish a beachhead settlement on the last of the habitable continents to be drawn into the realm of European imperialism. In its breadth and ambition, the announcement of the English expedition was every bit as monumental as the mission to land a man on the moon.

Soon the words 'Botany Bay' were on everybody's lips and the great publishing houses of London rushed to the principals in the endeavour. John Stockdale of Piccadilly signed up Governor Phillip and Captain John Hunter to produce accounts, while Cadell and Davies in The Strand got Judge-Advocate David Collins, and Debrett of Piccadilly retained chief surgeon John White. Botany Bay ballads were forming on the lips of singers, and broadsheets everywhere carried factual as well as fanciful accounts of the antipodes. From the very beginning the history of Sydney would be recorded in detail.

Some sense of the strength of the impression made by the expedition can be seen in the persistence of the name 'Botany Bay' for the new settlement. Botany Bay, in which James Cook had sheltered for a week in 1770, never was settled, for it had insufficient water and soil. The First Fleet stayed there a few days only before moving on to the more suitable Port Jackson; apart from the First Fleeters, no convict was ever sent to Botany Bay. The bay, however, has played an important role in Sydney's history. It was there, on the very day the First Fleet chose to abandon the place, that the ill-fated La Perouse Expedition, already years at sea, sailed into view. The French stayed six weeks, walking overland to visit Governor Phillip at Sydney Cove, but then sailed into oblivion. Decades later it was discovered that La Perouse's ships had foundered on a reef in what is now Vanuatu. Botany Bay, of course, is once again the gateway to the city, for with the passing of the great passenger liners that brought tens of thousands in through Sydney Heads, most visitors now step ashore beside Botany Bay at Sydney's Mascot Airport.

Unlike modern visitors, those sailing on the First Fleet were launching themselves into a great void, an isolation unimaginable today. While they were away the United States of America would ratify its constitution, France would have its revolution, King George III would go insane and then recover and Mozart would stage the first performance of *Don Giovanni*. Those lucky few destined to return from Sydney Cove would find a dramatically changed Europe, just as they themselves would irrevocably change Australia.

For half a century Sydney Cove was synonymous with European settlement in Australia in the European imagination, and because the settlement had such unusual beginnings it was under the microscope from the start. Enlightenment Europe was vitally interested in the moral and philosophical questions posed by the establishment of the colony. Could transportation redeem socially degraded felons? Could fallen women be made fertile and bounteous by the change of clime? Could the Aborigines be brought into the European fold, and could Europe itself be transplanted successfully into this strange antipodean world? Visitor after visitor penned opinions on these matters in everything from secret reports to popular books, while official documentation, letters, diaries and newspapers recorded how the city's inhabitants saw these issues. This book covers the first hundred-odd years of Sydney's life when such questions were urgent and the answers elusive. By the end of the nineteenth century, when Mark Twain made his triumphant visit to the city, and the journalist Nat Gould discovered that Sydney was the place to be on New Year's Eve, the character of the modern metropolis was largely formed.

Sydney thus represents the great experiment of the Enlightenment—the proving ground in which new philosophies and ideas were to be tested. What the savants of the Enlightenment did not have, however, was knowledge of the deep history of the region in which their experiment was being carried out, for geology is one of the newest of the natural sciences. This was a critical lack, for it was to be the mix of earth, water and people that was to determine the shape of the city.

One might imagine that Sydney was a purely British creation, but that would be quite wrong. Quite apart from the Aborigines who had been there for 50,000 years, the Maoris and Pacific Islanders, West Indians and Americans, Malays and Greeks put in early appearances, just to name a few. Within a few years, Muslim sailors would be constructing extravagant temples and filling the streets of the town with exotic Eastern festivals. It's important to remember that this great social experiment was taking place in a strange natural environment whose impact was to be profound, for the timeless interplay between earth, water, air and fire that helps shape all cities was felt in Sydney from the very first day. To understand how this interplay developed we need to see the world in a very different way.

Imagine if you can an utterly upside-down and inverted Sydney. The atmosphere is water and the sea is air. You are sitting in a boat afloat in the harbour, but you are on the wrong side of the line between air and water. Yes, you are a creature of the briny, approaching the land, fishing-line in hand, in hope of a meal. You cast your line out of the water and into the air, directing it to the bushes growing at the water's edge. What do you think will happen? How long will you wait for a meat-eating creature to come and seize the bait, and how long before you are snagged on some vegetation?

If you think about it you will see that this imagining reveals a great biological truth—that the ecosystems of the land and sea in the Sydney region are utter opposites, organised as mirror images of each other. The land forms a food pyramid whose broad base is made of plants. Feeding on these are fewer herbivores, and feeding on them in turn are even fewer carnivores. That's why you will get snagged land-fishing long before anything takes your bait. The seas are different because their food pyramid stands on a tiny base of plant life, which supports carnivores in huge numbers. Thus there is relatively little phytoplankton, algae and kelp existing at any one time. Balanced on this pinprick of plant life is a moderate number of marine herbivores, many of which are microscopic, though a few such as oysters and blackfish reach an edible size. On top of these herbivores in the theoretical food pyramid is balanced a vast number of carnivores. These include most of the fish recreational fishermen are familiar with—from jewfish to flathead and bream. Were it otherwise, fishing as we know it simply would not exist.

Sydney's sandstone region is an extreme kind of land environment, for it supports a plethora of plant species—indeed it stands in the top dozen or so environments on the planet for plant biodiversity—yet it supports fewer animals than most. Thus its food web structure is as different from the sea as any land ecosystem gets. Its soil is so poor that even the miserly koala has a hard time making a living, for most of the eucalypts growing on the sandstone produce leaves that are not nutritious enough to sustain it. Sydney's harbours and bays, in contrast, are relatively rich, for there fresh and salt waters meet, and rocky refuges abound. This difference between land and sea has meant that for as long as people have lived in the sandstone region they have looked to the sea for sustenance. The people of Sydney are and always have been a maritime people who do not fear to go to sea in their craft.

A very strange stone indeed lies in Sydney basements. The story of its origin and properties is an intriguing one. Imagine standing on a vast floodplain, bigger than any you've ever seen before. From horizon to horizon stretch meandering channels filled with ripples up to a metre high, testimony to the vast volume of water that sometimes flows here. The date is about 230 million years ago. The place—Bennelong Point, where Sydney's Opera House now stands. The significance? We are looking at the Hawkesbury sandstone in the making. It's the rock that will in turn make a city.

No city has been as profoundly influenced by its rocky foundation as Sydney, for its sandstone has given form and colour to its finest buildings, shaped its economy, guided its spread and protected its natural jewels—the rainforest gullies, coves and beaches made inaccessible to builders by its steep bluffs.

Sydney lies atop six kilometres of sandstone and shale, and all of it was laid down at a time when the world's first dinosaurs, mammals, ginkgos and pine trees were coming into existence. It was a temperate, wet world, a time when leafy swamps flourished. One day their debris would give the Sydney basin its coal mines.

Two hundred and thirty million years ago the Sydney area was hundreds of kilometres inland—as far from the coast as Broken Hill is today. It then lay in a vast valley, while to the east the highlands of what are now New Zealand and New Caledonia rose out of a prototypical Pacific Ocean. The entire continent lay well south of its present position and was firmly attached to Antarctica.

One of the enduring mysteries of the Sydney sandstone is just where the tiny grains of sand that constitute it came from. Geologists employ a handy trick in determining in which direction ancient rivers flowed (and thus from where they brought their sediment). They look for the remains of ancient ripple marks. These marks are very distinctive and are readily seen almost anywhere in the Sydney sandstone. They look like closely spaced lines running through the rock at an angle, something like this: \\\\\\\. These marks are left behind when the ripples move forward, just as waves do in water. Each ripple has a gentle slope (which faces upstream) and a steep side (downstream). The sand grains are pushed up the gentle slope and then fall down the steep side one by one. The lines in the rock are the steep faces, each covered by succeeding falls of sand.

Once you understand this you can never get lost in Sydney as long as you can see the rock. That's because the highest part of the lines you'll see always face approximately south, and the steeper the lines are the closer they are to facing true south. Even underground these ripples of the ancient river will guide you.

The ripples tell geologists that Sydney's sandstone must have originated in the south, but just how far south no-one quite realised until a sophisticated means of determining the ages and origins of sand grains became available. Dr Keith Sircombe, a geologist working at the Australian National University, has examined hundreds of grains from the Sydney sandstone using a technique called SHRIMP (Sensitive High Resolution Ion MicroProbe). Sircombe has discovered that most of the grains are derived from rocks that formed between 500 and 700 million years ago, far to the south of Australia in what is now the eastern Antarctic.

We can only imagine the river that brought these grains to rest, for it is long vanished. Its vast fossilised floodplain, however, indicates that it was the size of the Ganges or larger and its headwaters lay in the high mountains of Antarctica. As it flowed north along what is now the east coast of Australia it lost velocity. By the time it reached the Sydney area it was too feeble to transport sand grains more than a few millimetres in diameter, so the stone is composed of remarkably uniform grains of about that size.

David Roots, a geologist, explained to me that parts of the sandstone are such pure silica that were it not for iron stains it would be virtually clear. Imagine being able to see from the Harbour Bridge to Parramatta through crystal-clear rock. Several hundred million years ago the sands were buried deep in the earth's crust, where they were compressed and heated until they formed the solid stone we see today.

By 150 million years ago the great Antarctic river had stopped flowing past Sydney and the region was watered by streams whose headwaters lay in what is now New Zealand and New Caledonia. As they flowed past the Sydney area towards Australia's great inland sea (which then occupied the continent's heart) these ancient rivers cut into the sandstone to form channels, some of which are probably still occupied by waterways today.

These west-flowing rivers were also fated to be interrupted, for ninety million years ago the Pacific Ocean would finally come to Sydney as New Zealand and New Caledonia were torn from eastern Australia. Continents are broken up by a process called rifting. Heat from deep within the earth boils up along the line of the rift, causing a ribbon-like bulge in the land. Then the bulge collapses at its centre, forming a series of vast, rocky steps leading down to a central valley. As the land on either side pulls apart, this valley is eventually filled by the sea. In the Sydney area the remains of the steps formed during this process can still be seen today, along the Lapstone escarpment where the Blue Mountains jump up from the Cumberland Plain, and along the coast itself.

This process of bulging and collapse reversed the flow of the region's rivers (which now flowed east towards the newly created Tasman Sea), and cracked the sandstone in ways that dictated the position of harbours, coves, ridges and creeks. In essence, it laid Sydney out on a primitive, natural grid system that was profoundly to affect the city's development.

The Hawkesbury River, about forty-five kilometres from the harbour itself, is a most curious waterway, for its course describes a large semicircle that encloses the Sydney region. It follows this peculiar path in part because the direction of flow of the river has been in places reversed. Some of its headwaters still run westward, but its lower section now drains to the east, probably in a valley cut by west-flowing rivers over ninety million years ago.

The peculiar course of the Hawkesbury has deprived Port

Hacking, Botany Bay and Sydney Harbour of significant catchments, for all are hemmed between the sea and the narrow arc of the Hawkesbury's flow. Because of this, very little silt flows into the harbour and it remains remarkably clear and deep, even close to shore. It was a feature that was important to Aboriginal fishermen, who speared fish in the clear water, and it also attracted the attention of the first European settlers, who could anchor their ships metres from the land.

One other exceedingly peculiar characteristic of Sydney Harbour is that as one goes further downstream the cliffs become higher and the topography more rugged. Thus the land around Parramatta is formed of relatively gentle and rounded hills, while North Head forms a startling precipice. This is exactly the reverse of the common pattern for waterways, which usually originate in rugged mountains and terminate on plains. This peculiar characteristic of Sydney Harbour is probably due to the ancient tilting of blocks of the continent as they subsided during the rifting process.

Sydney Harbour's principal catchment is the insignificant Parramatta River, and geologists have long wondered how this tiny stream could have cut such a vast harbour out of the solid sandstone. The answer is time, for the stream has been on the job for tens of millions of years, removing the sandstone grain by grain until a huge chasm was created. Parts of the harbour are quite deep, and as streams can only cut into the rock at sea level or above, some of the cutting must have been done when the oceans were much lower, such as during the last ice age.

From this it is clear that Sydney Harbour has not always held seawater. The last time it was dry was just 15,000 years ago when so much water was frozen into ice at the poles. Then the ocean was 140 metres lower than at present and the sea lay thirty kilometres to the east of the heads. The harbour would have looked like a valley in the Blue Mountains or the wetlands of Kakadu. By then Aboriginal people had already occupied Australia for 30,000

years or more and they doubtless hunted on the grassy flats as the
sea withdrew, then fished over them as it flooded back in again.

We owe the construction of Sydney's Harbour Bridge, at least
in part, to ignorance of this ice-age history. In 1890 the commissioners charged with examining the options for linking the north
and south shores rejected a tunnel because 'so little is known as
to what the waters of the harbour hide from view'. Likewise
they rejected the option of placing piers in the water to support
a series of shorter and lower spans with a swing bridge in the
middle, because they lacked geological data on the nature of
the seabed. What worried the commissioners in both cases was
the depth and distribution of the ice-age sediments that filled
the old valley cut by the Parramatta River. And so they set about
the seemingly impossible task of constructing a single span
bridge tall enough to allow a ship with a sixty-metre mast to
pass underneath.

The Sydney Harbour Bridge appeared in the mind's eye long
before it was made a reality. Erasmus Darwin, Charles' grand-
father, was so moved by the potential of Port Jackson that in 1789
he wrote a poem eulogising the future bridge to adorn the future
city. Darwin (who, unlike his grandson, never visited Australia)
prophesied of the infant Sydney Cove:

> There, rayed from cities o'er the cultured land,
> Shall bright canals and solid roads expand.
> There the proud arch, Colossus-like, bestride
> Yon glittering streams, and bound the chafing tide;
> Embellished villas crown the landscape scene,
> Farms wave with gold, and orchards blush between.

It was not until 1923 that work commenced on the gargantuan
task of construction. The arch was finally closed on 30 August
1930 and the bridge opened for traffic on 19 March 1932, in the
midst of the deepest economic depression Australia has ever

known. In 1961 the structure was floodlit, and today Sydney is unimaginable without it.

Why did the harbour it spans form where it did, and not a few kilometres to the north or south? To answer this puzzle we must study cracks. Look at any flat, weathered surface of Sydney sandstone and you'll notice a series of narrow fissures in it. One curious feature of these hairlines is that they run predominantly in two directions; one lot paralleling the coast and running roughly northeast–southwest, the other crossing these at 90 degrees. These cracks sometimes form a pavement full of little squares, like a mosaic, a fine example of which can be seen below The Gap at South Head. This pattern is also repeated at a gigantic scale, and it is these very large cracks that have guided the flow of rivers and creeks. Warragamba Dam, west of Sydney, occupies one great coast-paralleling crack while its many tributaries, which meet it at 90-degree angles, fill the other set of fissures. The watercourses that followed such cracks eventually dug the harbour and its tributaries, giving the waterway the complexity that even twentieth-century development is forced to follow.

The vegetation the early Europeans found growing on the Sydney sandstone both delighted and appalled them. In 1770 Joseph Banks was amazed by its diversity, and James Cook changed the name of his new discovery from Stingray Bay to Botany Bay to celebrate the discoveries made there. Eighteen years later, however, when the First Fleet arrived, the hungry settlers realised in despair that this magnificent vegetation offered little sustenance. They found no significant fruits, roots or berries growing amidst the botanical profusion, and they never learned to suck the honey-filled flowers as did the Aborigines. To the First Fleeters the sandstone flora seemed to gratify all the senses but taste. It was a wet desert that left a man starving in a visual garden of Eden. Sandstone was even to figure in the vocabulary of these first European inhabitants, as the term was applied to convicts who could not endure their treatment in this harsh and weird environment.

Sydney gets about a metre of rain per year, yet the soils of its sandstone are often parched, for the water drains away almost as soon as it falls to ground. Where a layer of humus builds up the runoff is retarded, but here another factor comes into play. Rock beats water, but so does fire, for fire burns humus. For millions of years the infertile, rapidly draining sandstone has promoted the evolution of a hardy flora, which comprises one of the most intriguing botanic realms on the planet. There are 1500 species of plants growing within a 150-kilometre radius of the city, including the brilliant red waratah and gymea lily, whose blooms have been the pride of the bush since Aboriginal times. It's a region full of biological mysteries. Why, for example, should the gymea lily be absent from the area bounded by the harbour's north shore and the Hawkesbury, while it flourishes elsewhere? How did the wollemi pine survive its five-million-year seclusion, hidden in a single canyon in the region's northwest, and why do waratahs grow as patchily as they do? Tragically, given the present rate of development, changes in burning and the effect of introduced species, much of Sydney's flora will be dramatically altered before it becomes well studied.

The region's floral diversity and spectacular blooms have been nurtured by the sandstone's curious chemistry, for the soil it produces is so poor that it cannot support rapidly growing, dominant species. Instead, myriad specialists co-exist. Some grow only on ridges, some in slopes, some in wet gullies and some only on shale lenses. Some grow for only a few years after a fire, while others will disappear if a hot fire comes more than once a decade. In short, the flora is adapted to exploit a thousand ecological opportunities, each partitioned by time or space.

The Sydney sandstone is the heartland of those most characteristic of Australian trees, the eucalypts. One of the strongest arguments for the recent World Heritage nomination of the Blue Mountains area is the fact that over 140 species of eucalypt occur in the Sydney region, and they include representatives of all the major divisions of the genus. Some botanists take this as evidence that the sandstone was the cradle of this most emblematic group of Australian plants.

Where nutrients are scarce, plants can't afford to lose leaves to herbivores. As a result they defend their foliage with a deadly cocktail of toxins and it's these toxins that give the bush its distinctive smell—the antiseptic aroma of the eucalypts and the pungent scent of the mint bush. When the leaves of such plants fall to the ground the decomposers in the soil often find it difficult to digest them, for they are still laden with poisons. The dead leaves thus lie on the rapidly draining sand until a very hot spell. Then, fanned by searing north winds, there is fire.

Although fire is the one great natural terror the city must face today, it has not always been so. In 1790 the First Fleeters experienced the kind of summer that strikes fear into the heart of twentieth-century Australians. Temperatures rose into the forties and the wind blew from the north-west as if out of an oven. The heat was so extreme that birds fell dead into the streets and the Europeans succumbed to heat prostration. At one stage a great mob of flying foxes passed by, dropping from the air as they died. For all this, there is not one mention in the early journals of the threat of fire. The reason seems to be that the Aborigines' firestick farming, where they regularly burnt the bush to create pasture lands for the animals they hunted, had kept fuel loads down. Despite the tinder-dry conditions there was little to burn. Without these burning practices, there is every chance that the infant Sydney would have perished in flames. Given the difficulties with starvation and sickness the inhabitants of the settlement were experiencing it is unlikely that another attempt would have been made to settle Port Jackson for a long time.

Sydney has been repeatedly threatened by far less extreme conditions in the twentieth century. The most recent major fire occurred in January 1994 when hundreds of houses burned, principally in the southern suburbs of Como and Jannali. The risk has been made all the greater by appalling town planning. Many suburbs are laid out along the ridges, while the gullies are densely forested. Given current management of these gullies, it's probably best to think of the houses perched above them as temporary structures. Sooner or later they will find themselves sitting atop thousands of tonnes of fuel, with a fire raging their way. No-one has found a solution to this problem. No-one knows how to implement Aboriginal fire policy any more, and some botanists fear that frequent burning will lead to a decline in biodiversity.

Despite the supreme role fire plays on the sandstone, there are a few sheltered places around Sydney where water has beaten fire, and it is here that we find patches of rainforest. Sometimes the balance has been tipped by a slightly richer soil, and sometimes just by the shelter granted by a grand old Port Jackson fig. These figs are a signature plant for the city, for it is about the harbour that they reach their finest form. Growing along the water's edge, their twisted grey trunks support a dense canopy of leaves that are dark green on the upper side and a fiery rust colour underneath. The figs often start life on a bare rock where they are safe from fire, but as they grow they throw a dense shade and their basket-like roots hold humus. In the cool shade provided by the tree, and protected from fire, the humus rots to a rich soil. Then a stately red ash (or *murrung* to the Aboriginal people) might grow, its intricately mottled grey bark supporting orchids, moss and ferns. On the rocks below will spring up elkhorns, birds-nest ferns, cabbage palms and rock orchids with their spectacular yellow sprays, and there you have it—a rainforest in miniature.

Such places are true jewels in the botanical crown of Sydney. There are myriad coves around the harbour where you can sit in the shade of such a mini-rainforest, listening to the call of the whip bird or wonga pigeon while looking out over the impossibly blue waters of a tiny bay with its white sand beaches and sparkling waves.

When the *Endeavour* first sailed into Botany Bay in 1770 nothing amazed Captain James Cook as much as the stingrays he found basking in its shallows. What astonished him most was their abundance and size. Some were as broad across as a church pew, and these giants were not afraid to laze about right under the *Endeavour*'s keel. Ridiculously easy to hunt, they provided a free meal for the entire crew. The sailors harpooned the rays as they lay about the vessel, but found them so heavy that they had to be gutted before being hauled aboard with block and tackle. The largest, even without guts, weighed 200 kilograms! It doubtless took decades, perhaps centuries, for stingrays to grow to such prodigious proportions. Cook noted that stingray barbs were not used by the Aborigines for spear points and he mused, presciently as it turned out, that stingrays might be sacred to the people of the bay.

The First Fleeters knew the Aborigines of the region as the Eora. Their culture was rapidly altered after 1788, and today we know little of the beliefs and ways of these people before European contact. All that I have been able to gather about their feelings toward stingrays is that the Eora believed that it was death to eat one. Why, and what significance it had for the ecology of the region, remains unknown. It does seem possible though, given the Aborigines' frequent fights, that spears tipped with stingray barbs were just too dangerous to have about. An implicit policy of mutual deterrence may have outlawed the exploitation of these extraordinary marine creatures. Whatever the case the giants were eliminated by European hunting almost as quickly as Eora culture was changed by the settlement.

Ever since the end of the last ice age the waters of Botany Bay and Sydney Harbour have provided a living to Aboriginal people. When the British arrived its bays and coves were dotted with Eora canoes, and the smoke of Eora campfires filtered from its caves and rock shelters. Women paddling fragile canoes even ventured outside the Heads on fishing expeditions. Governor Phillip estimated that about 1500 Eora lived in the area between Botany Bay and Broken Bay. Some of those living on the northern shores of Sydney Harbour called themselves Cadigaleans, for *Cadi* was their name for Sydney Harbour, and *galeans* means 'the people of'.

The Eora spoke a language that formed part of the Pama–Nyungan language family, thought to have originated about 5000 years ago somewhere in eastern Arnhem Land. By the time of European settlement it had spread over all of mainland Australia except for parts of the north and west. Because of this, some individual words spoken by the Eora would have been recognisable right across the continent. Consequently it may yet be possible to reconstruct the now vanished Eora language. A handful of its words survive in English: *dingo*, *gin* (for Aboriginal woman) and the cry *coo-ee* are all of Eora origin.

The Cadigaleans and adjacent clans were a truly maritime people. Fish were their mainstay and they developed remarkable methods to catch them. They were one of very few Aboriginal groups to manufacture fishhooks, which they made by grinding down the shells of mud oysters. In late winter they journeyed into the bush to find suitable casuarina trees whose bark they used to build canoes up to five metres long. These they managed with astonishing dexterity. Mothers fished from them balancing infants on their shoulders, while men hunted with spears, their heads totally immersed in the water, as a friend counterbalanced the unstable craft. Often they would cook their meal at sea on a pad of clay, atop which sat a fire.

Another favourite fishing technique was to stand in the lee of a point with a spear poised over the still water, spitting chewed-up mussels into the water as berley. The fish of the harbour have been hunted in these ways for 15,000 years. Many have become well attuned to the human predator, especially the harbour bream. It has acute vision and immediately recognises the human shape. It is as crafty as a fish can get, and its sheer intelligence is a source of wonder.

In summer the waters of the harbour teem with life, and then it's easy even for an inexperienced angler to catch a meal. In winter, however, the fish leave for the ocean or retire to the deeper reaches, and commercial fishermen sometimes have difficulty making ends meet. Winter must have been a trial for the Aborigines, and early accounts indicate that starvation was routine during this lean period. It seems likely that by May many Eora left the harbour to find food elsewhere. Some probably travelled into rugged areas such as the Lower Hawkesbury. It was not easy to spear fish in its murky waters (making it an undesirable location in summer), but rock oysters abounded there. These shellfish, along with whatever could be gathered, sustained life until the fish returned in spring.

Cadi is a snug name for a snug harbour, so it's a pity that Captain Cook casually dropped the name Port Jackson on the map. Still, Sir George Jackson, a secretary of the Admiralty who lived to be ninety-three, seems not to have been a bad old stick. A worse fate befell the cove Governor Phillip chose to settle in, for in an act of political brown-nosing that is hard to forgive he named it after his next-door neighbour and patron, Viscount Sydney. Sydney had been a 'dissolute and philandering youth'. As secretary of state for the Home Department he was an incompetent bureaucrat, unequal to the most ordinary duties of his office.

I find it an embarrassment to live in a city named after such an eminently forgettable personage, and even Phillip appears to have had second thoughts, for at one stage he inclined to the name Albion, which would have doubtless pleased the Irish convicts no end. I suppose that Phillip, as the son of an immigrant, needed all the patrons he could get, despite their shortcomings. Yet I dearly wish that Phillip had asked the dignified old Eora man he met on his reconnaissance of Port Jackson what the cove was called. If he had, we might now be the proud inhabitants of Warran, or Werrong.

I have often wondered what the Eora thought about Werrong. It was clearly a strikingly beautiful location, for it was one of only a few places around the harbour with a permanent stream of water. Judge-Advocate Collins noted that a dense forest grew by the shore. This was probably composed of fire-sensitive rain-forest species such as Port Jackson figs, cheese trees and red ash. This, along with the exceptionally large size of the trees growing on the site and the fact that the freshwater brook, later to be known as the Tank Stream, flowed all year, suggests to me that the cove experienced a different fire regime, or had different soils from the surrounding areas.

Despite its beauty there is little mention of the Aborigines frequenting the place in the accounts of the First Fleeters. There may have been few if any shell middens there, for when oyster shells were required for mortar they had to be brought from adjacent coves. This apparent lack of use stands in striking contrast with nearby Farm Cove and Wallamola, now known as Woolloomooloo Bay, both of which were important gathering places for Eora initiation rituals and other purposes.

In some of these attributes Werrong bears a close resemblance to Aboriginal sacred sites recorded in other parts of Australia. These often had permanent water and were carefully burned around to exclude fire. Despite their being highly desirable locations, Aborigines rarely ventured into them and never camped in them, although important ritual sites might be found nearby. Was Werrong a sacred site, its margins burned around in spring by the Eora to prevent summer fires destroying the soil humus that fed the Tank Stream and the rainforest? Was it a place of spirits, and so an appropriate site for the apparently unearthly European invaders, whom the Eora may have believed to be their ghostly ancestors, to settle? We will probably never know the answers to these tantalising questions.

The harbour acted as a sort of dividing line between two Aboriginal groups, the Camerigal who lived between Botany Bay and the south shore, and the Cadigal, who largely dwelt between the north shore and Broken Bay. As with most neighbours, relations between the groups seem to have alternated between feasting and fighting. The opportunity for a feast came only rarely to the Eora, for it was difficult to find sufficient food to satisfy a large group for any length of time. A gift from the sea in the form of a stranded whale seems to have offered the most common opportunity. The discoverers of a stranded whale would light fires to broadcast news of the discovery, and then people would converge for days of feasting.

Young Cadigalean men were initiated during a ceremony known as *Yoo-lahng Erah-ba-daihng*. Surprisingly it was not held on their own land, but on Camerigal territory at Wallamola. There the tribes would gather and, after days of ceremony, the highlight came when the initiates had an upper incisor knocked out with a stone. The teeth were carefully kept by their Camerigal hosts, who returned them to the Cadigal at a ceremony some years later.

This practice of knocking out a front incisor, incidentally, was to have some significance for the Europeans, for Governor Phillip was lacking just such a tooth. The Aborigines clearly viewed him as an important person, perhaps as an initiated elder who had returned from the dead. They called him *Beeàna*—father.

The English found the Eora a stubborn and proud people, unwilling to conform to the habits the Europeans wished to force on them, such as the wearing of clothes and the adoption of a settled life. It is clear to me that the Eora did not view themselves as inferior to the Europeans in any way, and thus saw no reason to adopt their ways. It is not hard to imagine why, for early Sydney was a degenerate settlement, full of violent, starving and often immoral people. This must have been obvious to the Eora, many of whom—including Bennelong, a leading Eora whose name means 'great fish'—considered themselves to be distinctly superior to the Europeans in everything that mattered, including hunting, fighting and managing the land. Indeed, the superior intellects and morality of many Eora were evident even to some European observers such as Watkin Tench. Late in 1789 Bennelong, along with another prominent man Colbee, was kidnapped by the Europeans, who wished to open relations with the Eora. A few days later Colbee escaped but Bennelong, although at first enraged, soon took advantage of the opportunity his captivity afforded him and became a favourite of Governor Phillip and the other leading Europeans. He lived with them until May 1790. Watkin Tench says of him:

> His powers of mind were certainly far above mediocrity…Love and war seemed his favourite pursuits…Whenever he recounted his battles, 'poised his lance and shewed how fields were won', the most violent exclamations of rage and vengeance against his competitors in arms, those of the tribe called Cameeregal in particular, would burst upon him.

The Eora held to their traditional way of life for a surprisingly long time. As late as 1820, members of a Russian exploring expedition were surprised to find proudly traditional Eora wandering the streets of Sydney stark naked. One can't help but believe that they were making a statement, saying in effect, 'We're not bowed

yet by you Europeans.' Indeed, traditional Aboriginal life continued well into the 1830s in such rugged regions as the Lower
Hawkesbury. Doubtless the Aborigines were aided in their fight
for independence by the ruggedness of the sandstone country. To
the Europeans it was worthless, terrifying and confusing, while to
the Eora it was home.

Sydney Harbour is loved by modern Cadigaleans above all else,
for it is the centre—the great magnet—towards which the city is
turned. So memorable is its beauty and so distinctive are its land-
marks than one needs to travel it just once in order to develop a
clear mental map of it. In order to set the city in its context let's
take an imaginary tour up the harbour, beginning at the Heads
and ending at the bridge, visiting sites of historical and natural
significance. Until the 1950s this is how most overseas visitors
approached the city for the first time.

On entering the harbour on our right we pass North Head.
Rising abruptly from the restless ocean, its heathy summit is still
undisturbed by signs of European conquest, for it is one of
Sydney's great national parks. It is without doubt the most important remaining refuge for Sydney's wildlife, providing the last
redoubt for fauna including the harbour's last penguins, about
sixty of which still nest around its sandy beaches and in rock
crevices below the apartment buildings at Little Manly Bay.
Although severely threatened by irresponsible residents who
bring their pets to the park's beaches, at least for the moment you
can hear the penguins barking like dogs on a still day as they fish
in the harbour.

Just west of North Head lies that fine stretch of sand known as
Manly Cove. Today it is highly urbanised and boasts a ferry
terminal and aquarium, but in September 1790, fewer than two
years after settlement, it presented a very different scene. We can

imagine Governor Phillip approaching the strand in a longboat. On shore are hundreds of Aborigines feasting on the carcass of a beached sperm whale. They are formed into little groups, busy cutting up the blubber and roasting it over fires. Phillip, anxious to begin a conversation, steps ashore unarmed and calls for Bennelong, the only Aborigine he knows well.

Bennelong finally comes forward and, as one contemporary recounted,

> They discoursed for some time, Bennelong expressing pleasure to see his old acquaintance, and inquiring by name for every person whom he could recollect at Sydney; and among others for a French cook, one of the governor's servants, whom he had made the constant butt of his ridicule, by mimicking his voice, gait, and other peculiarities, all of which he again went through with his wonted exactness and drollery. He asked also particularly for a lady from whom he had once ventured to snatch a kiss; and on being told that she was well, by way of proving that the token was fresh in his remembrance, he kissed Lieutenant Waterhouse, and laughed aloud.

Things progressed well until an Aborigine, who had not seen Europeans before, arrived on the scene.

> He appeared to be a man of middle age, short of stature, sturdy and well set, seemingly a stranger, and but little acquainted with Bennelong and Colbee. The nearer the governor approached, the greater became the terror and agitation of the Indian. To remove his fear, Governor Phillip threw down a dirk which he wore at his side. The other, alarmed at the rattle of the dirk, and probably misconstruing the action, instantly fixed his lance in his throwing stick. To retreat, his Excellency now thought would be more dangerous than to advance. He therefore cried to the man, *Wee-ree, Wee-ree* (bad, you are doing wrong) displaying at the same time every token of amity and confidence. The words had, however, hardly gone forth when the Indian, stepping back with one foot, aimed his lance with such force and dexterity that,

striking the governor's right shoulder just above the collar-bone, the point, glancing downward, came out at his back, having made a wound many inches long. The man was observed to keep his eye steadily fixed on the lance until it struck its object, when he directly dashed into the woods and was seen no more.

A more distressing situation than that of the governor... cannot readily be conceived: the pole of the spear, not less than ten feet in length, sticking out before him and impeding his flight, the butt frequently striking the ground and lacerating the wound.

Phillip eventually recovered, and today the spear tip that inflicted the damage is a treasured item in the National Museum of Australia. To his great credit, Phillip did not take revenge for the spearing. In fact, the incident served to open greater dialogue with the Eora, who thereafter visited town frequently. Perhaps they realised that the Europeans—even *Beeàna*—were mortal after all.

On the south side of the harbour entrance lies South Head, and behind it a great sweep of sand backed by grass and stately Port Jackson figs. This is Watson's Bay, which has long offered the most sublime views of the city. The trip out along Old South Head Road, the first road built in the colony, was a favourite weekend jaunt in the early days and a compulsory sightseeing expedition for distinguished visitors who could then admire the city's lighthouse.

Proceeding along the southern shore we come to Rose Bay where Bungaree, the first Aboriginal circumnavigator of Australia and 'King of Sydney', was buried in 1830. Further on is Point Piper, where Captain Piper, the celebrated 'Prince of Australia', built his magnificent residence which was so favourably commented upon by many new arrivals. Next is Double Bay, now known colloquially as Double Pay because of its exclusive shopping precinct. It was here, in the 1870s, that the great Italian explorer of New Guinea, Luigi Maria D'Albertis, rented a cottage among the trees. In his journal, D'Albertis recorded the enormous pleasure he found in the pleasant, solitary weeks he spent on his verandah, peeping out through the foliage to the pristine sands and blue waters.

Just beyond is Rushcutters Bay, scene of a gruesome murder of two convicts by Aborigines in 1789, while west again is Woolloomooloo Bay, the key ritual site for the Eora. In the harbour nearby, a small castle appears as if floating on the water. Pinchgut is where convicts were exiled to starve, and where the bodies of particularly notorious malefactors were hung in chains until they rotted. Pinchgut was once a beautiful natural rock stack, and not everyone was pleased with its transformation into a fort. In 1841, Reverend John Dunmore Lang wrote, 'This natural ornament of the harbour, which no art could have equalled, this remarkable work of God, which has stood like a sentinel keeping watch for thousands of years, has been destroyed by the folly of man.'

We now approach the core of European settlement and three points that define it, named after a remarkable trio whose distinctive histories tell the story of the early city in miniature. The southern pylons of the Sydney Harbour Bridge rise from Dawes Point, named for one of the most interesting yet largely forgotten of the city's early residents. William Dawes spent a lifetime trying to build links between black and white. He arrived with the First Fleet as a lieutenant in the marines and was given charge of fortifications and astronomical observations. He built his observatory some distance west of the main camp so that fires would not obscure his view of the night sky. The relative solitude of the location seems to have given him a unique opportunity to interact with the Eora, who at first refused to enter Phillip's tent city.

Dawes strove hard to learn the Eora language, and the principal written record he left is two notebooks which document his attempt to do this. They make curious reading, for along the way he seems to have fallen in love with a girl called Patyegarang, whose name means great grey kangaroo. Dawes' notebooks hint at their growing love, recording events and phrases that haltingly chart its progress:

> I shall not become white: this was said by Patyegarang—after I had told her if she would wash herself often she would become white—at the same time throwing down the towel in despair...
>
> *miahug* = lover, sweetheart...
>
> you don't want my company?
>
> we two only...

In December 1790 an Eora man named Pemulwy speared the colony's 'game keeper', a man named McEntire. He had been transported for poaching, and in his new role in the colony he continued to practise his profession, only now he was doing it legally, and it was the Aborigines' game he was stealing. McEntire's reputation among the Eora was such that he was suspected of carrying out atrocities as well as killing the animals they hunted. Phillip, in an uncharacteristically bloody move, ordered a group of marines to bring him ten Aborigines to be made an example of. Lieutenant Dawes was ordered to participate, but at first refused. Such insubordination could have cost Dawes his life but the governor seems to have respected the man, and gave him a chance to reconsider. After consulting his pastor, Dawes agreed to participate, yet despite the fact that the raid was unsuccessful he was disgusted with himself for relenting, and made it known that he would never participate in such an action again. This left him in malodour with Phillip and, despite his desire to stay an additional three years, in 1792 Dawes was shipped out under a cloud. He eventually moved to the West Indies where he became a tireless campaigner against slavery.

Sydney grew up between Dawes Point and Bennelong Point, which today supports Danish architect Jørn Utzon's

incomparable Sydney Opera House. In November 1790, at a time
when almost all of the Europeans in the settlement were living
under canvas or wattle and daub, Governor Phillip ordered a
brick house to be built for Bennelong on this prized site. Bennelong himself chose the spot, and for many years it was the focus
of Eora activity in the colony. In 1795, however, Bennelong's
house was pulled down, and subsequently a series of other structures occupied the spot.

The fact that the Opera House stands on the point today is
largely due to the vision and determination of one man—Eugene
Goossens, conductor of the Sydney Symphony Orchestra and
director of the state conservatorium in the 1950s. Joe Cahill, the
New South Wales premier from 1952 to 1959, wanted to build the
new opera house above Wynyard Station but Goossens convinced
him to force the Maritime Services Board (which was keen to
build a new shipping terminal on the site) to relinquish its plans.
His gambit nearly went astray when Goossens was returning to
Sydney on one occasion and customs officers discovered porno-
graphic material in his luggage. Despite the fracas, Goossens' plan
went ahead.

Utzon won the competition to design the house in 1957.
During construction, costs spiralled from the original $7 million
projected by Utzon to $102 million and in response the state
instituted the Sydney Opera House Lottery. But by 1965 Utzon
had fallen out with both the state government and the construction engineers, so the building, finally opened in 1973, does
not strictly conform to his original design.

So remarkable is the structure, nonetheless, that an image of it
adorns the promo of a third-rate American television program
'Unsolved Mysteries of the World'. The program's usual staples
are lost treasures, hauntings, telepathy and extraterrestrial
visitations. Perhaps the greatest unsolved mystery about the
Opera House is just how the people of Sydney, who were busy

destroying the old Georgian heart of the city at the time, could have carried through, even imperfectly, such a brilliant and extraordinary plan.

A couple of decades later the opportunity existed to create an Opera House precinct every bit as majestic as the Opera House itself. That opportunity was lost with the construction, against enormous public opposition, of three blocks of flats commonly referred to disparagingly as 'the Toaster'. I must forbear from mentioning the official name of these structures, for by linking their construction with the Eora it conveys a gross insult to one of Sydney's most important Eora leaders. These flats occupy what could have been a magnificent open space linking Circular Quay, the Royal Botanic Gardens and the Opera House. The Toaster is perhaps the greatest act of environmental vandalism visited on Sydney in recent times.

Long before Utzon's astonishing structure was to adorn the site that commemorates his name Bennelong travelled to England where he met George III. Like almost all expatriate Sydneysiders he was miserable during his sojourn away, and he recorded with evident relief upon his return, 'I'm home now.' Bennelong died in 1813 at Kissing Point, just a year before Governor Phillip went to meet his maker. With their passing ended Sydney's first and most extraordinary age.

Just west of the Harbour Bridge is Blue's Point. You cannot miss it, for like the nose of Chaucer's miller it is marred by an outrageous wart. In this case the wart is an apartment block, Blues Point Tower, dominating an otherwise beautiful precinct. Tragically, similar developments are not hard to find throughout Sydney. They are the inheritance of an earlier age when the populace cared less for the beauty of their city, and when thefts of our common wealth by property developers were often called progress. Blues Point was named for Billy Blue, a Jamaican Negro who, for many years in the early nineteenth century, was the town's favourite son. Known as 'the Old Commodore', Billy and his European wife ran a sort of primitive ferry service, rowing people across the harbour at one of its narrowest points. He was also the town wag, cracking public jokes to the delight of all. Many visitors recalled seeing the locals in hysterics as Billy discomfited some high and mighty with a few well-chosen words. Some citizens, however, were not so amused, including one who called himself 'An Observer' in a letter to the *Sydney Gazette* in 1833.

> I intend putting up with the braggardism of Billy Blue no longer. It is a disgrace to our town police that this crying nuisance is not put down. Two very respectable ladies were bellowed about by this sweep and because they hurried on to get out of the reach of his tongue he made use of such language as must have shocked every modest person.

The editor of the *Gazette*, however, must have had a fondness for Billy, for he added, 'We think "An Observer" is hard upon the Old Commodore who has grown into a privileged position. Poor Billy is now nearly a hundred years old...he intends no harm.'

When Billy Blue died the following year, the editor eulogised his passing:

> The remembrance of the whimsicality of character which grew with him as he advanced to the end of his earthly pilgrimage will be treasured when the minions of ambition are forgotten in the dust...requiescat—we may never look upon his like again.

Blue, Bennelong and Dawes were all extraordinary people, notable for building links between races and cultures. They are testimony to the tolerance of diversity that has marked Sydney from its earliest times. Today, with rapid growth, cultural diversity and the development of ghettoes straining the social fabric of this city of about four million, we need to be reminded of this history more than ever.

Sydney's Aboriginal people were not beaten by superior European weapons, or indeed by superior European anything—except germs. As with Aboriginal people throughout Australia, their death rates from various epidemics such as smallpox, measles and pulmonary infections were appallingly high, while their birth rates were dismally low. The resulting demographic alone can probably account for their decline. This is hardly surprising, for the First Fleeters were probably the best source of contagion in the world, being drawn from London, one of Europe's great pestilential and insanitary port cities. The convicts had been living in filth for years and between them doubtless harboured enough diseases to eliminate every isolated human population on the planet. Certainly within three years, syphilis had made such progress in the infant town that Phillip despaired (quite correctly, it turns out) of ever ridding the place of it.

Despite all of their tribulations, some Eora have survived and today they play an increasingly important role in the life of the city. Some are leading environmental activists, while others contribute significantly to the arts and other spheres of endeavour.

The changes wrought on the wildlife of Sydney by the First Fleet were profound. The *gnar-ruck*, as the Eora knew the white-footed rabbit-rat (*Conilurus albipes*), was illustrated by a First Fleet artist, who noted that this delightful rodent was a considerable pest to the colony's storehouses. Sadly, the illustration is the first and last evidence that this now extinct creature ever inhabited the Sydney region.

Despite the demise of the *gnar-ruck*, new pillagers of the government store were not long in coming. By 1790 the First Fleeters were writing of the plagues of rats that swarmed about the settlement. I have examined the bones of many eighteenth and early nineteenth-century rats from archaeological excavations in Sydney and all are from the brown or Norway rat (*Rattus norvegicus*). In the 1780s this species was a newcomer to England, having arrived from Siberia only a few decades before, at about the time of the ascent of the Hanovers to the throne. To many loyal Britons the creatures were about as welcome as the German-speaking monarchs, and were soon known as Hanoverian rats.

Today Hanoverian rats are relatively uncommon in Sydney. They survive mostly around dockyards and drains, but elsewhere they have been replaced by a more recent invader, the black or plague rat (*Rattus rattus*). It's a species that belies its name, for it is often such an attractive creature, with its white belly and large eyes, that many people refuse to believe that it is not a native but a pest.

Given the contemporary reputation of Australia as a home of snakes it is curious that the First Fleeters encountered very few of the reptiles, and indeed many believed that there were no poisonous species in the area. By 1805, however, all of this had changed, and the public became alarmed at the number of fatalities occurring at the fangs of these creatures. So common had the reptiles become that in December 1808 an attack even occurred in the Sydney General Hospital. As the *Sydney Gazette* reported:

> A patient in the General Hospital on Tuesday was attacked by a snake, which twirled around one of his legs, and endeavoured repeatedly to inflict a wound that doubtless would have proved mortal; but was fortunately prevented from taking place by the woollen clothing that the poor man wore. As soon as disengaged the reptile endeavoured to make off, but was detained and killed.

Not only humans fell victim, for bullocks, horses, sheep, dogs and even caged birds succumbed to the scaly plague. The snakes, I suspect, were attracted by the outbreak of Hanoverian rats, which are an excellent food for the creatures. Already the ecology of the land was changing at the hands of the new invaders.

A surprising diversity of marsupials survived in the area that is now Sydney until quite late. Rock wallabies adorned Middle

Head until hunters eliminated them sometime after the 1860s. Bandicoots were so common in harbourside suburbs that they figure in the childhood memories of many Sydneysiders who grew up before the 1980s. Eastern quolls (cat-like spotted marsupial carnivores) also survived until recently. Once common on the mainland, they are now to be found only in Tasmania. Sydney was their last mainland stronghold, and they were common enough between Manly and Coogee for visiting American museum collectors to obtain specimens there in the 1930s. They made their last stand in the eastern harbourside suburb of Vaucluse, where as late as 1972 they were breeding in the sheds and outhouses of a few lucky local residents. It seems almost unbelievable that the people of Sydney would allow this last precious remnant to become extinct, but the quolls vanished without comment, probably as a result of the council 'cleaning up' Neilsen Park, as well as ever denser development.

Bandicoots are strange and ancient creatures. About the size of a rabbit, they eat insects and are valuable in keeping down garden pests, especially on lawns. They were once abundant, and in the early days provided Governor Phillip and the Eora alike with many a dainty repast. They are also remarkable in that they have the shortest gestation period of any mammal—a mere eleven days. So quickly do they breed that young females still suckling from their dams can be pregnant themselves. Unfortunately their rapid reproduction has not protected them from destruction, for of the three species that once occurred in the Sydney area only one is now left. The tiny remnant surviving around North Head are national treasures—the last land-dwelling marsupials in the Sydney area. They are particularly common on an area known as St Patrick's Estate, which is owned by the Catholic Church. Perhaps it's their predilection for early sex that has made them so unpopular with the Church. Whatever the case, their forty-million-year tenure on the estate seems to be drawing to a close, for the spirit of St Francis has given way to that of the medieval popes. The Church is determined to develop its land for housing.

Sydney's birds tell a different story. Their nadir came in the nineteenth century when virtually every man carried a gun and felt free to blast at any feathered thing that came within range. Emu, brolga and magpie-goose were lost to the city at this time, but since then it's the smaller birds that have suffered. Chats have vanished, while blue wrens have become increasingly rare. Black swans have also largely disappeared from the harbour. In their place, however, have come new arrivals. Sacred ibis colonised the city in the 1980s and today they are common in Sydney parks, where they scavenge from rubbish bins and take tidbits from the hands of toddlers.

In the late 1990s the wondrous channel-billed cuckoos returned in force. These great, pterodactyl-like birds were recorded by the First Fleeters, but have been scarce ever since. They fly to Australia from New Guinea each summer to lay their eggs in the nests of currawongs and crows, and it may be that Sydney's vast currawong population has been the lure for their return.

The large-scale ebbs and flows of species, however, do not tell the entire tale of Sydney's birds, for local events are also having profound impacts. Of prime importance is the intensifying density of development that is depriving many suburbs of their native vegetation. There are now areas where the only birds you're likely to see are introduced sparrows, rock pigeons and Indian mynahs. It's a phenomenon that will grow as concrete replaces trees.

In the early hours of one winter morning in 1999, Sydney Harbour received a blast from the past. For a few hours, before the ferries started running, and before the flotillas of boats started up, a solitary southern right whale passed between the Heads— the first of her kind to do so for about two centuries. She was probably looking for a safe place to calve or rest, just as countless thousands of her relatives did in the millennia before the arrival of the Europeans. Two months later, a second whale entered the harbour and this one frolicked in its waters for a week. She arrived a decade after the bicentenary of the visit of a less fortunate whale, which in July 1790 capsized a boat, drowning a midshipman and a marine. In revenge the whale was pursued and harpooned several times. A month later its carcass washed up dead on Manly beach. The Eora came to feast on it, and it was during this feast that Governor Phillip was speared.

If the returning whales offer some hope that wildlife and the city can coexist, there are precious few other indications that such a happy outcome can be achieved. Ever since first settlement, one species after another has been lost, and even today, despite the enacting of endangered species laws and various stops on developers, we continue to lose our precious biodiversity.

Sydney's sandstone keeps its European occupants oriented towards the sea, for its infertility and mountain barriers long prevented its people from developing a vast and wealthy hinterland. Instead, Sydney developed as a port city with its orientation towards the Pacific. From the very beginning, exotic peoples walked its streets: Tongan royals, tattooed Maoris, turbaned Malay Lascars, Chinese traders and Aborigines. In this it differs from all the other cities of Australia's south, for they were always turned towards a Europe made readily accessible across the Southern Ocean by the roaring forties.

The city began life as an armed camp ruled by a governor whose powers were so wide that everyone who arrived in the colony found themselves sold down from their liberty. The Home Office undoubtedly granted such wide powers to allow Phillip to deal with unrest and disquiet in a thief colony that was at best many months' sail from London.

The son of a Jew from Frankfurt who had migrated to England, Phillip was fifty when he sailed with the First Fleet and was often ill. Despite being a compassionate and just man, the difficulties he laboured under meant that he sometimes failed to live up to his ideals. He was assisted in his duties by the judge-advocate, David Collins, a strikingly handsome officer of the marines with no legal training but with a 'most cheerful disposition'. That disposition was to be sorely tested by his time in New South Wales. Spiritual guidance to the colony was provided by the Reverend Richard Johnson, one of a handful of First Fleeters to be accompanied by his wife. They seem to have been a lacklustre pair. Medical matters were supervised by the surgeon John White, an Irishman of uneven temper, who despite the burden of his office managed to document the flora and fauna of the new land.

The First Fleet sailed under the protection of the marines, at whose head stood the cantankerous and treacherous Captain Robert Ross. In March 1788 he placed most of his subordinates (including Lieutenant Watkin Tench) under arrest over a trivial matter, and technically they remained so until they returned to England. It is in these second ranks of command within the service that we find the truly luminous minds in the colony. To me, Tench stands out above them all, for he was able to take an overarching view of the settlement that encompassed both black and white. His friend William Dawes was perhaps the most morally upright man in the colony. Poor Ralph Clark took months to adjust to life in Sydney Cove, but even he left us intriguing insights into the new colony.

On the other side of the invasion stood the Eora. The names of many remain unknown to us, for the smallpox epidemic of 1789 carried them off before much could be learned of them. Bennelong stands out, however, as a great warrior and as a bridge between the colonists and his own people. Arabanoo, who preceded him in living among the colonists, was a gentler soul, while Colbee seems to have been an important traditional leader. Those who stood aloof from the settlers, such as the resistance fighter Pemulwy, are also less well known, but deserve recognition for the role they played in battling the invasion of their land.

Nowhere, perhaps, are the colony's peculiar characteristics as plainly evident as in the city's first newspaper, the *Sydney Gazette*. First published in 1803, the broadsheet was the megaphone of government. Don't look in its pages for dissenters' voices or incisive political analysis, for the *Gazette* was fiercely censored, and with each new administration it subtly changed its style. Some governors, however, seem to have tolerated gossip, tidbits and humour, and the paper is leavened with both intentional and accidental comedy. A careful reading of the *Gazette* reveals much about Sydney. Through it we learn details of its streetscape, changing architecture, its crimes and its social preoccupations.

Even the convict camp of this early period possessed a few articles of refinement. The printing press that produced the *Sydney Gazette* arrived with the First Fleet, as did a pianoforte. It belonged to surgeon's second mate and later naval surgeon George Worgan, who upon departing the colony in 1792 passed it on to Elizabeth Macarthur. In Mrs Macarthur we find a remarkable woman, for in this wilderness she educated her children, managed a farm, and formed a magnet for the educated souls who clung to civilisation in this most testing of places.

During these years the inhabitants of Sydney often lived in fear of a revolt by such hardened types as the Irish Defenders. But when it came the revolt sprang not from the felons but from within the group ostensibly dedicated to preserve order: the New South Wales Corps. The Rum Corps, as everybody called this junta, thrived by monopolising trade, especially in ardent spirits, which then acted as the colony's currency. In January 1808 the Corps overthrew Governor Bligh, whose ill-fated trip on the *Bounty* must have acted as a rehearsal for his undoing in Sydney.

Bligh was left a bitter man by his experiences in Sydney, quipping that half of the residents had been transported—and that the other half should have been.

With the arrival of Governor Macquarie in 1810 some semblance of order was restored and the city began to move away from its military roots. Despite his reputation as a reformer Macquarie was not above using grog monopolies for his own ends, and Sydney's new hospital was built on the profits from a monopoly on rum imports granted by the governor. Under Macquarie the *Gazette* began publishing exhortations to its readers to enter the state of matrimony, whereas earlier the paper had carried advertisements by elderly love-seekers that seemed to lampoon wedded bliss. Regularity and morality were the order of the day under Macquarie as lists of official street names and diverse proclamations filled the paper.

It is important to remember just how tiny Sydney was during this time. As late as 1800 there were fewer than 5000 Europeans in all of New South Wales, while by 1810 the population of Sydney was only 10,000, rising to just 30,000 by 1820. It was during Macquarie's reign that prosperous ex-convicts (known as eman-cipists to the chagrin of Wilberforce and other anti-slavery campaigners) began to be looked upon as respectable members of society. By the 1830s, horrifying traditionalists like James Mudie, they started to play important roles in the life of the colony.

After the first decades of multicultural mixing, Sydney became ever more British. From the 1830s onwards visitors increasingly commented on the quintessentially English character of the settle-ment. For some, it was only when they sat down to a meal including tropical fruits or kangaroo that they realised they were not in England. The more astute, however, realised that something was amiss when they heard street calls and music that were popular in London a quarter of a century earlier.

The truth is that the colony had become an awful parody of

England, a parody that was predicated upon convictism—the issue of whether you had left your country for your country's good, or had come to New South Wales for your own reasons. It was the yardstick against which all social standing was measured, thus all social status in the colony was defined in terms of the convict present. The problem was that as the city grew it became impossible to know who was an ex-convict and who was not. In this crazy society the most extreme social niceties were of the utmost importance in keeping one from 'convict pollution'. It was simply not possible, for example, to approach someone in the street and address them, even if you had been introduced in polite society the night before. 'Upon my life, I don't know you, sir!' was the bellowed response to such a threatened breakdown of the precarious social order.

The height of this absurd society came with the publication in 1837 of James Mudie's *Felonry of New South Wales*. In the preface to his privately published and scandalous work Mudie coined his term 'felonry'. Like gentry and yeomanry, felonry was meant to denote a class of persons, but Mudie made it clear that this class distinction was immutable. Once a member of Mudie's felonry, you could never become anything else.

The transportation of convicts to Sydney ceased in 1840, but the threat of renewal continued until 1850, when this sick society was finally smashed apart by the discovery of gold. The old animosities were buried under an avalanche of immigration, and not even the slightest pretence at punishment could be kept up in sending convicts to a land of Ophir. The rush of the 1850s totally changed Sydney. Eyewitness accounts of the city reveal what appears to have been an almost instantaneous change, from a city of prisoners with an oppressive administration to a metropolis somewhat similar to the one we know today. Gold was not an unalloyed blessing, however, for it also brought competitors. Melbourne rose almost overnight on the banks of the Yarra, and

for decades it was a larger, richer and more important place than
its northern neighbour.

This stage of colonial development coincided with increasing
degradation of the Sydney environment and the arrival of inconveniences unknown to earlier settlers. Among the most
distressing of these new irritants were the winds known as 'brickfielders'. These dust-filled gales resulted from the denudation of
the Sydney region. (There was, at this time, not a single tree in
Hyde Park.) The bare ground seemed to increase the intensity of
the windstorm and allowed it to carry grit and dust in enormous
volume. As if the brickfielders were not enough, Sydney
summers were now heralded by squadrons of flies and mosquitoes. The Australian bush fly is a hairy and irritating creature
that breeds in offal and faeces, and both food sources then
abounded in the city. The mosquito, previously uncommon,
doubtless benefited from poor drainage; and these factors, along
with a disrupted ecosystem, allowed the pests to proliferate and
disrupt every outdoor activity in a way unimaginable to Sydney's
inhabitants in both 1788 and 1988. Like the pestilential snakes of
an earlier age, their rise bespoke a sick ecosystem. Sydney's
society was also beginning to show signs of strain. Young men
were gathering in public places and irritating passers-by. Soon
they would transform themselves into larrikin gangs known as
'pushes' and begin threatening lives.

The first visitor of consequence to come to Sydney and speak
of it with nothing but admiration was perhaps Anthony Trollope. In his widely read book the prominent author represented
Sydney as a distinctive, beautiful and cultured city capable of
rivalling any in Europe. Trollope went into raptures over the
harbour, and his words changed the nature of Sydney's visitors
from predominantly scientists and administrators, to tourists.

Sydney's first century encompassed its infancy. Its dependence upon London, the unselfconsciousness of many of its early chroniclers and its embryonic physical state are all concordant with this notion. Puberty came in the 1880s, for by then the city had left childhood behind and had taken on, in general outline, its adult form. Sydney had grown into a city of 400,000 people. It was no longer an isolated European outpost at the ends of the earth. The city's second century may be thought of as its teenaged phase, for mixed together are sparks of genius, jejune gestures and downright destructiveness. From the Sydney Push with its bohemian ambitions to the push of the developer's bulldozers, the century has a loutish feel about it.

At the dawn of Sydney's third century what trends can we detect? I think I see an overweight adult, drowning in its excrement and suffocating in its own lard, for the city has now grown so large that the quality of life of its inhabitants is suffering. Anyone who must take to the roads or trains in peak hour will know what I am talking about. Anyone who has watched the last bandicoots and penguins dwindle, who has seen green space after green space disappear under housing, and who has seen the summer air thicken ever more with smog, knows of the theft of life that comes with each new phase of growth. The tragedy is, you see, that the best things Sydney has to offer—its weather, beaches and parks—are free. They're not making them any more, yet each year there are more and more people who want a piece of them.

This book is an exploration of what makes Sydney special. It's a search for the origin of that unique mix that gave birth to the city, for an understanding of the natural world upon which it was grafted. In assembling this anthology I have tried to let those who were on the spot during the moments of Sydney's infancy tell us how it was, and I've included reports from the city's distinguished

visitors, everyone from François Peron to Charles Darwin, from
the Spaniard Francisco Xavier de Viana to the Frenchman
Hyacinthe de Bougainville. I've also tried to tell the story of what
happened to early Sydney's favourite sons and daughters such as
Watkin Tench, Bennelong, Phillip, Collins, Bungaree and others.

Above all, my eye has been drawn to accounts which record
the irrepressible life of the city. Near the end of *The Birth of
Sydney* is a yarn by Mark Twain. In it he relates a tall story
concerning a shark, a sharp businessman and a wool stockpile
that he reputedly heard while visiting Sydney in 1895. Yet at the
core of Twain's fable lies a kernel of truth—that curious fabrica-
tion of myth from fragile history that lives at the heart of all great
cities. The history of Sydney, to borrow Twain's marvellous
words, 'does not read like history, but like the most beautiful lies.
And all of a fresh new sort, no mouldy old stale ones. It is full of
surprises, and adventures, and incongruities, and contradictions,
and incredibilities; but they are all true, they all happened.'

★

Where necessary, I have modernised punctuation and spelling,
silently corrected a handful of obvious errors, inserted the occasional explanatory date, and sometimes added a word or two of
clarification in a footnote, marked by a dagger (†). The original
authors' own footnotes are indicated by an asterisk (*). Otherwise, their writings are presented as they were first printed, with
any omissions of text indicated by an ellipsis (…).

JAMES COOK

A Port Passed By

In May 1770 Captain James Cook anchored the *Endeavour* for a week in a 'capacious, safe and commodious' harbour he first called Stingray Bay. Then, in honour of the treasure trove of plant specimens collected there by Joseph Banks and Daniel Solander, he changed the name to Botany Bay. It was to become the most famous place-name in Australia.

Anxious to continue mapping the east coast, Cook weighed anchor, and a few hours later he spied an entrance to another harbour. Cook sailed by, but gave the place its first European name.

6 May 1770—During our stay in this harbour I caused the English colours to be displayed ashore every day and an inscription to be cut in one of the trees near the watering place setting forth the ship's name, date, &c. Having seen everything this place afforded we at daylight in the morning weighed with a light breeze at NW and put to sea, the wind soon after coming to the

southward. We steered alongshore NNE and at noon we were by observation in the latitude of 33° 50' S about two or three miles from the land and abreast of a bay or harbour wherein there appeared to be safe anchorage which I called Port Jackson.

PHILIP GIDLEY KING

A Great Shout of Admiration

The First Fleet, eleven vessels in all carrying around 1500 people, commanded by Governor Arthur Phillip, arrived in Botany Bay in January 1788, thirty-six weeks after its departure from Portsmouth. Phillip was intent on establishing a convict colony in the place Cook had so amply praised. As the English officers explored the bay their meetings with the Eora people were frequent, but few were as curious as this one recorded by the plain-spoken Lieutenant Philip Gidley King, a twenty-nine-year-old Cornishman.

King was struck by 'the ridiculous figure we must appear to those poor creatures, who were perfectly naked'; and when the Aborigines seemed uncertain about whether the clean-shaven Europeans were men or women he didn't hesitate to order one of his company to give them the ocular proof. And so, as Robert Hughes put it, 'the first white cock was flashed on an Australian beach'. The identity of the exhibitor who received a 'great shout of admiration' remains unknown.

20 January 1788—At ten o'clock the governor, lieutenant-governor and Captain Hunter went over to the south side of ye bay, a little within Point Sutherland, and I was ordered, with Lieutenant Dawes of the marines, to explore all ye south side of ye bay, and trace the two inlets on the south side as high as possible.

I ran up the southern shore till I rounded — Point, off which lies a long shoal, which is in many places quite dry at low water. We ran up the first inlet about a mile, when we came to the head of it. I returned down again and crossed over to a point; which from what happened there I gave it the name of Lance Point.

Perceiving that it was the highest hill hereabout, I imagined it was probable that we should find some good water there. On landing I ascended the hill, and found ye soil an exceeding fine black mould, with some excellent timber trees and very rich grass. Arrived at ye top of the hill, we perceived a red fox-dog, and soon after discovered a number of ye natives, who hollered and made signs for us to return to our boats. Having only three marines with me and Lieutenant Dawes, I advanced before them unarmed, presenting some beads and ribbands. Two of the natives advanced armed, but would not come close to me. I then dropped ye beads and baize which I held out for them and retreated.

They took it up, and bound the baize about their head. They then in a very vociferous manner desired us to be gone, and one of them threw a lance wide of us to show how far they could do execution. The distance it was thrown was as near as I could guess about forty yards, and when he took it out of the ground where it struck it required an exertion to pull it out. As I took this for a menace that more would be thrown at us if we did not retreat, and being unwilling to fire amongst them, there being twelve of them, I retreated, walking backwards till I came to the brow of the hill where I halted and again offered them presents, which they refused.

On descending the hill they showed themselves on the top of it, and were ten times more vociferous, and very soon after a lance was thrown amongst us, on which I ordered one of the marines to fire with powder only, when they ran off with great precipitation. I embarked, and Governor Phillip joined me from the south side of ye bay, where he had found ye natives very sociable and friendly. We relanded on Lance Point, and ye same body of natives appeared, brandishing their lances and defying us. However, we rowed close in shore, and ye governor disembarked with some presents, which one of them came and received.

Thus peace was re-established, much to the satisfaction of all parties. They came round ye boats, and many little things were given them, but that they wanted most was ye greatcoats and clothing, but hats was more particularised by them, their admiration of which they expressed by very loud shouts whenever one of us pulled our hats off. When they found us so very friendly, they ran up to the man who had thrown the lance and made very significant signs of their displeasure at his conduct by pointing all their lances at him and looking at us, intimating that they only waited our orders to kill him. However, we made signs for them to desist, and made the culprit a present of some beads &c...

I gave two of them a glass of wine, which they no sooner tasted than they spit it out. We asked them the names of a number of articles, which they told us, and repeated our words, and had already learnt so much English as to express their want for anything by putting their finger on it, gently looking me in the face, and saying 'No?' I must do them the justice to say that I believe them to be conscientiously honest. When they found we were not disposed to part with any more things, they entered into conversation with us, which was very fully interpreted by very plain signs.

They wanted to know of what sex we were, which they explained by pointing where it was distinguishable, as they took us for women, not having our beards grown. I ordered one of the people to undeceive them in this particular, when they made a great shout of admiration, and pointing to the shore, which was but ten yards from us, we saw a great number of women and girls, with infant children on their shoulders, make their appearance on the beach, all *in puris naturalibus—pas même la feuille de figueur.*[†]

Those natives who were round the boats made signs for us to go to them, and made us understand that their persons were at our service.

However, I declined this mark of their hospitality, but showed a handkerchief, which I offered to one of the women. Pointing her out, she immediately put her child down and came alongside ye boat and suffered me to apply the handkerchief where Eve did ye fig leaf. The natives then set up another very great shout and my female visitor returned on shore. As ye evening was coming on fast, and we were twelve miles from ye fleet, it was time to return. We wished the natives *good bi wi ye*, which they repeated. We got on board about midnight, when we found the governor preparing to go the next morning at daybreak in some longboats to explore Broken Bay and Port Jackson.

Watkin Tench

The Little Boy and the Old Gentleman

Lieutenant Watkin Tench was as wide-eyed as a puppy at the novelties that Botany Bay had to offer. Hailed as 'the most cultivated mind in the colony' he seems to have been an eternal optimist and everybody's favourite. He was particularly fascinated by the Eora, several of whom were to become close friends. We see him here with a child in hand—and who but Tench would have thought of giving the lad a walk on the beach?—as he meets his first 'Indian'. The convicts, meanwhile, remained cooped up on the fleet.

[†] Naked—not even a fig leaf.

21 January 1788—I went with a party to the south side of the harbour and had scarcely landed five minutes when we were met by a dozen Indians, naked as at the moment of their birth, walking along the beach. Eager to come to a conference, and yet afraid of giving offence, we advanced with caution towards them. Nor would they, at first, approach nearer to us than the distance of some paces. Both parties were armed, yet an attack seemed as unlikely on their part as we knew it to be on our own.

I had at this time a little boy, of not more than seven years of age, in my hand. The child seemed to attract their attention very much, for they frequently pointed to him and spoke to each other; and as he was not frightened I advanced with him towards them, at the same time baring his bosom and showing the whiteness of the skin. On the clothes being removed they gave a loud exclamation and one of the party, an old man with a long beard, hideously ugly, came close to us. I bade my little charge not to be afraid and introduced him to the acquaintance of this uncouth personage. The Indian, with great gentleness, laid his hand on the child's hat and afterwards felt his clothes, muttering to himself all the while. I found it necessary, however, by this time to send away the child, as such a close connection rather alarmed him, and in this, as the conclusion verified, I gave no offence to the old gentleman.

JOHN WHITE

The Finest Harbour in the Universe

On 21 January Governor Phillip left Botany Bay to explore the hitherto unknown Port Jackson. Whatever his expectation about what he would find, he and his officers were amazed by the harbour they discovered, and Phillip at once determined to move the settlement there. Five days later the entire fleet set out for its new home. John White, chief surgeon to the colony, decided no praise was too high for Sydney Harbour. The work of building the new town began at once.

Phillip's decision meant that, apart from the First Fleeters, no convicts were ever sent to Botany Bay. The popularity of the name in ballads and poems is due to the enormous impact the departure of the First Fleet had on the public imagination.

26 January 1788—At ten o'clock the *Sirius*, with all the ships, weighed, and in the evening anchored in Port Jackson, with a few trifling damages done to some of them, who had run foul of each other in working out of Botany Bay.

Port Jackson I believe to be, without exception, the finest and most extensive harbour in the universe, and at the same time the most secure, being safe from all the winds that blow. It is divided into a great number of coves, to which his Excellency has given different names. That on which the town is to be built is called Sydney Cove. It is one of the smallest in the harbour, but the most convenient, as ships of the greatest burden can with ease go into it and heave out close to the shore. Trincomalé, acknowledged to be one of the best harbours in the world, is by no means to be compared to it.[†] In a word, Port Jackson would afford sufficient and safe anchorage for all the navies of Europe.

The *Supply* had arrived the day before, and the governor, with every person that could be spared from the ship, were on shore, clearing the ground for the encampment. In the evening, when all the ships had anchored, the English colours were displayed; and at

---

[†] Trincomalé: on the east coast of Sri Lanka.

the foot of the flagstaff his Majesty's health, and success to the settlement, was drank by the governor, many of the principal officers, and private men who were present upon the occasion.

27 January—A number of convicts from the different transports were landed to assist in clearing the ground for the encampment. His Excellency marked the outlines and, as much as possible to prevent irregularity and to keep the convicts from straggling, the provost-marshal, aided by the patrol, had orders to take into custody all convicts that should be found without the lines, and to leave them in charge of the main or quarter guard.

The boats sent this day to fish were successful. Some of the natives came into the little bay or cove where the seine was hauled, and behaved very friendly. Indeed they carried their civility so far, although a people that appeared to be averse to work, as to assist in dragging it ashore. For this kind office they were liberally rewarded with fish, which seemed to please them and give general satisfaction.

RALPH CLARK

Without You I Cannot Live

When Lieutenant Ralph Clark sailed with the First Fleet he left behind a beautiful young wife Betsey Alicia, and an infant son he affectionately called Ralphie. He had sought permission to bring his family with him, but Phillip refused. Clark was consigned to travel to Botany Bay on the *Friendship*, a vessel full of whores and other convict women. Surrounded by 'debauchery', Clark carried a locket with him that enclosed an image of his darling wife, and this he kissed each morning until he feared that constant use would wear it out. He then restricted himself to kissing it on Sundays.

The journal Clark kept is one of early Sydney's great documents: intimate, spontaneous and revelatory, it gives a glimpse of the fears and desires that were amplified by this new and strange place. His headlong, slapdash expression has all the immediacy of living speech. Here, in a rare moment of happiness, we find him enchanted with the site for the new settlement.

Sunday 27 January 1788—Kist your dear Pictour as Usual on this day and read the lessons for the day...Sent the men beloning to Capt. Tench Company on board the *Charlotte* to be landed from ther—dinned by myself all the rest dinned out—I am Quite charmed with the place—oh that if you was only here and our dear Boy my Alicia I Should not wish to come home if the place agreed with our health but without you I would not Stay if it was the best place under the face of heaven no that I would not my dear Beloved wife for without you I cannot live. The Tents look a pretty amonst the Trees—I hope to be on Shore to morrow if Please good

Munday 28—Got up early this morning and Sent all the Convicts on Shore except them that were Sick—thank God that they are all out of the Ship hope in God that I will have nothing to doe with them any more—at 10 Debarkt with all the Marines and there Baggage Except my own—I never Saw So much confusion in all the course of my life as there was in the three compys. disembark—after I had Pitchd it twice but thank God I Sleept very well but reather cold.

JOHN WHITE

True Camp Dysentery

With the disembarkatian of the male convicts, Surgeon White was kept busy from the first. If it was not dysentery, scurvy or the pox that demanded his attention, it was flayed backs and autopsies. He was to see more 'pitiable objects' over the coming months than he could have imagined.

29 January 1788—A convenient place for the cattle being found, the few that remained were landed. The frame and materials for the governor's house, constructed by Smith in St George's Fields, were likewise sent on shore, and some preparations made for erecting it.

This day Captain Hunter and Lieutenant Bradley began to take a survey of the harbour. In the course of the last week, all the marines, their wives and children, together with all the convicts, male and female, were landed. The laboratory and sick tents were erected, and, I am sorry to say, were soon filled with patients afflicted with the true camp dysentery and the scurvy. More pitiable objects were perhaps never seen. Not a comfort or convenience could be got for them, besides the very few we had with us.

His Excellency, seeing the state these poor objects were in, ordered a piece of ground to be enclosed, for the purpose of raising vegetables for them. The seeds that were sown upon this occasion, on first appearing above ground, looked promising and well, but soon after withered away, which was not indeed extraordinary, as they were not sown at a proper season of the year.

The sick have increased since our landing to such a degree that a spot for a general hospital has been marked out and artificers already employed on it. A proper spot, contiguous to the hospital, has been chosen, to raise such vegetables as can be produced at this season of the year; and where a permanent garden for the use of the hospital is to be established.

WILLIAM BRADLEY

The Ladies Kept Their Distance

Surveying the harbour, William Bradley, first lieutenant on the *Sirius*, had some rare opportunities to observe the Aborigines as they lived before European contact altered their ways. Perhaps with tales of the maidens of Tahiti in mind, he seems to have been particularly interested in the Eora women, who alas were too well chaperoned for the liking of the young sailor.

Tuesday 29 January 1788—Landed on a point forming the NW or middle branch to which we were followed by several of the natives along the rocks, having only their sticks which they use in throwing the lance with them. A man followed at some distance with a bundle of lances; they pointed with their sticks to the best landing place and met us in the most cheerful manner, shouting and dancing. The women kept at a distance near the man with the spears.

This mark of attention to the women, in showing us that although they met us unarmed they had arms ready to protect them, increased my favourable opinion of them very much. Some of these people having pieces of tape and other things tied about them, we concluded them to be some of those people whom the governor had met here before. These people mixed with ours and all hands danced together. From here we went to Grotto Point, moored the boats for the night and made a tent fore and aft the longboat, in which we all slept.

A.M. Went over to Shell Cove and left this branch, taking it as reported by those who examined it when the boats first came into this harbour. As we left this branch we met several canoes with one man in each of them; they had so much confidence in us as to come close alongside our boats. After fixing the place of the rock and extent of the shoalwater round it we went into the north arm.

As we were going in to the first cove on the east side called Spring Cove, we were joined by three canoes with one man in each. They hauled their canoes up and met us on the beach leaving their spears in the canoes. We were soon joined by a dozen of these and found three amongst them with trinkets &c. hanging about them that had been given to them a week before by the governor on his first visit to this place. Our people and these mixed together and were quite sociable, dancing and otherwise amusing them. One of our people combed their hair with which they were much pleased; several women appeared at a distance, but we could not prevail on the men to bring them near us.

We had here an opportunity of examining their canoes and weapons: the canoe is made of the bark taken off a large tree of the length they want to make the canoe, which is gathered up at each end and secured by a lashing of strong vine which runs amongst the underbrush. One was secured by a small line.

They fix spreaders in the inside; the paddles are about two feet long, in shape like a pudding stirrer; these they use one in each hand and go along very fast sitting with their legs under them and their bodies erect and although they do not use outriggers I have seen them paddle through a large surf without over-setting or taking in more water than if rowing in smooth water. From their construction they are apt to leak when any weight is in them; the man nearest that point of the canoe, where the water lies, heaves it out behind him with a piece of wood in the hollow of his hand, still keeping his body erect as when rowing.

They are by far the worst canoes I ever saw or heard of. I have seen some so small as eight feet long and others twice that length. In these canoes they will stand up to strike fish, at which they seem expert. The lances which they had here with them were one sort about twelve feet in length with four barbed prongs made of bone and fastened on to the prong by a stiff gum. These four prongs are secured to the stick and spread equally, about a foot in length; a smaller one of the same kind and one with a single stick barbed at and above the point. The long spears are indented at the end, for to receive a peg which is fixed on a stick two or three feet long and which they apply to throw the lance any considerable distance. The other end of this stick has a sharp hard shell fixed on it which serves for opening shellfish, getting them off the rocks and various other purposes.

The governor's plan with respect to the natives was, if possible, to cultivate an acquaintance with them without their having an idea of our great superiority over them, that their confidence and friendship might be more firmly fixed. We could not persuade any of them to go away in the boat with us.

Having occasion to measure another base line we landed at the upper part of the north arm for that purpose. While we were about it two of the natives came down, seemed pleased to meet us and much astonished at what we were doing. These people passed on to the place where our fire was and mixed with our people; they were neither of them armed. Soon after and as we were going along the beach a man and a very old woman met us. They stopped with us a short time and then walked on to the place our people were at—this was the first woman that came among us.

She appeared feeble with old age, very dark and ugly; we could not from her judge what the younger ones might be, but we had now some hopes that by the old woman coming to us that the others who we saw on the beach close by the woods would allow us an interview. As we approached them they ran away and as soon as we retired they showed themselves again and had a party of very stout armed men near them. We used many entreaties without effect. The ladies still kept their distance.

When we had done what we had to do, we returned to the boat leaving two of the officers on shore with the people who were cooking, that nothing improper might be done by them as we had now many of the natives assembled about us and armed and several more coming along the beach. Two muskets were handed to our people on shore and the other arms kept ready in the longboat. These people all came among us and laid their lances down on the beach. The old woman made herself very comfortable and was with us from our first meeting with her.

She and her companions expressed a wish to know whether we were men or women. These people wanted everything from us that they saw us make use of or that we had about us. We did not give them anything, in hopes of bringing the women among us by keeping what articles we had to give them and signified to the men that we would give all to the women if they would come from the woods where they were sitting looking at us.

Wednesday 30 January, P.M.—This scheme at last succeeded, for as we left the beach to dine in the boats, which lay close to, the women came, having a party of armed men with them who had each a green bough in his hand which they waved as they advanced. They came near us and sat down amongst our other visitors. The party of armed men stood by them and never laid down their spears.

We made signs to them that if they would stay we would bring them ashore some things which we showed to them. We took every precaution to prevent improprieties being committed by ordering the people out of the small boat, and Captain Hunter and the three officers went in her from the longboat to go on shore, leaving the muskets in the longboat loaded in case there might be occasion to use them.

As we approached the shore the women retired, on which we immediately put back to the longboat making the same signs as we had done before. An old man then called to the women and the greatest part of them returned and came to the old man who walked close down to the waterside as we approached. The armed men with the boughs posted themselves together just by and every one of the men now took up their spears and kept them poised ready for throwing, standing close to the edge of the beach and rocks. When the boat landed, the old man came to the side of her and wanted the things which we had held out to the women to take to them; which we refused and signified to them that we must give the things to the women ourselves.

The old man, finding us determined, spoke to the women and one of them came in to the water to the side of the boat. We ornamented this naked beauty with strings of beads and buttons round her neck, arms and wrists. She appeared rather frightened although she affected a laugh and seemed pleased with her presents. When she retired several of the other women came to the side of the boat, attended by the old man. We ornamented these the same as the first: some came without fear, others trembling and laughing, hesitating before they would come and some just near enough to reach the things. Two of them could not be persuaded to come within two or three yards of the boat—to those we threw some things and gave the old man some for them.

The whole of this time the men who kept their lances ready were silent and attentive to what was doing. Two men were placed on a separate rock we supposed to keep a lookout upon the longboat. After having disposed of our trifling presents we went off to the longboat. As soon as we put off the men held their spears carelessly and began shouting, laughing and dancing. We counted seventy-two besides women and children: this was more than twice the number ever yet seen together before, either in this harbour or Botany Bay.

The men we met with here were in general stout and well-limbed. The women excepting the very old woman, were young and in general shorter than the men; very straight-limbed and well featured, their voice a pleasing softness, they were all entirely naked, old and young. The men had their beards long and very bushy; their hair hangs about their heads clotted with dirt and vermin. Some of them had the teeth of some animal and pieces of bone stuck in their hair with gum. They are so dirty that it is hard to tell the real colour of their hides, which I think is nearly black. Their noses somewhat flat and all those that we noticed had a hole bored, through which they sometimes put a stick or small bone but of all this party only one wore it.

Most of these men had lost one of the fore teeth and their skins are much scarred, not like those commonly seen from wounds, this as well the lop of a particular tooth is a custom observed amongst them that we cannot yet learn the reason for. They walk very upright and very much with their hands behind them.

RALPH CLARK

What a Terrible Night

Sydney's violent summer storms traumatised Ralph Clark. He was the only First Fleet diarist to record his dreams, and his dear Alicia appeared in most of them, in the role of lover or hussy or both. Here she allows herself to be seduced by a certain Kempster, of whom history records nothing else but that he was Alicia's imaginary lover and a haunter of dockyards.

Thursday 31 January 1788—what a Terrible night it was last of thunder lighting and Rain—was obliged to get out of my tent with nothing one but my shirt to Slacking the tent Poles—dreamt of You my dear Sweet woman and that I was in bed with you and that I dreamt also that I was very Angry with You and that I wanted to run Kempster throu for a Breach of Friendship—remarkably hott have nothing to Sleep but a Poor Tent and a little grass to Sleep on...

Friday 1 February—...in all the course of my life I never Slept worse my dear wife than I did [last] night—what with the hard cold ground Spiders ants and every vermin that you can think of was crauling over me I was glad when the morning came—my poor Poutch was my Pillow—dreamt that I was in the dockyard and that a Gentleman a stranger told me that the things that I Saw were Kempsters which he had bought as a Saile—went out with my Gun and Kild only one Parrot—they are the most beatifuless birds that I ever Saw—when it is please god that I am to Return to you my dear woman I will bring Some of them home for you.

ARTHUR BOWES SMYTH

The Tempest Came On

While the male convicts were put ashore at the first opportunity, it was the best part of two weeks before Phillip gave the order for the women to disembark. There were 189 of them out of a total of 732 convicts. Many arrived on the *Lady Penrhyn*, the vessel on which

Arthur Bowes Smyth served as surgeon. So relieved was its captain to be shot of the women that, upon their leaving the ship, he issued an extra ration of rum to the crew in celebration. The results, amid another massive electrical storm, were predictable.

The following day, as the convicts sat in the mud encircled by soldiers, Phillip opened the red leather cases that carried his commissions and read them to the shagged-out assembly, who learned that their governor held absolute power in this micro-society. Phillip's announcement that even such petty criminals as chicken thieves would be hanged must surely have given due warning of what was to come. Two days later a pair of Eora elders visited the new settlement at the place they called Werrong, or Warran. They were to be the last visitors for some time.

6 February 1788—At five o'clock this morning all things were got in order for landing the whole of the women and three of the ships longboats came alongside us to receive them. Previous to their quitting the ship a strict search was made to try if any of the many things which they had stolen on board could be found, but their artifice eluded the most strict search and about six o'clock p.m. we had the long wished for pleasure of seeing the last of them leave the ship.

They were dressed in general very clean and some few amongst them might be said to be well dressed. The men convicts got to them very soon after they landed, and it is beyond my abilities to give a just description of the scene of debauchery and riot that ensued during the night. They had not been landed more than an hour before they had all got their tents pitched or anything in order to receive them, but there came on the most violent storm of thunder, lightning and rain I ever saw. The lightning was incessant during the whole night and I never heard it rain faster.

About twelve o'clock in the night one severe flash of lightning struck a very large tree in the centre of the camp under which some places were constructed to keep the sheep and hogs in. It split the tree from top to bottom, killed five sheep belonging to Major Ross and a pig of one of the lieutenants...

The sailors in our ship requested to have some grog to make merry with upon the women quitting the ship. Indeed the captain himself had no small reason to rejoice upon their being all safely landed and given into the care of the governor, as he was under the penalty of £40 for every convict that was missing—for which reason he complied with the sailor's request and, about the time they began to be elevated, the tempest came on.

The scene which presented itself at this time and during the greater part of the night beggars every description: some swearing, others quarrelling, others singing, not in the least regarding the tempest, though so violent that the thunder [that] shook the ship exceeded anything I ever before had a conception of. I never before experienced so uncomfortable a night expecting every moment the ship would be struck with the lightning: the sailors almost all drunk and incapable of rendering much assistance had an accident happened and the heat was almost suffocating.

7 February—This morning at eleven o'clock all who could leave the ships were summoned on shore to hear the governor's commission read, and also the commission constituting the court of judicature. The marines were all under arms and received the governor with flying colours and a band of music—he was accompanied by the judge-advocate, lieutenant-governor, clergyman, surveyor-general, surgeon-general &ca.

After taking off his hat and complimenting the marine officers, who had lowered their colours and paid that respect to him as governor which he was entitled to, the soldiers marched with music playing drums and fifes and formed a circle round the whole of the convict men and women who were collected together.

The convicts were all ordered to sit down on the ground. All gentlemen present were desired to come into the centre where stood the governor, lieutenant governor, judge-advocate, clergyman, surgeon &ca &ca. A camp table was fixed before them and two red leather cases laid thereon, containing the commissions &ca which were opened and unsealed in the sight of all present and read by the judge-advocate (Captain Collins) constituting Arthur Phillip esq. governor general, commander-in-chief over all those territories, belonging to his Britannic Majesty George III, king of Great Britain, France and Ireland and called New South Wales and parts adjacent with full power and authority to build forts, castles and towns, and to erect batteries &ca &ca as shall seem to him necessary, with full power also to appoint and constitute officers of every kind as he shall judge proper.

In short I shall not attempt to follow the commission through its various parts, I shall only observe that it is a more unlimited one than was ever before granted to any governor under the British Crown.

After the commission was read the governor harangued the convicts, telling them that he had tried them hitherto to see how they were disposed; that he was now thoroughly convinced there were many amongst them incorrigible and that he was persuaded nothing but severity would have any effect upon them to induce them to behave properly in future.

He also assured them that if they attempted to get into the women's tents of a night there were positive orders for firing upon them; that they were very idle; not more than 200 out of 600 were at work; that the industrious should not labour for the idle; if they did not work they should not eat. In England thieving poultry was not punished with death; but here, where a loss of that kind could not be supplied, it was of the utmost consequence to the settlement, as well as every other species of stock, as they were preserved for breeding. Therefore stealing the most trifling article of stock or provisions would be punished with death.

That, however, such severity might militate against his humanity and feelings towards his fellow-creatures yet though justice demanded such rigid execution of the laws and they might implicitly rely upon justice taking place; their labour would not be equal to that of an husbandman in England, who has a wife and family to provide for. They would never be worked beyond their abilities, but every individual should contribute his share to render himself and community at large happy and comfortable as soon as the nature of the settlement will admit of. That they should be employed erecting houses for the different officers, next for the marines, and lastly for themselves.

After this harangue they were dismissed in the same form as they were assembled; after which the governor retired to a cold collation, under a large tent erected for that purpose to which the general officers only were invited, and not the least attention whatever was paid to any other person who came out from England...[†]

9 February—This day two of the natives came down very near the camp. They came to within a small distance of the governor's house but could not by any entreaty be prevailed upon to go into the camp. They were both men pretty much advanced in life; had each of them long spears in their hands.

The governor went to them attended by several officers and presented one of them with an hatchet and bound some red bunting about their heads with some yellow tinfoil. They sat down under a tree and could not be prevailed upon to go any further. They appeared to express very little surprise at the governor's house, which was very near them.

[†] The B-list didn't miss out on much—the feast was flyblown.

They sit in the same form in which the tailors in England sit and one of them while in this attitude sharpened the point of his spear with an oyster shell (rubbed to an edge and fastened into a stick about a foot long) on the bottom of his foot.

While I was standing by them a black boy belonging to one of the ships in the fleet came up to look at them. They appeared pleased to see him, felt his hair, opened his shirt bosom and examined his breasts and by signs expressed a wish to have a lock of his hair, which I made the boy let me cut off and presented to them and in return I cut off some of their hair.

They put the boy's hair carefully by in a wreath of grass twisted round one of the spears. They stayed here at least an hour then betook themselves into the woods, and nobody has been near the camp since.

RALPH CLARK

The Nightmare Begins

Using a large 'X' as code for the rutting of convicts, Ralph Clark began to understand the true nature of the dislocated society in which he found himself and in which he would spend at least the next three years of his life. Now his real nightmare began. Governor Phillip may have had the power of a dictator but the chaos of nature in this crazed place seemed far more awesome to Clark.

Saterday 9 February 1788—Satt my dear wife as one of Members of the court Martial to troy Prisoners when Brimage was Sentanced to Receive 200 lashes on his bare back for stricking one of the convict women because She would not goe up in the woods with him and to X—also Sentanced Green both marines one hunder lashes for been drunk on Guard...

Sunday 10—mounted the Govenours Guard to day by which I could not attend prayers but kist your dear Pictour as Usual on this day—was very much frightened by the Lightening as it brock very near my as I was Sitting in my tent on Guard—it is nothing else but the Lightening that has burnt all the trees but it— my dear woman I return my God thanks that You did not come out for I should have gone mad if you for fear that the lightening would have hurted you or our dear boy—I could not Stay longer than the three Years for the world—I wish that I could get home now I should goe mad for you would be so frightened with the thunder and Lightening—

ARTHUR BOWES SMYTH
Kangaroos and Cabin Boys

Arthur Bowes Smyth was also terrified by the sexual anarchy of the new settlement, and the discovery of a cabin boy in the women's tents convinced him the colony now held the world record for debauchery.

Fear seems to have driven curiosity entirely from Smyth's mind, for all he tells us of that great novelty— the first kangaroo to be shot in the colony—is that it reputedly tasted almost as good as venison. Perhaps Bowes was excluded from this feast too. He was certainly sensitive to the military's grumblings about favourable treatment being given to the convicts. This was a society which estimated privilege by counting strokes of the lash.

11 February 1788—This day Captain Shea shot a kangaroo and it was brought into the camp. It is said to be nearly equal in goodness to venison.

This day our carpenter, one of our sailors, and a boy belonging to the *Prince of Wales* were caught in the women's tents. They were drummed out of the camp with the Rogue's March playing before them and the boy had petticoats put upon him—they had all of them their hands tied behind 'em.

The anarchy and confusion which prevails throughout the camp, and the audacity of the convicts, both men and women, is arrived to such a pitch as is not to be equalled, I believe, by any set of villains in any other spot upon the globe. The men seize upon any sailors on shore who are walking near the women's camp, beat them most unmercifully and desire them to go on board.

This day Thomas Bramwell, a marine (lately servant to Lieutenant G. Johnstone in our ship) got amongst the women and beat one of them (Elizabeth Needham, a most infamous hussy) with whom he had had connections while on board us, and this day he received 100 lashes and is to have 100 more.

One of the convicts who had struck a sentry on duty received only 150 lashes. The severity shewn to the marines and lenity to the convicts has already excited great murmuring and discontent among the corps and where it will end, unless some other plan is adopted, time will discover.

RALPH CLARK

God Keep Me from Them

Lieutenant Clark was a God-fearing man, deeply in love with his wife, and had been without sex for the best part of a year. The 'Seen of Whordome' he glimpsed through the flashes of lightning in early February seems to have roused fierce passions in his breast. Would even Ralph Clark, dreaming of Betsey, succumb to the dubious charms of the convict women's camp?

Toothache would soon serve to increase the woes of our Botany Bay Job. What could be worse: Clark's realisation that 'we brought nothing but thefs out' and found 'nothing but thefs' in the new land, or his terrifying experience of Georgian dentistry? A week later he witnessed the price a thief would pay at Port Jackson when a certain Thomas Barrett was launched 'into the other world' for stealing food. He was the first to suffer capital punishment on the fatal shore.

Munday 11 February 1788—Several of the convicts were married Yesterday and amongst them that were have left wives and familes at home—a good God what a Seen of Whordome is going on there in the womans camp—no Sooner has one man gone in with a woman but a nother goes in with her—I hope the Almighty will keep me free from them as he has heather to done but I need not be affraid as I promised you my Tender Betsey I will keep my word with you—I never will have any thing any woman what ever except your Self my dear wife I will be true to my Betsey my love for you will keep me...

Tuesday 12—…the Patroles caught 3 Seamen and a Boy in the womans camp and they were drumd out of our the male convicts and woman camps—the Boy was the handsomest that I ever Saw Except our dear Boys—the Majr Sent for one of the womens peticoats and put it on the Boy who cut the droles appearents that I ever Saw—I hope this will be a warning to them from coming into the whore camp—I would call it by the Name of Sodem for ther is more Sin committed in it than in any other part of the world—

Wednessday 13—dreamt my Belovd Betsey that I was with you and that I thought I was going to be arrested and that You was in the greatest concern for me that could be—I also after dreamt that I thought that you was Sitting on a Stool and that I did X with you my dear wife—

Munday 18 February—was very ill with the Tooth eack all last night—got up early and went to the Hospital and had it puld out Buy Mr Consident—oh my God what pain it was it was So fast in and the Jaw bone very fast to one of the prongs the Tooth would not come out without breacking the Jaw bone which he did—I thought that half of my head would have come off—there is a piece of the Jaw bone remaining to the Tooth—the Pain was So great my dear wife that I fainted away and was very ill the remainder of the day but I could not let Consident report to Majr Ross that I was ill but would goe on Picket—my gum Keep Bleeding all the day—

Tuesday 19—having the Picket lay with my cloaths on and had but little Sleep as my Jaw paind me very much but in the course of the little I did Sleep I dreamt that I was with you my Tender woman and I thought that I Saw Your head was drest out and Small Sparks of fire in your hair that you often told me was Malice—I hope to god that you are only well and that of our dear Boy and I don't cear for any bodys Malice—went on Guard over the Governors to day wher I have done nothing but thinking of You and our dear Son—oh my beloved Betsey oh my dr. woman how tenderly I love you both—my face very much Sweld and the Pain at times very great—the Govr told me that the indians had gone to the number of 20 over to the Island wher the *Sirius Gardian* and where there is only 3 men and the half had come up and were very Kind to the three men while the others Stole what they could lay there hands on but one of the men Seing them carring of ane Axe and Spade he fired at the man that had the Spade with small Shot and struck him about the legs when they dropt the spade but they carried of the other things—they are the Greatest thefs that ever lived—I think that we are in a fine stat we brought nothing but thefs out with use to find nothing but thefs...

Wednesday 27 February—a Criminal court Sits to day for the Trayer of Such Prisoners as may be brought befor them—amons the Number to be tryd is two that came out of the Ship with me Heny. Lovell and one Ryan—at 1 oClock there Centance was read the charge being clearly Proven of their Stealing Butter Pease and Pork—Thomas Barrit Heny. Lovell Josh. hall and Ryan the three former Received Centance of death and the Latter to Receive 300 Lashes—at 5 oClock PM the Battalion was order under arms for the centance of the Land to be put into Excution and soon after we mach to the place of Execution which was a Tree between the male and female convicts Camp—at a Quarter after 5 the Unhappy men wair brought to the place of Where they were to Suffer when after the Parson had done prayers with them—the Provos Martial put the halter a bout the neck Thos. Barret and he mounted the Ladder—from his going I dont think that he had the least thought that was to Suffer but when the Provos Martial put a handkerchiff a bout his head he turned as white as a sheet—when Soon after the Ladder was puld from under him and he Lanched into the other world without a gron...

JOHN WHITE

The Anomalous Hornbill

Somehow, despite the burden of his work, Surgeon White found time to study the creatures of this new land. His descriptions of the channel-billed cuckoo ('the anomalous hornbill') and the wattled bee-eater ('the wattle-bird') have the wonderful freshness of new discovery about them. The words 'saw this day' would occur ever more frequently in White's journal as Sydney's marvellous fauna was revealed to him. White's natural history collections have been dispersed and some lost, but some of his botanical specimens can still be seen in the Academy of Natural Sciences in Philadelphia.

White was to learn that, although they avoided the settlement, the Aborigines were not passive in the face of the invasion. We travel with him to Rushcutters Bay to investigate a grisly murder. A month or so later White was in an expansively celebratory mood on the occasion of the King's birthday: he was now living not only on the shore of the finest harbour in the universe but in the largest county in the world. It must have been the largest county of thieves too, as White was to discover. His claim that Phillip intended to call the colony Albion receives little support from other witnesses; just one other diarist records it.

16 April 1788—About four o'clock in the afternoon we came to a steep valley, where the flowing of the tide ceased, and a freshwater stream commenced. Here, in the most desert, wild and solitary seclusion that the imagination can form any idea of, we took up our abode for the night, dressed our provisions, washed our shirts and stockings, and turned our inconvenient situation to the best advantage in our power.

Saw this day the Anomalous Hornbill...This bird is so very singular in its several characteristics that it can scarcely be said to which of the present known genera to refer it. In the bill it seems most allied to the hornbill, but the legs are those of a toucan, and the tongue is more like that of a crow than any other. It must therefore be left to future ornithologists to determine the point, resting here satisfied with describing its external appearance.

The size of the body is not much less than that of a crow: the bill is very large and bent, particularly at the tip of the upper mandible; the nostrils and space round the eyes are bare and red; the head, neck, and all beneath, are of a pale grey, crossed over the thighs with dusky lines; the back and wings dusky lead-colour, with the end of each feather black; the tail is long and wedge-shaped, the feathers white at the ends, near which is a bar of black. The bill and legs are brown; the toes are placed two before and two behind, as in the parrot or toucan genus...

17 April—The next morning we hid our tents and the remains of our provisions, and, with only a little rum and a small quantity of bread, made a forced march into the country, to the westward, of about fourteen miles, without being able to succeed in the object of our search, which was for good land, well-watered. Indeed, the land here, although covered with an endless wood, was better than the parts which we had already explored. Finding it, however, very unlikely that we should be able to penetrate through this immense forest, and circumstanced as we were, it was thought more prudent to return. We, accordingly, after an expeditious walk, reached the stream from whence we had set out in the morning, and, taking up the tents and provisions which we had left, proceeded a little farther down, to the flowing of the tide, and there pitched our tents for the night, during which it rained very heavily, with thunder and lightning.

The Wattled Bee-eater...fell in our way during the course of the day. This bird is the size of a missel thrush but much larger in proportion, its total length being about fourteen inches. The feathers on the upper part of the head, longer than the rest, give the appearance of a crest; those of the under part are smooth; the plumage for the most part is brown, the feathers long and pointed, and each feather has a streak of white down the middle; under the eye, on each side, is a kind of wattle, of an orange colour; the middle of the belly is yellow; the tail is wedge-shaped, similar to that of the magpie, and the feathers tipped with white; the bill and legs are brown. This bird seems to be peculiar to New Holland, and is undoubtedly a species which has not hitherto been described.

18 April—We began our progress early in the morning, bending our course down the river…We all went on board the boats, and fell down the river till we got to a pleasant little cove, where we dined, with great satisfaction and comfort, upon the welcome provisions which were sent in the boats by the governor's steward. After having refreshed ourselves, we again embarked, and about six o'clock in the evening arrived in Sydney Cove.

30 April—Captain Campbell of the marines, who had been up the harbour to procure some rushes for thatch, brought to the hospital the bodies of William Okey and Samuel Davis, two rush-cutters, whom he had found murdered by the natives in a shocking manner.

Okey was transfixed through the breast with one of their spears, which with great difficulty and force was pulled out. He had two other spears sticking in him to a depth which must have proved mortal. His skull was divided and comminuted so much that his brains easily found a passage through. His eyes were out, but these might have been picked away by birds.

Davis was a youth, and had only some trifling marks of violence about him. This lad could not have been many hours dead, for when Captain Campbell found him, which was among some mangrove trees, and at a considerable distance from the place where the other man lay, he was not stiff nor very cold; nor was he perfectly so when brought to the hospital. From these circumstances we have been led to think that while they were dispatching Okey he had crept to the trees among which he was found, and that fear, united with the cold and wet, in a great degree contributed to his death.

What was the motive or cause of this melancholy catastrophe we have not been able to discover, but from the civility shewn on all occasions to the officers by the natives, whenever any of them were met, I am strongly inclined to think that they must have been provoked and injured by the convicts.

We this day caught a Yellow-eared Flycatcher...This bird is a native of New Holland, the size of a martin, and nearly seven inches in length; the bill is broad at the bottom and of a pale colour; the legs dusky; the plumage is mostly brown, mottled with paler brown; the edges of the wing feathers yellowish; the under part of the body white, inclining to dusky about the chin and throat; the tail is pretty long and, when spread, seems hollowed out at the tip; beneath the eye, on each side, is an irregular streak, growing wider and finishing on the ears, of a yellow or gold colour.

Early the next morning the governor, lieutenants G. Johnston and Kellow, myself, six soldiers, and two armed convicts, whom we took as guides, went to the place where the murder had been committed, in hopes, by some means or other, to be able to find out either the actual perpetrators or those concerned. As most of their clothes and all their working tools were carried off, we expected that these might furnish us with some clue, but in this we were disappointed. We could not observe a single trace of the natives ever having been there...

4 June—This being the anniversary of his Majesty's birthday, and the first celebration of it in New South Wales, his Excellency ordered the *Sirius* and *Supply* to fire twenty-one guns at sunrise, at one o'clock, and at sunset.

Immediately after the King's ships had ceased firing, at one o'clock, the *Borrowdale, Friendship, Fishburne, Golden Grove,* and *Prince of Wales* fired five guns each. The battalion was under arms at twelve and fired three vollies, succeeded by three cheers.

After this ceremony had taken place, the lieutenant-governor, with all the officers of the settlement, civil and military, paid their respects to his Excellency at his house. At two o'clock they all met there again to dinner, during which the band of musick played 'God Save the King' and several excellent marches.

After the cloth was removed, his Majesty's health was drank with three cheers. The Prince of Wales, the Queen and royal family, the Cumberland family, and his Royal Highness Prince William Henry succeeded. His Majesty's ministers were next given; who, it was observed, may be pitted against any that ever conducted the affairs of Great Britain.

When all the public toasts had gone round, the governor nominated the district which he had taken possession of, Cumberland County; and gave it such an extent of boundary as to make it the largest county in the whole world. His Excellency said that he had intended to have named the town, and laid the first stone, on this auspicious day, but the unexpected difficulties which he had met with, in clearing the ground and from a want of artificers, had rendered it impossible; he therefore put it off till a future day. Its name, however, we understand, is to be Albion…

His Excellency ordered every soldier a pint of porter, besides his allowance of grog, and every convict half a pint of spirits, made into grog, that they all might drink his Majesty's health; and, as it was a day of general rejoicing and festivity, he likewise made it a day of forgiveness…

At night every person attended an immense bonfire that was lighted for the occasion, after which the principal officers of the settlement, and of the men of war, supped at the governor's, where they terminated the day in pleasantry, good humour and cheerfulness.

The next morning we were astonished at the number of thefts which had been committed, during the general festivity, by the villainous part of the convicts, on one another, and on some of the officers, whose servants did not keep a strict lookout after their marquees.

DANIEL SOUTHWELL

They Despise Our Imbecility

In his early twenties, Daniel Southwell came to Sydney as a mate on the *Sirius*. His description of a meeting of Governor Phillip with a group of Eora in Manly Cove is the most detailed to survive. The fight he witnessed was possibly a low-key conflict which, given the reaction of the Eora women present, may have been triggered by a sexual peccadillo. The Aborigines may have interpreted the departure of the whites as a form of cowardice which warranted a volley of spears. This, however, is purely speculative, and Southwell's diffidence in explaining Aboriginal motives reveals that he was well aware of how different Eora culture was from his own. In another age, he would have made a fine anthropologist.

24 August 1788—On the day appointed we accordingly went down the harbour to Manly Cove, accompanied by the governor's boat and two marines in each. When there, we came to a grappling two boats' length from the beach, having received an injunction not to land on any account, but to wait there till sunset.

The people were now more numerous than usual, upwards of two hundred, as I judge, being in sight. The major part of them were sitting in the long grass a little inland from the sandy beach; and this either by way of sunning themselves, or to view the Europeans and their canoes. We were sufficiently near to talk with them; and several of them came close by the waterside under the stem of our boats. A good while was spent in telling them the names of a variety of things, many of which, it is no less true than remarkable, they pronounced with as much ease and propriety as ourselves, and were mightily well pleased to see us so completely foiled, as we often were, in attempting to master some of their 'throttlers' or gutturals.

They wanted us much to come on shore, which was impracticable. Indeed, so intent seemed they on persuading us to it that after several waggish intimations from our people that a sight of their ladies would be very agreeable, they caused about twenty of them to pass close by us, to which, indeed, they seemed not at all averse.

They were preceded by an ill-favoured old Beldam of so disagreeable an aspect that we could not determine whether a short harangue she made on the occasion was a kind invitation to land, or a sarcastic volley of abuse for what she might take it in her head to deem our idle curiosity. Some of the young damsels looked well enough, all things considered. They were quite facetious and, so far as our slender knowledge of their dialect extended, kept up a very warm, animated, and amorous discourse. However, they did not forget now and then to give a side glance at their countrymen, with whose grand foible they were no doubt well acquainted; and when they retired seemed to do it rather from a fear of giving them offence than from any inclination of their own.

After this, when all had for some time been quiet and still, sitting quite hush in the grass, we were not a little surprised to hear a great tumult which proceeded from some who sat farther back among the trees. At first the noise was simply that of men's voices wrangling with the most barbarous dissonance and savage agitation; but now the clashing of spears and the strokes of lances against the target was very distinctly heard. Looking that way, therefore, we saw several of them engaged in warm combat, darting at each other with true savage fierceness. All now ran and seized their weapons which, by the way, must have been deposited in the grass, as till now they had kept them out of our sight, and a scene of great noise and confusion ensued on all sides.

The women, who hitherto had all huddled together a little way from our boats' station, came running down with every appearance of terror, and calling to us repeatedly. Some stayed behind, anxiously looking out from between the trees as if to observe the event and wait the decision, and the children every- where were clinging to them and squalling pitiably. What those females meant who thus precipitately came down to us I am at a loss to conclude, but they seemed to supplicate our assistance.

The battle continued long, and was now and then interrupted with noisy expostulations, in the midst of which the contending parties would, however, frequently launch a spear at each other with all the rage of madmen. They are dexterous to a degree in the use of the target and during the affray, which lasted an hour, I did not see one of them completely disabled, though frequently forced to quit the field. I mean not by this to say there was really no execution done, but the thickness of the trees greatly impeded our view.

Four of our people affirmed that they saw one man carried off the field with a lance fast in his side. It is hard indeed to suppose but that during so long a contest some must be wounded, and in fact we see few of these people anywhere, or of any age, but have many scars and marks of weapons on their bodies.

'Tis odd that the warriors in question would frequently all at once desist from the attack, and talk together as though nothing at all had happened, and some others of the multitude would come down and gaze at us just as before. The women were less discomposed, and many of the men, though a part of their corps were still as warmly engaged as ever, came down on the shore to discourse with us in the usual way, and apparently regardless of what was going on among the rest.

I must not omit that in one of their expostulations, in which the women now and then endeavoured to assist, our old Jezebel, the matron, to use an homely sea phrase, 'got herself capsized heels over head', a sign, perhaps, that they pay no great respect to the decisions of the ladies, at least on such occasions; and I rather took it as a rude mode of suggesting a hint that they deemed the business she had engaged in as impertinent and officious—in short, no concern of hers.

But, in truth, the whole proceedings of this afternoon were so equivocal as to leave me, I must confess, incapable of giving any positive opinion concerning the variety of their manoeuvres. It strikes me, however, that one of the following conjectures may be right:—
1. It is possible, when any of these uncivilised beings happen to fall out, that instead of deciding the matter by fisticuffs, as with us boxing Britons, they instantly obey the first dictates of passionate resentment, aiming for the time at nothing less than the life of their immediate antagonist;
2. As they seem much to dread our decisive superiority to them in arms, they might perhaps hope to impress us with formidable sentiments of their native savage bravery by thus making a fiery display of prowess in a sharp engagement, acted to the very life, in which, therefore, the most bitter animosity and every corroborating appearance of cruelty was most artfully managed, as I have above attempted to show; or
3. Lastly, the whole exploit might be a stratagem to draw us on shore at any rate, whether by the supposed invincible attraction of female blandishments, or by the repeated show of terror and distress so naturally exhibited, as I have observed, by the women and children.

I have only to add that, when seemingly tired either with the reality or the strong semblance of fighting with each other, they took it into their heads to begin with us by throwing several spears from behind the trees that fell little short of our boats. I was unwilling to exert the power we had over these poor wretches, and finding they still continued to lurk behind the trees with every appearance of hostility, I thought proper, the sun being just on the horizon, to haul farther out from the beach, contenting myself with now and then presenting a musket when I perceived any of them preparing to aim from behind the thicket.

This never failed to strike them with a panic, and sent them off with all the heel they had. But still, so depraved are their sentiments (if I may thus hazard that respectable word), or so little do they reflect on motives or effects, that forbearance, instead of having the use intended, only led them to despise our seeming imbecility. On going away they came down and hooted, as, I presume, in contempt of our menaces. Whenever their spears were thrown a barbarous yell was raised in applause, as I concluded, of the warrior; and in this horrid exclamation the voice of the sooty sirens was very distinguishable, who not long before had endeavoured to allure us to their inhospitable beach in vain.

Deprived of Tea

The anonymous female convict who wrote this letter speaks bitterly of the difficulties the few women in the settlement faced. None, however, seem to have affected her as severely as the lack of tea, which she mentions three times in her missive. Perhaps she enjoyed a relatively privileged life, such as might be lived by a woman under the protection of a lieutenant of the marines?

14 November 1788—I take the first opportunity that has been given us to acquaint you with our disconsolate situation in this solitary waste of the creation. Our passage, you may have heard by the first ships, was tolerably favourable; but the inconveniences since suffered for want of shelter, bedding &c., are not to be imagined by any stranger. However, we have now two streets, if four rows of the most miserable huts you can possibly conceive of deserve that name. Windows they have none, as from the governor's house &c., now nearly finished, no glass could be spared; so that lattices of twigs are made by our people to supply their places.

At the extremity of the lines, where since our arrival the dead are buried, there is a place called the churchyard; but we hear, as soon as a sufficient quantity of bricks can be made, a church is to be built, and named St Phillip, after the governor. Notwithstanding all our presents, the savages still continue to do us all the injury they can, which makes the soldiers' duty very hard, and much dissatisfaction among the officers. I know not how many of our people have been killed.

As for the distresses of the women, they are past description, as they are deprived of tea and other things they were indulged in in the voyage by the seamen, and as they are all totally unprovided with clothes, those who have young children are quite wretched. Besides this, though a number of marriages have taken place, several women, who became pregnant on the voyage, and are since left by their partners, who have returned to England, are not likely even here to form any fresh connections.

We are comforted with the hopes of a supply of tea from China, and flattered with getting riches when the settlement is complete, and the hemp which the place produces is brought to perfection. Our kangaroo rats are like mutton, but much leaner; and there is a kind of chickweed so much in taste like our spinach that no difference can be discerned. Something like ground ivy is used for tea; but a scarcity of salt and sugar makes our best meals insipid.

The separation of several of us to an uninhabited island was like a second transportation. In short, everyone is so taken up with their own misfortunes that they have no pity to bestow upon others. All our letters are examined by an officer, but a friend takes this for me privately. The ships sail tomorrow.

ROBERT ROSS

Hardships, Mortifications, Cruelties

Lieutenant-Governor Ross, commander of the marines, was a cantankerous and duplicitous old fogey. Ralph Clark called him 'without exception the most disagreeable commanding officer I ever knew'. Ross made life for Phillip and those under his command hell, and to be rid of him the governor sent him to Norfolk Island, to join a small settlement there. Ross's famous grumble in this letter to Under Secretary Nepean that 'here, nature is reversed' is part of a wider diatribe against the new country. Later he was to declare that it would be less trouble and expense to keep all the kingdom's felons at the best London hotel for the duration of their sentences.

16 November 1788—I do not feel myself at all at ease with respect to you, as I much fear you expect to hear from me by every ship which sails from here. The truth of the matter is that I have no one thing to communicate to you that can give you either pleasure or satisfaction, for, unless I attempted to give you a description of this country and of the hardships, mortifications, and I had almost

said cruelties, we are obliged to submit to, I have no subject worth taking up your time with.

From our governor's manner of expressing himself, for he communicates nothing to any person here but to his secretary (Captain Collins), he has, I dare say, described this country as capable of being made the Empire of the East. But notwithstanding all he may from interested motives say—and as this letter is only for your own private perusal—I do not scruple to pronounce that in the whole world there is not a worse country than what we have yet seen of this.

All that is contiguous to us is so very barren and forbidding that it may with truth be said here nature is reversed; and if not so, she is nearly worn out, for almost all the seeds we have put into the ground has rotted, and I have no doubt but will, like the wood of this vile country when burned or rotten, turn to sand. This latter is a fact that has been proved, and will, I much fear, be fatally felt by some of its present inhabitants. I say the present, because if the minister has a true and just description given him of it he will not surely think of sending any more people here.

If he does, I shall not scruple to say that he will entail misery on all that are sent and an expense of the mother country that in the days of her greatest prosperity she was not equal to, for there is not one article that can ever be necessary for the use of man but which must be imported into this country. It is very certain that the whole face of it is covered with trees, but not one bit of timber have we yet found that is fit for any other purpose than to make the pot boil. Of the general opinion entertained here of the wretched prospect we have before us I cannot, I think, give you a more convincing proof than that every person (except the two gentlemen already mentioned, whose sentiments I am perfectly unacquainted with) who came out with a design of remaining in the country are now most earnestly wishing to get away from it.

ARTHUR PHILLIP

The Contemplation of Order

Some months after setting foot in the cove he named after Lord Sydney, Governor Arthur Phillip penned this official report. In it we are given a vision of the city's progress, of the imposition of order upon a chaotic wilderness. 'Future regularity is clearly discerned,' wrote Phillip, referring as much one suspects to his hopes for the conduct of his charges as to the development of the settlement.

The nature of Phillip's 'future town' is made clear by its topography. The main roads terminate at the 'governor's house, the main guard, and the criminal court'. The settlement also conforms to a much older pattern of human occupation in the Sydney region: like many Aboriginal campsites it lies near water on a north-facing shore where it catches the winter sun and is sheltered from the chilling southerly and westerly winds.

There are few things more pleasing than the contemplation of order and useful arrangement, arising gradually out of tumult and confusion; and perhaps this satisfaction cannot anywhere be more fully enjoyed than where a settlement of civilised people is fixing itself upon a newly discovered or savage coast.

The wild appearance of land entirely untouched by cultivation, the close and perplexed growing of trees, interrupted now and then by barren spots, bare rocks, or spaces overgrown with weeds, flowers, flowering shrubs, or underwood, scattered and intermingled in the most promiscuous manner, are the first objects that present themselves; afterwards, the irregular placing of the first tents which are pitched, or huts which are erected for immediate accommodation, wherever chance presents a spot tolerably free from obstacles, or more easily cleared than the rest, with the bustle of various hands busily employed in a number of the most incongruous works, increases rather than diminishes the disorder, and produces a confusion of effect, which for a time appears inextricable, and seems to threaten an endless continuance of perplexity. But by degrees large spaces are opened, plans are formed, lines marked, and a prospect at least of future regularity is clearly discerned, and is made the more striking by the recollection of the former confusion.

To this latter state the settlement at Sydney Cove had now at length arrived, and is so represented...Lines are there traced out which distinguish the principal street of an intended town, to be terminated by the governor's house, the main guard and the criminal court. In some parts of this space temporary barracks at present stand, but no permanent buildings will be suffered to be placed, except in conformity to the plan laid down. Should the town be still further extended in future, the form of other streets is also traced in such a manner as to ensure a free circulation of air. The principal streets, according to this design, will be two hundred feet wide; the ground proposed for them to the southward is nearly level and is altogether an excellent situation for buildings.

It is proposed by Governor Phillip that when houses are to be built here, the grants of land shall be made with such clauses as will prevent the building of more than one house on one allotment, which is to consist of sixty feet in front, and one hundred and fifty feet in depth. These regulations will preserve a kind of uniformity in the buildings, prevent narrow streets, and exclude many inconveniences which a rapid increase of inhabitants might otherwise occasion hereafter. It has been also an object of the governor's attention to place the public buildings in situations that will be eligible at all times, and particularly to give the storehouses and hospital sufficient space for future enlargement, should it be found necessary.

The first huts that were erected here were composed of very perishable materials, the soft wood of the cabbage palm, being only designed to afford immediate shelter. The necessity of using the wood quite green made it also the less likely to prove durable. The huts of the convicts were still more slight, being composed only of upright posts, wattled with slight twigs, and plastered up with clay. Barracks and huts were afterwards formed of materials rather more lasting. Buildings of stone might easily have been raised, had there been any means of procuring lime for mortar. The stone which has been found is of three sorts: a fine free stone, reckoned equal in goodness to that of Portland; an indifferent kind of sandstone, or firestone; and a sort which appears to contain a mixture of iron. But neither chalk, nor any species of limestone has yet been discovered.

In building a small house for the governor on the eastern side of the cove...lime was made of oyster shells, collected in the neighbouring coves; but it cannot be expected that lime should be supplied in this manner for many buildings, or indeed for any of great extent. Till this difficulty shall be removed by the discovery of chalk or limestone, the public buildings must go on very slowly, unless care be taken to send out those articles as ballast in all the ships destined for Port Jackson. In the meantime the materials can only be laid in clay, which makes it necessary to give great thickness to the walls, and even then they are not so firm as might be wished. Good clay for bricks is found near Sydney Cove and very good bricks have been made. The wood, from the specimens that have been received in England, appears to be good; it is heavy indeed, but fine grained, and apparently strong and free from knots. The imperfections that were found in it at first arose probably from the want of previous seasoning.

The hospital is placed on the west side of the cove, in a very healthful situation, entirely clear of the town; and is built in such a manner as to last for some years. On the high ground between the hospital and the town, if water can be found by sinking wells, it is the governor's intention to erect the barracks, surrounding them with proper works. These were to have been begun as soon as the transports were cleared, and the men hutted, but the progress of work was rendered so slow by the want of an adequate number of able workmen that it was necessary to postpone that undertaking for a time. The ground marked out for a church lies still nearer to the town, so that this edifice will form in part one side of the principal parade.

The design which demanded the most immediate execution was that of a storehouse, which might be secure from the danger of fire. In a country exposed to frequent storms of thunder and lightning, it was rather an uneasy situation to have all the provisions and other necessaries lodged in wooden buildings, covered with thatch of the most combustible kind. On the point of land that forms the west side of the cove, and on an elevated spot, a small observatory has been raised under the direction of Lieutenant Dawes, who was charged by the Board of Longitude with the care of observing the expected comet...

A small house, built by the lieutenant-governor for himself, forms at present the corner of the parade; the principal street will be carried on at right angles with the front of this building. Instead of thatch, they now use shingles made from a tree in appearance like a fir, but producing a wood not unlike the English oak.[†] This, though more secure than thatching, is not enough so for storehouses. For these, if slatestone should not be found, tiles must be made of the clay which has been used for bricks. The principal farm is situated in the next cove to the east of the town, and less than half a mile from it.[‡] When the plan was drawn it contained about nine acres laid down in corn of different kinds. Later accounts speak of six acres of

[†] A species of casuarina.
[‡] Farm Cove: now the Royal Botanic Gardens.

wheat, eight of barley, and six of other grain, as raised on the public account, and in a very promising way.

Sydney Cove lies open to the north-west, and is continued in a south-west direction for near a thousand yards, gradually decreasing from the breadth of about one thousand four hundred feet, till it terminates in a point, where it receives a small stream of fresh water. The anchorage extends about two thousand feet up the cove, and has soundings in general of four fathoms near the shore, and five, six, or seven, nearer the middle of the channel. It is perfectly secure in all winds; and, for a considerable way up on both sides, ships can lie almost close to the shore: nor are there, in any part of it, rocks or shallows to render the navigation dangerous. Such a situation could not fail to appear desirable to a discerning man.

WATKIN TENCH

An Extraordinary Calamity

Watkin Tench was a professional soldier. He had fought in the War of American Independence before enlisting to sail with the First Fleet in 1787. Despite his bellicose profession he was a compassionate man, and the devastation wrought among the Aborigines by the smallpox epidemic of 1789 appalled him. The death of Arabanoo was both a personal blow to Tench (who regarded the Eora man as a friend) and a disaster for the colony, for without him there was little hope of relations improving between black and white.

Arabanoo had been kidnapped at Manly Cove in December 1788 and until they could learn his name the English called him 'Manly'. By April 1789, and partly as a consequence of the ravages of this new disease, Phillip felt that Arabanoo was sufficiently comfortable among Europeans and released him from the restraints that had hitherto kept him in the settlement.

The origin of the smallpox epidemic has continued to baffle historians. Some think the disease was introduced by Asian visitors to northern Australia and arrived in Sydney via a continental route. Watkin Tench noted that 'variolous matter' (scabs collected from mild cases of smallpox and used for immunisation) was carried with the First Fleet, but that it had remained sealed in a bottle. He also speculated that the French La Perouse expedition carried the disease to Botany Bay. Aboriginal oral history, as recorded by Obed West a century later, supports this. A low-population density and the rigorous quarantine enforced by the Eora may explain why it took smallpox fourteen months to appear at Port Jackson after its release at Botany Bay. Whatever the origins of the epidemic, there is no evidence that the disease was deliberately introduced or spread by the Europeans.

April 1789—An extraordinary calamity was now observed among the natives. Repeated accounts, brought by our boats, of finding bodies of the Indians in all the coves and inlets of the harbour, caused the gentlemen of our hospital to procure some of them for the purposes of examination and anatomy.

On inspection, it appeared that all the parties had died a natural death. Pustules, similar to those occasioned by the smallpox, were thickly spread on the bodies; but how a disease to which our former observations had led us to suppose them strangers could at once have introduced itself, and have spread so widely, seemed inexplicable. Whatever might be the cause, the existence of the malady could no longer be doubted.

Intelligence was brought that an Indian family lay sick in a neighbouring cove. The governor, attended by Arabanoo and a surgeon, went in a boat immediately to the spot. Here they found an old man stretched before a few lighted sticks and a boy of nine or ten years old pouring water on his head from a shell which he held in his hand. Near them lay a female child dead, and a little farther off, her unfortunate mother. The body of the woman showed that famine, superadded to disease, had occasioned her death.

Eruptions covered the poor boy from head to foot, and the old man was so reduced that he was with difficulty got into the boat. Their situation rendered them incapable of escape and they quietly submitted to be led away. Arabanoo, contrary to his usual character, seemed at first unwilling to render them any assistance, but his shyness soon wore off, and he treated them with the kindest attention. Nor would he leave the place until he had buried the corpse of the child. That of the woman he did not see from its situation and as his countrymen did not point it out the governor ordered that it should not be shown to him.

He scooped a grave in the sand with his hands, of no peculiarity of shape, which he lined completely with grass and put the body into it, covering it also with grass; and then he filled up the hole and raised over it a small mound with the earth which had been removed. Here the ceremony ended, unaccompanied by any invocation to a superior being, or any attendant circumstance whence an inference of their religious opinions could be deduced.

An uninhabited house near the hospital was allotted for their reception and a cradle prepared for each of them. By the encouragement of Arabanoo, who assured them of protection, and the soothing behaviour of our medical gentlemen, they became at once reconciled to us and looked happy and grateful at the change of their situation. Sickness and hunger had, however, so much exhausted the old man that little hope was entertained of his recovery.

As he pointed frequently to his throat at the insistence of Arabanoo, he tried to wash it with a gargle which was given to him; but the obstructed, tender state of the part rendered it impracticable. *Bàdo, bàdo* (water) was his cry. When brought to him he drank largely at intervals of it. He was equally importunate for fire, being seized with shivering fits, and one was kindled. Fish were produced to tempt him to eat, but he turned away his head with signs of loathing. Nanbaree (the boy), on the contrary, no sooner saw them than he leaped from his cradle and eagerly seizing them, began to cook them. A warm bath being prepared, they were immersed in it; and after being thoroughly cleansed they had clean shirts put on them and were again laid in bed.

The old man lived but a few hours. He bore the pangs of dissolution with patient composure and, though he was sensible to the last moment, expired almost without a groan. Nanbaree appeared quite unmoved at the event and surveyed the corpse of his father without emotion, simply exclaiming, *bò-ee* (dead). This surprised us, as the tenderness and anxiety of the old man about the boy had been very moving. Although barely able to raise his head, while so much strength was left to him, he kept looking into his child's cradle. He patted him gently on the bosom and, with dying eyes, seemed to recommend him to our humanity and protection. Nanbaree was adopted by Mr White, surgeon-general of the settlement, and became henceforth one of his family.

Arabanoo had no sooner heard of the death of his countryman than he hastened to inter him. I was present at the ceremony, in company with the governor, Captain Ball and two or three other persons. It differed, by the accounts of those who were present at the funeral of the girl, in no respect from what had passed there in the morning, except that the grave was dug by a convict. But I was informed that when intelligence of the death reached Arabanoo, he expressed himself with doubt whether he should bury or burn the body, and seemed solicitous to ascertain which ceremony would be most gratifying to the governor.

Indeed, Arabanoo's behaviour during the whole of the transactions of this day was so strongly marked by affection to his countryman and by confidence in us that the governor resolved to free him from all farther restraint and at once to trust to his generosity, and the impression which our treatment of him might have made, for his future residence among us. The fetter was accordingly taken off his leg...

May 1789—I feel assured that I have no reader who will not join in regretting the premature loss of Arabanoo, who died of the smallpox on the 18th instant, after languishing in it six days. From some imperfect marks and indents on his face we were inclined to believe that he had passed this dreaded disorder. Even when the first symptoms of sickness seized him, we continued willing to hope that they proceeded from a different cause. But at length the disease burst forth with irresistible fury. It were superfluous to say that nothing which medical skill and unremitting attention could perform were left unexerted to mitigate his sufferings, and prolong a life which humanity and affectionate concern towards his sick compatriots unfortunately shortened.

During his sickness he reposed entire confidence in us. Although a stranger to medicine and nauseating the taste of it, he swallowed with patient submission innumerable drugs, which the hope of relief induced us to administer to him.* The governor, who particularly regarded him, caused him to be buried in his own garden and attended the funeral in person.

The character of Arabanoo, as far as we had developed it, was distinguished by a portion of gravity and steadiness which our subsequent acquaintance with his countrymen by no means led us to conclude a national characteristic. In that daring, enterprising frame of mind which, when combined with genius, constitutes the leader

---

* Very different had been his conduct on a former occasion of a similar kind. Soon after he was brought among us he was seized with a diarrhoea, for which he could by no persuasion be induced to swallow any of our prescriptions. After many ineffectual trials to deceive or overcome him, it was at length determined to let him pursue his own course and to watch if he should apply for relief to any of the productions of the country. He was in consequence observed to dig fern-root and to chew it. Whether the disorder had passed its crisis, or whether the fern-root effected a cure, I know not; but it is certain that he became speedily well.

of a horde of savages, or the ruler of a people, boasting the power of discrimination and the resistance of ambition, he was certainly surpassed by some of his successors who afterwards lived among us. His countenance was thoughtful but not animated. His fidelity and gratitude, particularly to his friend the governor, were constant and undeviating and deserve to be recorded.

Although of a gentle and placable temper, we early discovered that he was impatient of indignity and allowed of no superiority on our part. He knew that he was in our power, but the independence of his mind never forsook him. If the slightest insult were offered to him, he would return it with interest. At retaliation of merriment he was often happy, and frequently turned the laugh against his antagonist. He did not want docility, but either from the difficulty of acquiring our language, from the unskilfulness of his teachers, or from some natural defect, his progress in learning it was not equal to what we had expected.

For the last three or four weeks of his life, hardly any restraint was laid upon his inclinations, so that had he meditated escape, he might easily have effected it. He was, perhaps, the only native who was ever attached to us from choice, and who did not prefer a precarious subsistence among wilds and precipices to the comforts of a civilised system.

DAVID COLLINS
Caesar Renders unto Himself

As judge-advocate, David Collins had every crime committed in the colony paraded before him. Despite an obvious lack of legal training he handled most of his onerous duties well. Yet his 'cheerful and social disposition' suffered greatly from what he saw and experienced in the colony, and by the time he died in Hobart in 1810 he was weighed down by the injustices of the world. Collins believed that 'nature intended and fashioned me to ascend the pulpit', and he sometimes does seem like a cleric in a Regency novel. His *Account of the English Colony in New South Wales* is an often gloomy but fascinating litany of the failings of humanity in an outpost of empire.

Here we find him confronted with the 'incorrigibly stubborn' Caesar, a Negro convict. Caesar's threat to 'create a laugh' by playing a trick upon the executioner if hanged seems to have disturbed Collins, for if hangings were a joking matter then the entire colony must have been a farce. The play Collins writes of, George Farquhar's comedy *The Recruiting Officer*, was the first to be performed in Sydney. In one scene the recruits march off merrily singing 'over the hill and far away'. Like everyone in the colony they too must leave their loved ones behind.

May 1789—Towards the end of the month, some convicts having reported that they had found the body of a white man lying in a cove at a short distance from the settlement, a general muster of the convicts at Sydney was directed; but no person was unaccounted for except Caesar, an incorrigibly stubborn black, who had absconded a few days before from the service of one of the officers, and taken to the woods with some provisions, an iron pot and a soldier's musket, which he had found means to steal.

Garden robberies, after Caesar's flight, were frequent and, some leads belonging to a seine being stolen, a reward of a pardon was held out to any of the accomplices on discovering the person who stole them; and the like reward was also offered if, in five days, he should discover the person who had purchased them; but all was without effect. It was conjectured that they had been stolen for the purpose of being converted into shot by some person not employed or authorised to kill the game of this country.

The weather during the latter part of this month was cold; notwithstanding which a turtle was seen in the harbour.

4 June—The anniversary of his Majesty's birthday, the second time of commemorating it in this country, was observed with every distinction in our power; for the first time, the ordnance belonging to the colony were discharged; the detachment of marines fired three volleys, which were followed by twenty-one guns from each of the ships of war in the cove; the governor received the compliments due to the day in his new house, of which he had lately taken possession as the government house of the colony, where his Excellency afterwards entertained the officers at dinner, and in the evening some of the convicts were permitted to perform Farquhar's comedy of *The Recruiting Officer*, in a hut fitted up for the occasion. They professed no higher aim than 'humbly to excite a smile', and their efforts to please were not unattended by applause...

Caesar, being closely attended to, was at length apprehended and secured. This man was always reputed the hardest-working convict in the country; his frame was muscular and well calculated for hard labour; but in his intellects he did not very widely differ from a brute; his appetite was ravenous, for he could in any one day devour the full ration for two days. To gratify this appetite he was compelled to steal from others, and all his thefts were directed to that purpose. He was such a wretch, and so indifferent about meeting death that he declared, while in confinement, that if he should be hanged he would create a laugh before he was turned off, by playing off some trick upon the executioner. Holding up such a mere animal as an example was not expected to have the proper or intended effect; the governor, therefore, with the humanity that was always conspicuous in his exercise of the authority vested in him, directed that he should be sent to Garden Island, there to work in fetters; and in addition to his ration of provisions he was to be supplied with vegetables from the garden.

RALPH CLARK

A Child for a Hat

Ralph Clark's journal from 10 March 1788 to 15 February 1790 is lost. Here, as he resumes his narrative, we encounter a very different man. Gone are the erotic dreams, the adulation of Alicia's image and the skittish fear of thunder and insects. Instead Clark has become vitally interested in this new land and is trusted by the Eora people.

At some time during the missing interval Clark had succumbed to 'whordome' and had taken up with Mary Branham, a convict, who bore him a daughter named Alicia. In 1792 Clark was reunited with his family in England but, inexplicably, he sailed again the following year to fight the French in the West Indies, taking young Ralph with him. On 18 June 1794 Clark died of yellow fever, and his son eleven days later. Unknown to Clark, his wife Alicia had died in childbirth a short time earlier.

Munday 15 February 1790—Fine clear weather—went up the Harbour in my Boat and went into Lane Cove where I was Yesterday to See Dourrawan and Tirriwan the two Natives that I exchanged the hatchet with Yesterday for there two Spears— I had not gone far up the cove before I Saw the Smook of there fires for which I rowd not Seeing any thing of them— I Cald to them for I was certain that they could not be a great way from me—they Soon Answerd me I then got out of the Boat (Davis) my Convict Servant who was in the Boat with me begd of me not to goe on Shore—he is one of the greatest Cowards living—

I cald to them again when I got to ther fire for they had run into the bush on there Seing the Boat pulling towards them—they could See me although I could See nothing of them—on there Seing that it was me who had given them the Hatchet Yesterday they came down to me—they had left Some Muscle on the fire to roast which they both begd of me to eat Some of—before I left the Boat I disired Ellis and (Squirs) my other convict Servant that Should they attempt to throu any of their Spears at me or them to fire without waiting for my Orders but when they found that I had offerd them no harm yesterday they came to me without any weapens—I made Ellis, Davis and Squirs come on Shore to them—Davis trembled the whole time—

I herd the crying of children close to me—I asked them for to goe and bring me there (*Dins*) which is there woman and I would give there woman Some bits of different coulerd cloath which I had brought on purpose to give to them—they made me to understand that there were no women there... Dourrawan went and brought a Boy a bout 3 Years old on his Shoulder—the child was as much frightend at use as Davis was at them—I then desired Tirriwan to goe and bring me down one of his children as Dourrawan informd me that he was the father of the Child he had brought down and that his woman the mother of his child was (*poc*) dead of the (*mittayon*) Small Pox—

Tirriwan brought also down a Boy much a bout the same age as the other—Tirriwan child was not quite Recoverd from the Small Pox—I asked him for his (*din*) he Said that She was up in the wood given a Young child the (*nipan*) the Breast—I gave each of the children a bit of Red cloath—I asked them if they would give me the children for my hatt which they Seemd to wish most for but they would not on any account part with there children which I liked them for—the Governour has often asked me as the Natives Seemd not So much affraid of me as they are of every body else to take one of them and bring them in—

Yesterday and to day I might with great ease and without running any danger have taken these two men but as I told Ellis when he asked me if I did not intend to take them I told him that it would be very Ungenerous to take them for after they had place Such confidence in us that I could not think of doing it for if I had taken them both what would have become of there young children they must have Starved...

The Barefoot Colony

This anonymous letter describing the condition of the marines two years after their landing in Sydney reveals details passed over in the official journals. It was written when things were at their lowest ebb. News had just arrived of the wreck of the *Sirius*, the colony's principal lifeline to the outside world. This left the tiny tender *Supply* as the sole vessel available to the settlement.

Around this time Surgeon White lamented to his friend in London Mr Skill, 'dealer in hams, tongues and salt salmon', that just enough four-year-old salt pork and flour remained to 'enable us to drag out a miserable existence for seven months', if supplied as half-rations. 'In the name of heaven,' White continued, 'what has the ministry been about? Surely they have quite forgotten or neglected us...It would be wise...to withdraw the settlement, at least such as are living...The *Supply*, tender, sails tomorrow for Batavia, in hopes the Dutch may be able to send in time to save us; should any action happen to her, Lord have mercy on us!'

As the writer of this letter (possibly Watkin Tench) informs us, dignity vanished as the staples ran out. That Tench continued to maintain his marvellous journal through this hell-like period is cause for admiration.

14 April 1790—By the time this reaches you, the fate of this settlement, and all it contains, will be decided. It is now more than two years since we landed here, and within less than a month of three since we left England. So cut off from all intercourse with the rest of mankind are we, that, subsequent to the month of August 1788, we know not of any transaction that has happened in Europe, and are no more assured of the welfare or existence of any of our friends than of what passes in the moon. It is by those only who have felt the anguish and distress of such a state that its miseries can be conceived...the dread of perishing by famine stares us in the face...

Our present allowance is a short one: two pounds of pork (which was cured four years ago, and shrinks to nothing if boiled), two pounds and a half of flour, a pound of rice and a pint of pease per week is what we live upon. Now, on this ration, reduced as it is, I have no fear of being able to crawl on for many months to come; so that if Heaven be but favourable to the voyage of the *Supply* (and, thank God, she is ably commanded and navigated as any ship in the King's service) all things will yet do, for when I spoke of only eight weeks' provisions in the stores, I meant at full allowance, whereas what we are at at present is but a third.

Again, to help us out, we use every means to get fish, and sometimes with good success, which is an incredible relief. On the fishing service, the officers, civil and military, take it in turns every night to go out for the whole night in the fishing boats; and the military, besides, keep a guard at Botany Bay, and carry on a fishery there, taking it three days and three days, turn and turn about.

Were the ground good, our gardens would be found of infinite use to us in these days of scarcity, but with all our efforts we cannot draw much from them; however, they afford something, and by industry and incessant fatigue mine is one of the best. Were you to see us digging, hoeing and planting, it would make you smile.

As to parade duties and show, we have long laid them aside, except the mounting of a small guard by day and a picket at night. Our soldiers have not a shoe, and mount guard barefoot. 'Pride, pomp, and circumstance of glorious war are at an end.' After having suffered what we do, I shall be grievously hurt, on landing in England, to meet the sneers of a set of holiday troops, whose only employ has been to powder their hair, polish their shoes and go through the routine of a field-day, though I must own that our air, gait and raggedness will give them some title to be merry at our expense.

RICHARD JOHNSON

The Smell Was So Offensive

The arrival of the Second Fleet in June and July 1790 should have brought relief to the starving inhabitants of Sydney. When the *Justinian* transport entered the Heads on 20 June laden with stores, the crisis seemed to be over—until a week later a floating catastrophe arrived. Not only had the *Guardian* supply ship been holed by an iceberg in December 1789 and her cargo lost, but the state of the male convicts, who were shipped to Port Jackson on the *Neptune*, *Scarborough* and *Surprize*, beggared belief. Many were dead or dying upon arrival and the beautiful harbour was soon dotted with bodies that had been thrown overboard as if they were cattle.

Surgeon White left no record of his reaction to the fleet's arrival, but we can guess at the fury and helplessness that he must have felt. Here the colony's pastor, Richard Johnson, gives us an unforgettably vivid account of the arrival of that floating hell. Added to the smallpox, starvation and criminality already existing in the settlement, it was a reminder of how Enlightenment Europe manifested itself in Australia. It also forcibly reminds us that mateship was yet to develop in this nascent society.

July 1790—The *Lady Juliana* brought out from England 226 women convicts, out of which she had only buried five, though they had been on board for about fifteen months. The case was much otherwise with the other three ships.

There were on board:

	Died on board	Sick landed
The *Neptune*, 520	163	269
The *Scarborough*, 252	68	96
The *Surprize*, 211	42	121

The short calculation or account given me will account for what I am going to relate.

Have been on board these different ships. Was first on board the *Surprize*. Went down amongst the convicts, where I beheld a sight truly shocking to the feelings of humanity, a great number of them laying, some half and others nearly quite naked, without either bed or bedding, unable to turn or help themselves. Spoke to them as I passed along, but the smell was so offensive that I could scarcely bear it.

I then went on board the *Scarborough*; proposed to go down amongst them, but was dissuaded from it by the captain. The *Neptune* was still more wretched and intolerable, and therefore never attempted it.

Some of these unhappy people died after the ships came into the harbour, before they could be taken on shore—part of these had been thrown into the harbour, and their dead bodies cast upon the shore, and were seen laying naked upon the rocks. Took an occasion to represent this to his Excellency, in consequence of which immediate orders were sent on board that those who died on board should be carried to the opposite north shore and be buried.

The landing of these people was truly affecting and shocking; great numbers were not able to walk, nor to move hand or foot; such were slung over the ship side in the same manner as they would sling a cask, a box or anything of that nature. Upon their being brought up to the open air some fainted, some died upon deck, and others in the boat before they reached the shore. When come on shore many were not able to walk, to stand or to stir themselves in the least, hence some were led by others. Some creeped upon their hands and knees, and some were carried upon the backs of others.

The next thing to be considered was what was to be done with all these miserable objects. Besides the sick that were in the hospital previous to the arrival of the fleet, there were now landed not less than 486 sick; but the hospital erected here is not sufficient to hold above sixty or eighty at most; what then must be done with the rest?

It was fortunate that a new hospital was brought out in the *Justinian*. This was set up with all speed; a great number of tents, in all ninety or a hundred, were pitched. In each of these tents there were about four sick people; here they lay in a most deplorable situation. At first they had nothing to lay upon but the damp ground, many scarcely a rag to cover them. Grass was got for them to lay upon, and a blanket given amongst the four of them. Have been amongst them for hours, may say days together, going from one tent to another, from one person to another, and you may imagine that what I here beheld was not a little affecting.

The number landed sick were near five hundred, most at the hospital, and some few dispersed here and there throughout the camp. The misery I saw amongst them is unexpressible; many were not able to turn, or even to stir themselves, and in this situation were covered over almost with their own nastiness; their heads, bodies, cloths, blanket, all full of filth and lice. Scurvy was not the only nor the worst disease that prevailed amongst them (one man I visited this morning, I think, I may say safely had 10,000 lice upon his body and bed). Some were exercised with violent fevers, and others with a not less violent purging and flux.

The complaints they had to make were no less affecting to the ear than their outward condition was to the eye. The usage they met with on board, according to their own story, was truly shocking; sometimes for days, nay, for a considerable time together, they have been to the middle in water chained together, hand and leg, even the sick not exempted—nay, many died with the chains upon them. Promises, entreaties, were all in vain, and it was not till a very few days before they made the harbour that they were released out of irons…

You will, perhaps, be astonished when I tell you a little of the villainy of these wretched people. Some would complain they had no jackets, shirts, or trousers, and begged that I would intercede for them. Some by this means have had two, three, four—nay, one man not less than six different slops given him, which he would take an opportunity to sell to some others, and then make the same complaints and entreaties. When any of them were near dying, and had something given them as bread or lillipie (flour and water boiled together), or any other necessaries, the person next to him or others would catch the bread &c. out of his hand and, with an oath, say that he was going to die, and therefore it would be of no service to him.

No sooner would the breath be out of any of their bodies than others would watch them and strip them entirely naked. Instead of alleviating the distresses of each other, the weakest were sure to go to the wall. In the night-time, which at this time is very cold, and especially this would be felt in the tents, where they had nothing but grass to lay on and a blanket amongst four of them, he that was strongest of the four would take the whole blanket to himself and leave the rest quite naked.

DANIEL SOUTHWELL

A Great Whale

Daniel Southwell spent many a lonely month in New South Wales, for he was left to tend the distant signal station on South Head and without a boat was a virtual prisoner on the promontory. His interminable boredom was occasionally enlivened with moments of terror, such as when three of his colleagues were drowned after encountering a whale. James O'Hara, an eyewitness, wrote that the errant creature was a 'spermaceti [sperm] whale' and elaborated that, on finding the beast in the harbour, 'those who were best acquainted with the nature of this enormous animal were not without a degree of alarm...He differs, it seems, much from his dull kindred in the north seas, and in nothing more than in a disposition to mischief. Several boats were gallantly put off with harpoons, but from the unskilfulness of the adventurers returned with the sole success of having escaped him.'

27 July 1790—My next tale of woe is, alas! a recent one...Having long been without a boat (which by the by is cruel), we are at times glad to meet with a conveyance up to Sydney Cove. How pleasant and shining was the day when our much esteemed and sadly regretted companion and messmate Mr Jno. [James] Ferguson, as we wanted provision, took the opportunity of a boat which had been down the harbour fishing! He also had with him Jno. Bates (a marine), a man who from his good conduct had deservedly become a favourite with us...

It was Friday the 23rd when, having breakfasted here, these two got into a little flat-bottomed boat originally calculated for shuting in shoalwater (called by us a pont). Besides these were two marines who had been trying their luck all night, and called in here, as we had given them leave (for they were good lads) anytime to do.

They had not got above one third of the way, being a short mile below Point Bradley, and nearly in the mid-stream, when a great whale appeared (for the first time since we have been here) in the harbour, spouting and dashing about in their usual manner. This monstrous creature, either through being mischievous or playful, no sooner espied the boat than he pursued and never left her till he had overturned and sent her to the bottom.

For more than ten minutes were these unfortunates a prey to inexpressible anguish and horror. At first, in rising, he half filled the boat, and with their hands against the whale did they bear the boat off. In vain they threw out their hats, the bags for our provisions and the fish they had caught in hopes to satisfy him or turn his attention. It seemed bent on their destruction, and with one sudden and tremendous gambol consigned three of their number to their hapless fate and an endless eternity.

Neither of those I've mentioned by name could swim; the survivor's comrade could, even the best, but through being heavily clad went down, after having several times complained of his inability to hold up, the other affectionately encouraging him, but in vain; they were friends, and greatly attached.

One gained the rocks a small distance below Rose Bay with much difficulty, and returning to the Look-out related this afflicting circumstance. The poor fellow was sadly affected, and indeed disordered.

WATKIN TENCH
Spearing the Governor

The whale which overturned the fishing boat and drowned Daniel Southwell's friend was pursued by those bent on vengeance, and harpooned several times.

It eventually died of its wounds, and its carcass washed up in Manly Cove. Aborigines came to feast on it from near and far, including Bennelong and Colbee. When Governor Phillip arrived on the scene he was greeted by these old friends. At that moment a stranger, a man named Wileemarin appeared. He had almost certainly never seen a European before. As Phillip approached him, Wileemarin panicked.

7 September 1790—The tremendous monster, who had occasioned the unhappy catastrophe just recorded, was fated to be the cause of farther mischief to us.

On the 7th instant, Captain Nepean of the New South Wales corps, and Mr White, accompanied by little Nanbaree and a party of men, went in a boat to Manly Cove, intending to land there and walk on to Broken Bay. On drawing near the shore, a dead whale in the most disgusting state of putrefaction was seen lying on the beach, and at least two hundred Indians surrounding it, broiling the flesh on different fires and feasting on it with the most extravagant marks of greediness and rapture. As the boat continued to approach they were observed to fall into confusion and to pick up their spears, on which our people lay upon their oars and Nanbaree, stepping forward, harangued them for some time assuring them that we were friends.

Mr White now called for Bennelong who, on hearing his name, came forth and entered into conversation. He was greatly emaciated, and so far disfigured by a long beard that our people not without difficulty recognised their old acquaintance. His answering in broken English, and inquiring for the governor, however, soon corrected their doubts. He seemed quite friendly. And soon after Colbee came up, pointing to his leg to show that he had freed himself from the fetter which was upon him when he had escaped from us.

When Bennelong was told that the governor was not far off, he expressed great joy and declared that he would immediately go in search of him, and if he found him not, would follow him to Sydney. 'Have you brought any hatchets with you?' cried he. Unluckily they had not any which they chose to spare; but two or three shirts, some handkerchiefs, knives and other trifles were given to them, and seemed to satisfy. Bennelong, willing to instruct his countrymen, tried to put on a shirt, but managed it so awkwardly that a man of the name of McEntire, the governor's gamekeeper, was directed by Mr White to assist him.

This man, who was well known to him, he positively forbade to approach, eyeing him ferociously and with every mark of horror and resentment. He was in consequence left to himself, and the conversation proceeded as before. The length of his beard seemed to annoy him much, and he expressed eager wishes to be shaved, asking repeatedly for a razor. A pair of scissors was given to him, and he showed he had not forgotten how to use such an instrument, for he forthwith began to clip his hair with it...

Our party now thought it time to proceed on their original expedition, and having taken leave of their sable friends, rowed to some distance, where they landed and set out for Broken Bay, ordering the coxswain of the boat in which they had come down to go immediately and acquaint the governor of all that had passed. When the natives saw that the boat was about to depart, they crowded around her, and brought down, by way of a present, three or four great junks of the whale, and put them on board of her, the largest of which Bennelong expressly requested might be offered, in his name, to the governor.

It happened that his Excellency had this day gone to a land-mark, which was building on the South Head, near the flagstaff, to serve as a direction to ships at sea, and the boat met him on his return to Sydney. Immediately on receiving the intelligence he hastened back to the South Head, and having procured all the firearms which could be mustered there, consisting of four muskets and a pistol, set out attended by Mr Collins and Lieutenant Waterhouse of the navy.

When the boat reached Manly Cove the natives were found still busily employed around the whale. As they expressed not any consternation on seeing us row to the beach, Governor Phillip stepped out unarmed and attended by one seaman only, and called for Bennelong, who appeared but, notwithstanding his former eagerness, would not suffer the other to approach him for several minutes. Gradually, however, he warmed into friendship and frankness and, presently after, Colbee came up.

They discoursed for some time, Bennelong expressing pleasure to see his old acquaintance, and inquiring by name for every person whom he could recollect at Sydney; and among others for a French cook, one of the governor's servants, whom he had constantly made the butt of his ridicule by mimicking his voice, gait, and other peculiarities, all of which he again went through with his wonted exactness and drollery. He asked also particularly for a lady from whom he had once ventured to snatch a kiss and, on being told that she was well, by way of proving that the token was fresh in his remembrance, he kissed Lieutenant Waterhouse, and laughed aloud...

Matters had proceeded in this friendly train for more than half an hour, when a native with a spear in his hand came forward, and stopped at the distance of between twenty and thirty yards from the place where the governor, Mr Collins, Lieutenant Waterhouse and a seaman stood. His Excellency held out his hand and called to him, advancing towards him at the same time, Mr Collins following close behind.

He appeared to be a man of middle age, short of stature, sturdy and well set, seemingly a stranger and but little acquainted with Bennelong and Colbee. The nearer the governor approached, the greater became the terror and agitation of the Indian. To remove his fear, Governor Phillip threw down a dirk, which he wore at his side. The other, alarmed at the rattle of the dirk, and probably misconstruing the action, instantly fixed his lance in his throwing-stick.

To retreat his Excellency now thought would be more dangerous than to advance. He therefore cried out to the man, *Weè-ree, Weè-ree* (bad, you are doing wrong), displaying at the same time every token of amity and confidence. The words had, however, hardly gone forth when the Indian, stepping back with one foot, aimed his lance with such force and dexterity that, striking the governor's right shoulder just above the collarbone, the point glancing downward, came out at his back, having made a wound of many inches long.* The man was observed to keep his eye steadily fixed on the lance until it struck its object, when he directly dashed into the woods and was seen no more.

Instant confusion on both sides took place. Bennelong and Colbee disappeared and several spears were thrown from different quarters, though without effect. Our party retreated as fast as they could, calling to those who were left in the boat to hasten up with firearms. A situation more distressing than that of the governor, during the time that this lasted, cannot readily be conceived. The pole of the spear, not less than ten feet in length, sticking out before him and impeding his flight, the butt frequently striking the ground and lacerating the wound.

In vain did Mr Waterhouse try to break it; and the barb which appeared on the other side forbade extraction until that could be performed. At length it was broken, and his Excellency reached the boat, by which time the seamen with the muskets had got up and were endeavouring to fire them, but one only would go off, and there is no room to believe that it was attended with any execution.

When the governor got home, the wound was examined. It

---

* His Excellency described the shock to me as similar to a violent blow, with such energy was the weapon thrown.

had bled a good deal in the boat and it was doubtful whether the subclavian artery might not be divided. On moving the spear, it was found, however, that it might be safely extracted, which was accordingly performed...

From this time until the 14th, no communication passed between the natives and us. On that day, the chaplain and Lieutenant Dawes, having Abaroo with them in a boat, learned from two Indians that Wileemarin was the name of the person who had wounded the governor. These two people inquired kindly how his Excellency did, and seemed pleased to hear that he was likely to recover. They said that they were inhabitants of Rose Hill, and expressed great dissatisfaction at the number of white men who had settled in their former territories. In consequence of which declaration, the detachment at that post was reinforced on the following day.

ELIZABETH MACARTHUR

Every Bird, Insect, Flower

Elizabeth Macarthur arrived in Sydney on 28 June 1790, one of the first women to travel to the colony under her own free will. She accompanied her husband, Lieutenant John Macarthur of the New South Wales Corps, which had arrived to relieve the marines. Elizabeth soon became a nucleus around which a cultured core formed in the young settlement, and her coterie included lieutenants Watkin Tench and William Dawes. Here she writes to a friend in England, the grace of her letter providing a sharp contrast to other accounts of the colony. She might never have imagined that she would need to travel to Port Jackson to learn to play the piano.

March 1791—On my first landing, everything was new to me—every bird, every insect, flower &c.—in short, all was novelty around me, and was noticed with a degree of eager curiosity and perturbation that after a while subsided into that calmness I have already described…

We are in that habit of intimacy with Captain Tench that there are few days pass that we do not spend some part of together. Mr Dawes we do not see so frequently. He is so much engaged with the stars that to mortal eyes he is not always visible. I had the presumption to become his pupil, and meant to learn a little astronomy. It is true I have had many a pleasant walk to his house (something less than half a mile from Sydney), have given him much trouble in making orrerys and in explaining to me the general principles of the heavenly bodies; but I soon found I had mistaken my abilities, and blush at my error.

Still, I wanted something to fill up a certain vacancy in my time which could neither be done by writing, reading, or conversation. To the two first I did not feel myself always inclined, and the latter was not in my power, having no female friend to unbend my mind to, nor a single woman with whom I could converse with any satisfaction to myself, the clergyman's wife being a person in whose society I could reap neither profit nor pleasure.

These considerations made me still anxious to learn some easy science to fill up the vacuum at many a solitary day, and at length, under the auspices of Mr Dawes, I have made a small progress in botany. No country can exhibit a more copious field for botanical knowledge than this. I am arrived so far as to be able to class and order all common plants. I have found great pleasure in my study: every walk furnished me with subjects to put in practice that theory I had before gained by reading…

I shall now tell you of another resource I had to fill up some of my vacant hours. Our new house is ornamented with a pianoforte of Mr Worgan's. He kindly means to leave it with me, and now, under his direction, I have begun a new study; but I fear, without my master, I shall not make any great proficiency. I am told, however, I have done wonders in being able to play off 'God Save the King', and Foot's minuet, besides that of reading the notes with great facility.

In spite of music I have not altogether lost sight of my botanical studies. I have only been precluded from pursuing that study by the intense heat of the weather, which has not permitted me to walk much during the summer. The months of December and January have been hotter than I can describe—indeed, insufferably so, the thermometer rising from 100 to 112, which is, I believe, thirty degrees above the hottest day known in England.

The general heat is to be borne; but when we are oppressed by the hot winds we have no other resource but to shut ourselves in our houses, and to endeavour to the utmost of our power to exclude every breath of air. This wind blows from the north, and comes as if from an heated oven; it is generally succeeded by a thunderstorm, so severe and awful that it is impossible for one who has not been a witness to such a violent concussion of the elements to form any notion of it. I am not yet enough used to it to be quite unmoved, it is so different from the thunder we have in England.

WILLIAM DAWES

Gatu Piryala—We Two Are Talking to Each Other

Of all the educated minds on the First Fleet that of Lieutenant William Dawes, who fascinated Elizabeth Macarthur, remains the most mysterious, for he left

behind almost nothing except two unpublished notebooks containing a vocabulary and grammar of the Eora
language. Dawes' seclusion in his observatory gave him
both privacy and access to the Eora, who were fearful of
going into the main camp. He seems to have spent most
of his spare time getting to know them and learning their
language. At some time during 1790 or 1791 Dawes met
a young Eora woman called Patyegarang. As he tran-
scribed her language he perhaps unconsciously recorded
their increasing closeness. That Dawes cared deeply for
Patye cannot be doubted. Whether she was his lover or
simply a young female friend remains unclear.

Dawes refused to participate in the first retaliatory raid
ordered by Phillip against the Eora when the governor
demanded ten Aborigines be executed to avenge the murder
of McEntire. Nothing came of the venture. In later life
Dawes became an anti-slavery campaigner. He had intended
to stay at least three more years in New South Wales, but
was forced to leave in 1791 because of the governor's
displeasure at his refusal to participate in the raid.

Here, published for the first time, are annotated fragments of conversations with Patye in the Eora tongue.

Be-re-wal-gal   The name given to us by the natives.
Berewal   A great distance off.

★

No-tu-lu-brie-law-low-ne-lie   Sung on seeing a flock
Gnoo-roo-me, la-tie, na-tie, na-tie   of pelicans.
No-tu-lu-brie-law-low-ne-lie
Gnoo-roo-me, la-tie, na-tie, na-tie
Tar wane-nolie lar-rah-wuo

★

Dje-ra-bar or *Je-rab-ber*   The name given to the musket. The
natives frequently called us by the name they give the musket.

★

War-ran-jain-ora   I am in Sydney Cove.

★

Tāgarán, Túba, Patyegaráng,   The names of Patyegarang.
  Kanmagnál

★

Question from me to Patyegarang sometime after she had hurt
her finger.
Márrà búdjul?   Is your finger better?
Bíal, karágan   No, (I suppose) worse.

★

Gonangubye [was] desiring to wear one of Patyegarang's petticoats. I told her it was too long for her, on which she said
Gūlbagabou which Patye explained as 'I will hold it up.'

★

Gan widátye teara   Who was that drinking tea
  wúra wurá   with you?

★

Patyegarang after telling me she was very warm said *Pīnmíly-
ibaou panáwá* 'I will cool myself in the rain.' NB It then rained
quite fast.

★

Matigarbárgun náigaba   We shall sleep separate.

★

Metcoarsmadyēmínga   You winked at me.

★

Taperabárrbowaryaou   'I shall not become white.' This was
said by Patyegarang—after I had told her if she would wash
herself often she would become white—at the same time throwing
down the towel as in despair.

★

Putuwá   To warm one's hand by the fire and then to squeeze
gently the fingers of another person.

★

Wanadyemínga?   'You will not have me?' Or 'You don't want
                            my company?' Of course.

Wanadyu-inea   I don't desire your company.

★

Wúral. Wúralbadyaóu.   'Bashful. I was ashamed.' This was
said to me by Patyegarang after the departure of some strangers,
before whom I could scarce prevail upon her to read '25 Sept.
1791'.

Gwago patabágun or *Gwágun patába*   We will eat presently.

★

Goredyú tágarin   'I more it' (that is, I take more of it) 'from
cold' (that is, to take off the cold). At this time Patyegarang was
standing by the fire naked, and I desired her to put on her clothes,
on which she said *Goredyú tágarín* the full meaning of which is 'I
will or do remain longer naked in order to get warm sooner, as the
fire is felt better without clothes than if it had to penetrate
through them.' (This is a mistake. *Goredyú* signifies something
else.) *Gore* to warm.

[Dawes] *Nímadyíme, me?*   What's the matter, what?

[Patye] *Tienmilye bunín*   I am come from play.

Having sung '*Ngalgear mutigoré*' and Ngalgear being very angry
at it; I asked Patye:

[Dawes] *Minyin gūlara-ngalgear?*   Why is Ngalgear angry?

[Patye] *Beríadwarin*   Because you sung.

On singing the same again at some distance from Ngalgear,
Patyegarang said *Kamarāta heriádinye*, 'My friend, he sings
about you.'

★

[Dawes] *Minyin gyíní,*	Why don't you (learn to)
bial piyabúri whiteman?	speak like a whiteman?
[Patye] *Mangabuníga bíal*	

Not understanding this answer I asked her to explain it which she did very clearly, by giving me to understand it was because I gave her victuals, drink, everything she wanted, without putting her to the trouble of asking for it.

I then told her that a whiteman had been wounded some days ago in coming from Kadi to Waráng. I asked her why the black man did it.

[Patye] *Gulara*	(Because they are) angry.
[Dawes] *Mínyin gūlara Eora?*	Why are the black men angry?
[Patye] *Injaim galawdi w.on*	Because the white men
Tapérun kamerigal	are settled here. The
	kamarigals are afraid.
[Dawes] *Mínyi taperun kamarigal?*	Why are the kamarigals
	afraid?
[Patye] *Gánin*	(Because of the) guns.

★

[Dawes] *Minyin bial mangadyime?*	Why don't you sleep?
[Patye] *Kandulīn*	(Because of the) candle.

ARTHUR PHILLIP

Giving Away Whose Land?

James Ruse was the first person ever to coax a successful crop from the recalcitrant Australian soil. The grant of land made to him by Governor Phillip in 1792 was the first act in a tragedy of dispossession for Aboriginal Australia. It would take 200 years exactly for the country to acknowledge that Phillip's declaration was a sham. In 1992 the High Court of Australia, in delivering its *Mabo* judgment, overturned the legal fiction of *terra nullius*— the concept that no-one owned the land the British took possession of in 1788.

22 February 1792—Whereas full power and authority for granting lands in the territory of New South Wales to such persons as may be desirous of becoming settlers therein is vested in me, his Majesty's captain-general and governor-in-chief over the said territory and its dependencies, by his Majesty's instructions under the royal sign manual, bearing date respectively the twenty-fifth day of April, one thousand seven hundred and eighty-seven, and the twentieth day of August, one thousand seven hundred and eighty-nine.

In pursuance of the power and authority vested in me as aforesaid, I do by these presents give and grant unto James Ruse, his heirs and assigns, to have and to hold for ever, thirty acres of land, in one lot, to be known by the name of Experiment Farm, laying on the south of the ponds, at Parramatta, the said thirty acres of land to be had and held by him, the said James Ruse, his heirs and assigns, free from all fees, taxes, quit-rents, and other acknowledgments, for the space of ten years from the date of these presents. Provided that the said James Ruse, his heirs or assigns, shall reside within the same, and proceed to the improvement and cultivation thereof, such timber as may be growing or to grow hereafter upon the said land which may be deemed fit for naval purposes to be reserved for the use of the Crown, and paying an annual quit-rent of one shilling after the expiration of the term or time of ten years before mentioned.

In testimony whereof, I have hereunto set my hand and the seal of the territory, at Government House, Sydney, in the territory of New South Wales, this twenty-second day of February, in the year of our Lord one thousand seven hundred and ninety-two.

FRANCIS GROSE

No Place I Like Better

Francis Grose, commander of the New South Wales Corps, arrived in Sydney in 1792. His soldiers were to replace the marines led by Captain Robert Ross, and Grose himself took control of the city for two years after Phillip's departure. An 'unassertive, affable and easy-going man', Grose was delighted by his new home, even if rather more than a shipful of corn and black cattle was needed to set things aright. Nonetheless, Grose was one of the first cheery and contented immigrants to Australia since the Aborigines, tens of thousands of years earlier, decided it was the place for them.

2 April 1792—I am at last, thank God, safely landed with my family at this place, and, to my great astonishment, instead of the rock I expected to see, I find myself surrounded with gardens that flourish and produce fruit of every description. Vegetables are here in great abundance, and I live in as good a house as I wish for. I am given the farm of my predecessor, which produces a sufficiency to supply my family with everything I have occasion for. In short, all that is wanting to put this colony in an independent state is one ship freighted with corn and black cattle. Was that but done, all difficulties would be over.

Everybody at Home seems to have an unfavourable opinion of this place, and I am certain no one could possibly be more prejudiced against it than myself. I am glad to have it in my power to change my opinion, and be able to assure you that since I have left England I have seen no place I like better than this.

FRANCISCO XAVIER DE VIANA

Spanish Chocolate

The Spanish corvettes *Descubierta* and *Atrevida*, led by Alexandro Malaspina, spent five years circling the globe, mapping and carrying out scientific research. The ships arrived in Sydney in March 1793, the first European expedition to visit following British settlement, and Francisco Xavier de Viana, an officer on the Malaspina expedition, recorded in his diary the cordial welcome the Spanish received at Port Jackson. After months at sea Viana was clearly delighted to be among Europeans again. In gratitude the Spanish set up a pavilion in which they served the ladies of Sydney chocolate and other delicacies. Meanwhile, sailors from the two vessels, in a tradition honoured to the present day, were discovering the tricks the city's prostitutes could get up to.

11 March 1793—A neat, well-equipped launch had already gone alongside the Descubierta and approached the Atrevida. In it came a city official who greeted us on behalf of the interim governor, Major Grose, and offered in his name every assistance the colony afforded... For an observatory, we chose a promontory on the east, a cable and a half distant from our ships, preferring it to the observatory of Mr Dawes, because it was furthest from the town and nearest the ships and the seacoast. Shops for our coopers and blacksmiths could also be set up right next to this observatory; canvas and tackle were hauled taut, everything was made ready to begin watering the following day; both botanists obtained a fairly good place on land for caring for their plant specimens; and finally, the necessary instructions were given on board so that whatever might eventuate, everything would contribute towards the continuation of cordial relations.

These measures mainly came down to these: that a marine officer from each ship was daily in charge of watering, now that it was necessary to get water in town; that in the boat selected for fishing, a sergeant or some other soldier should go to prevent any surprise attack from the natives (a very timid lot, according to information from the colony); that by night the observatory should be guarded by an officer and two of our soldiers, who would exchange passwords with the sentinels on board the two ships; that for absolutely no reason would women be allowed on board; that two roll-calls a day be taken to punish severely anyone not present for whatever reason; that no convict be allowed in the boats or ships; that from the very beginning all drunkenness or disorderliness among the crew should be avoided; and, more than anything else, there should be no letdown in neatness of dress; finally, after 8 p.m. no boats could bring any visitors aboard, unless the order was countermanded after first making an agreement with the city...

The *Descubierta*'s launch was dispatched to Botany Bay to establish a geometric plane, and from there to bring a well-ordered series of triangulations all the way back to the observatory itself along the bays within the harbour.

Don Juan Ravenet combined with this expedition another of his own overland to Botany Bay, accompanied by Captain Johnston and Lieutenant Prentice, in order to have a better chance of finding some natives and to draw them with their weapons and in their native dress. Don Antonio Tovar went hunting a couple of times; Don Fernando Brambila sketched a few landscapes in perspective; the botanists went inland toward Parramatta and Toongabbie; the work at the observatory continued; and both of us commanders resolved to stay on board for the first two days of Easter to be hosts to Major Grose and the most distinguished citizens of the colony.

Previously, they had agreed to let us have the pleasure of the ladies' company at lunch in a little pavilion set up for the purpose in the neighbourhood of the observatory, where we could serve chocolate and other delicacies from Spain...

During these last days, the conduct of our men ashore had not been as orderly as formerly, not because we believed it was difficult for them to resist the continuous seductive advances of the women prisoners—who were degraded by vice, or rather greed, and who were so uninhibited in their conduct that the women of Teneriffe described by Mr White in his diary would seem chaste by comparison—but because they led them on into drinking some concoctions solely for the purpose of doping them and afterwards robbing them of the little money they had. There was one crewman of the *Atrevida* who failed to show up for roll-call for four consecutive days. In the *Descubierta*, also, five crewmen failed to appear for a time; and although Major Grose took active measures to punish these robberies, even though they were slight ones, and to cut off such disorders at their source, not only was it impossible to stop them but daily they became worse.

This was a new reason for us to speed up the departure of the ships, which was set for the early morning of the eleventh. On the eighth we all said farewell to the governor, whose table and continued hospitality we nevertheless still enjoyed up to the last moment; and the remaining days were filled so well on both sides, in extending and deepening friendships, compatibility, and appreciation which drew us ever closer, that the thought of our imminent departure and the vastness of the distance that was to separate us greatly saddened our hearts.

ALEXANDRO MALASPINA

A Secret Study

The leader of the Spanish expedition Alexandro Malaspina managed to collect a great deal of information about Sydney during his month in the city. This extract, with its strange analysis of the kangaroo and its caustic observations of the female convicts, its shrewd assessment of the English colonists and its fascination with the Aborigines, forms part of a secret report on the new and potential rival settlement for the Spanish government. Although full of misunderstandings, it provides a valuable and candid outside view of the settlement.

Malaspina was dogged by ill-fortune. After returning triumphant to Spain in 1794 he fell victim to court intrigues and was jailed for eight years. An account of the expedition was not published until nearly a century later, while the secret report remained buried until an English translation was published in 1990.

March 1793—A colony composed of 4000 Europeans of both sexes, in which are counted individuals of all arts and offices, a nation as enlightened as the English, which has not encountered natives but to vanquish them, nor other kinds of resistance but to overthrow them, which the properties of the soil, a government which extends whatever help is required, a climate moderately temperate, where if one experiences some sudden variation in temperature it is not of a kind which causes visible damage to health, would promise rapid progress, is admired by the uninstructed in the circumstances of a wise Europe, but nothing further removed from this is what was presented to us at Sydney Cove: land ill-cleared, fields little worked, wretched houses, and everywhere the marks of oppression and disgust.

The town of Sydney, designed to be the centre of commerce and administration, contains about 300 houses, the greater part constructed and roofed with brick and tile (a third part still with straw), gathered together, it would appear, in disorder but fulfilling, according to those informed persons who told us, a plan formed beforehand and suitable to the terrain; I managed to examine it and do not know how it operates; meanwhile the colony will not progress infinitely...

Up to six species of trees, infinite shrubs, and an immensity of plants either new or rare to botany compose all the vegetation...The quadrupeds are not less rare, Mr White has copied up to six species, which have been domesticated and tamed. The squirrels and marmots are very varied; there are different species of them which can fly, and those which carry their young and newborn in a pouch. But the most abundant and most useful is that which Cook named kangaroo, even though this name, which may be used in another part of the island, was not known among these natives.[†]

Its shape is very different from that depicted by that voyager, the body just like that of a dog, a big head and greyhound's muzzle, long and pointed ears, the hind legs of a hare with cloven hooves, the hands short and with claws, the neck long and not as furry as depicted by that voyager, it moves by bounding, and on its hind legs its ordinary posture is erect like a monkey, observing dangers attentively. It extends itself as much as possible to delay discovery, is never caught, and always procures its escape by its agility. Its claws and teeth are a regular defence when it finds itself attacked, but it only defends itself from dogs and views man with terror.

[†] The word 'kangaroo' is from Cooktown. Its meaning is unclear, and the Eora were mystified by it. When Watkin Tench showed Colbee some cows brought to Sydney in the *Gorgon*, he asked if they were kangaroos.

In spite of its clumsy posture on two legs and its leaping gait, it has the speed of a hare, and leaps over the branches and obstacles which oppose its flight. The greyhounds are hard worked, and ordinarily lose them in the field if the ball of the hunter does not come to their help. They apparently breed much and are docile. Five years of hunting has neither reduced nor increased them; the chase of this species of animal is a frequent diversion, and of utility to the colonists: it is done with European greyhounds which have already been accustomed to it, but requires much agility and nimbleness by the hunter, who at times must pursue them running for five or six miles.

Its meat is very good sustenance, inferior to veal, but better than many others, substantial, tender without the gameyness of goat, nor as greasy as mutton, very superior to that of guanaco and to that of hare. In the colony there is a great consumption of it, it is almost the only one which is eaten; there were very few times that it was missing from our table, and it always made several meals. I do not know if there will always be the abundance of this season, but a consumption so excessive and the progress of population must winnow them: perhaps an attempt to domesticate them would have the desired effect. There are some living in several houses, and they do not pine in captivity: especially a species which ever increases and is so tame as to come to one's hand when called...

The English nation, sober in its pleasures, taciturn by character, haughty even though enlightened and reflective, and prone to vehement passions, observes inviolably its customs in every corner of the universe. Incapable of varying them, or of giving them up even in their abuses, they discredit with several despicable features the brilliance of this beautiful picture. Their society recalls by its harshness the national pride. It reveals itself in loose talk: they will never talk of nor show their works without praise, they know too well the progress of their country, and this love of fatherland from which their nation draws so many advantages, only makes them disgusting to others. Their swordsmen, their frequent, at times baseless duels, the continued abuse of liquor, and the inferior treatment with which they degrade the amiable sex, are other such testimonies which accuse an insular ferocity still not well domesticated...

The variability of the weather does not happen to be at all harmful to the health. The perpetual abuse of liquor, frequent humidities and clearing of trees bring about inflamed dysenteries, which is the local sickness, whose cure has not been ascertained and which exhausts the colony. Intermittent fevers are also quite frequent, but not fatal. These and the abuses brought about by the dissoluteness of manners are the only ones which are known...

The class of public prostitutes, which comprehends all the women of the colony (if one excepts some few who are the lawful wives of the officials) contributes infinitely to these disorders. It is incredible the licentiousness to which leads a lack of habitual modesty and the haughty disdain with which the men treat them. Almost always they approach announcing the price at which they sell their favours, and it is common to claim a small increase to indulge in other detestable vices apparently frequent in the colony...

The negritos of New Holland described by Captain Cook are the most miserable and least advanced nation which exists on earth. We are not able to give an idea of their customs or rites, nor of their state of society, as we would wish: our deficiency in the European language of the country and the lack of opportunities for informing ourselves constantly hindered our investigation; but we will explain simply and with our habitual impartiality whatever occasion has permitted us to observe of them in person at the times when we have had dealings with them, which did not happen to be frequent. We quite realise that one can conclude nothing from investigations undertaken at haphazard nor without a set plan, but will confidently attempt to permit to our imagination a freer field than that which our eyes have beheld.

The English nation, disposed towards these kinds of observations by inclination and by character, have already advanced in the subject as much as one could desire: we lack that information and only promise to advance some ideas which may serve as a check on the way we look at things, exposed always to the errors of the weakness of our imagination, and of confusing the indigenous customs with those which have been imperfectly adapted from the Europeans.

This wandering nation, without agriculture and industry, and without any product which would attest their rationality, frugal by necessity and timid by character, received the first Europeans without surprise albeit with some admiration, but neither the strangeness of colour, nor clothes, nor arms, nor whatever means devised by Captain Cook to arouse their cupidity, nor the efforts of European artfulness, excited their imagination or covetousness, and at the end of many days he saw with surprise that they abandoned the same articles which they had been made gift of. Doubtful of their rationality and at the same time confusing them by their shape with the orangutans of Africa, he redoubled his efforts to gain a meeting, with little result.

Having a lively character, a language exceedingly soft, and enough sharpness, they do not make any exertion of their talent and at the same time are the only nation which does not manifest in either of the sexes seen any shyness, nor of having acquired viciousness in exchange for their original grace. Completely naked, without a single thread on their bodies, neither has the continued contact with Europeans succeeded in increasing their dislike as far as horror of this custom. Men, women, youths, children, all present themselves in the streets, or by themselves or in groups, in the same fashion in which they were born, and if sometimes they are seen evincing some repugnance to wearing clothes, they nevertheless love clothing when it is cold, but stupidly throw it away or put it aside when it hinders them.

The figure in both sexes is quite refined: the men are small, of a burnt black colour, the skin roughened by the weather, a little hairy, the head thickly covered with curly hair, but not lank, beard curly and badly parted, eyes black, round and penetrating, features coarse, nostrils quite wide, the mouth large and thickly whiskered, a weak musculature with little strength, a large belly, thighs and calves short, slender and bowed, the arms and shoulders adorned with seams made in the skin arranged in disorder.

The women, without a better body than the men, enjoy it would appear a more robust constitution: the faces finer, breasts perfectly formed, almost rounded, elastic and separated, the belly equally rounded, thighs and calves generally more robust and better proportioned than the men's, hips much narrower and regular than those of our European women, their skin in contrast tanned in all parts, and in addition those who have given birth do not remain wrinkled and ravaged like our women; the pubis extremely deep and with a thick growth of hair, and that figure they owe perhaps to a practice, used only by licentiousness among other nations, of leaving to the females the superior position in copulation.

From girlhood they cut off one of the little fingers, and their fecundity appears to be much in advance of the other sex. In them one sees how much the beautiful formation of unaided nature exceeds that of art. A well-formed European woman put to examination without any greater adornment than the islander would be made to see what disorders a dress laced up viciously from infancy is capable of causing in our scheme of things.

Their rites are composed of various superstitions, upon which we are not informed. It appears that they are allowed only one wife and several concubines, requiring of them respect for the others. Each family, comprising one man, his wives and his children, form a separate tribe. We do not know how far the faculties of the chief extend, nor at what stage of life the sons proceed to form a new family. Jealousy does not appear to be a passion known in these regions: the females prostitute themselves easily (perhaps this is a vice acquired from contact with Europeans). They are allowed to go freely wherever they wish, and they themselves make all the efforts to offer themselves: for my part I have seen them in this case only twice, on both there were no young men of their kind there, and the offer of all of them fell always on the youngest, I do not know whether in order to consider advantages in that circumstance, or in order not to allow this liberty to their husbands.

But it would require a total depravity of sensibilities to suffer the smell, the slovenliness and the roughness of their gross caresses: few women in the universe could present themselves in conditions which would cause an effect so contrary to their desires. However, it happens that such is the desire for novelty and the depravity of tastes in a free country where prostitution is so common, and where nothing is as easy as the means of satisfying every kind of voluptuous passion, that the English lower orders do not disdain them, and each night a large number of them are gathered in the quarters of the troops...

In spite of their simplicity they live happily: ordinarily one comes across them dancing. Alike in this to the Guineans, they express the sensuality of their desires in their songs and attitudes. The vibration of their knees, the vigorous rubbing of the most sensitive parts, and the other movements of each sex, with the ardour which may be observed in their features, are other such unequivocal signs of what they express...

They keep generally good harmony with the Europeans: punishment has made them cautious in this regard; there are very few tribes which do not maintain a strict subordination to the English, and the inequality in arms has extinguished or removed the discontented. The mere sight of a musket, the appearance of the uniform of a soldier, would scatter an army of natives, who with signs of peace and submission take pains to capture their goodwill—in contrast to their behaviour towards the unarmed citizen travelling by himself, several of whom have been the victims of their lack of precaution...

The stupidity of the natives is such that they are unable to draw any profit for themselves, contact with the Europeans having merely contributed to increasing their needs without thereby stimulating them to supply the means of satisfying them; they take and solicit what one gives them without any labour. At the most some serve as domestics but without any ability, and work less than it takes to keep them clothed.

When we arrived they could not understand that we spoke another language than English, and the most they could comprehend was that we did not understand how to speak...Their language is exceedingly soft, each word consists of many vowels, they pronounce it with incredible volubility, and in an agreeable tone, which seems more like well-composed music.

THOMAS WATLING

A Country of Enchantments

More than anyone else, Thomas Watling, through his numerous paintings and illustrations, has given us a clear idea of what early Sydney was like. Convicted of forgery, which he denied, he was transported in 1791. Upon his arrival in 1792 he was assigned to Surgeon White, who made extensive use of his artistic skill.

Watling's *Letters from an Exile at Botany Bay to His Aunt in Dumfries* were published about 1794. They reveal a thoughtful man who respected the Aborigines, and whose sensuous visual imagination was equal to the richness of his strange environment. I can imagine Colbee sitting silently beside Watling for hours on end, observing minutely his work, as he paints the scenes of his new home.

12 May 1793—The landscape painter may in vain seek here for that beauty which arises from happy-opposed off-scapes. Bold rising hills, of azure distances, would be a kind of phenomena. The principal traits of the country are extensive woods, spread over a little-varied plain. I however confess that, were I to select and combine, I might avoid that sameness and find engaging employment. Trees wreathing their old fantastic roots on high, dissimilar in tint and foliage, cumbent, upright, fallen, or shattered by lightning, may be found at every step, whilst sympathetic glooms of twilight glimmering groves, and wildest nature lulled in sound repose, might much inspire the soul—all this I confess...

In the warmer season, the thunder very frequently rolls tremendous, accompanied by a scorching wind, so intolerable as almost to obstruct respiration—whilst the surrounding horizon looks one entire sheet of uninterrupted flame. The air, notwithstanding, is in general dry. Fifteen months have been known to elapse without a single shower but, though thus dry, the transitions of hot and cold are often surprisingly quick and contrasted without any discernible injury to the human system. I have felt one hour as intensely warm as if immediately under the Line, when the next has made me shiver with cold, yet have I not experienced any harm there from; owing, without a doubt, to the dryness and salubrity of the atmosphere.

The vast number of green frogs, reptiles, and large insects, among the grass and on the trees, during the spring, summer, and fall, make an incessant noise and clamour. They cannot fail to surprise the stranger exceedingly, as he will hear their discordant croaking just by, and sometimes all around him, though he is unable to discover whence it proceeds; nor can he perceive the animals from whence the sounds in the trees issue, they being most effectually hid among the leaves and branches.

Should the curious ornithologist, or the prying botanist, emigrate here, they could not fail of deriving ample gratification in their favourite pursuits in this luxuriant museum. Birds, flowers, shrubs and plants; of these many are tinged with hues that must baffle the happiest efforts of the pencil—quadrupeds are by no means various, but we have a variety of fishes, the greater part of which are dropped and spangled with gold and silver, and stained with dyes transparent and brilliant as the arch of heaven.

One great error in many of our voyagers is the giving prematurely a decided opinion of what falls within the circle of their observation. That the inhabitants of N. S. Wales are centuries behind some other savage nations in point of useful knowledge may be fact; but in this there is no criterion of judging mental ability...

In imitation they are extremely apt, particularly in mimicry; and they seem also in many other respects to be capable of much improvement; but they are so very unsteady and indolent that it would be almost next to a miracle to bring them to any degree of assiduity or perseverance...

Bedaubing, or streaking themselves in various forms with red or white earth they would prefer to the most tawdry birthday suit whatever. The same want of taste keeps them honest this way—but victuals, knives, or hatchets, vanish with them in a twinkling.

It pays no small compliment to poesy and painting that they are affected by the most unenlightened as well as the most refined countries. The natives are extremely fond of painting and often sit hours by me when at work. Several rocks round us have *outre* figures engraven in them; and some of their utensils and weapons are curiously carved, considering the materials they have to work with...

It were presumption in me to speak of their language, with which I am but little acquainted. Glossaries have been attempted by some of our pretending and aspiring gentry who, I am conscious, are as much ignorant of it as myself...One thing they have in common with more refined communities, that marks a clannish propinquity of kindred; which is a similarity in the termination of their surnames: Terribilong, Bennelong, Byegong, Wyegong, Colbee, Nanbaree, etc. etc., are full as striking as Thomson, Johnson, and Robson.

As it is impossible for me to be so particular as I could wish, the barbarian New Hollander must give place to a few other remarks, I would inform you of ere I finish my letter...the whole appearance of nature must be striking in the extreme to the adventurer, and at first this will seem to him to be a country of enchantments. The generality of the birds and the beasts sleeping by day, and singing or catering in the night, is such an inversion in nature as is hitherto unknown.

The air, the sky, the land are objects entirely different from all that a Briton has been accustomed to see before. The sky clear and warm; in the summer very seldom overcast, or any haze discernible in the azure; the rains, when we have them, falling in torrents, and the clouds immediately dispersing. Thunder, as said, in loud contending peals, happening often daily, and always within every two or three days, at this season of the year. Eruscations and flashes of lightning, constantly succeeding each other in quick and rapid succession. The land, an immense forest, extended over a plain country, the maritime parts of which are interspersed with rocks yet covered with venerable majestic trees, hoary with age, or torn with tempests.

RICHARD JOHNSON

The Middle of My Discourse

The Reverend Richard Johnson was accompanied to Port Jackson by his wife Mary, whose conversation bored Elizabeth Macarthur, and he made himself unpopular with the officers of the colony by forever complaining to influential people in London about the conditions under which he was compelled to preach. He held the first divine service in Sydney 'under a great tree' on 3 February 1788 and five years later still lacked a church to call his own. His sermons were in the interim thinly attended by both convicts and soldiers. This was, Johnson protested, because he was compelled to preach 'wholly exposed to the weather'. As a result, he claimed, he himself had 'contracted a deafness'.

Finally, in 1793, he erected a church at his own expense, the cost being £67 12s. 11½d. This independent action offended Lieutenant-Governor Grose—during whose rule, Johnson asserted, godliness and decency were absent from the colony. But the cleric's admitted preference for long sermons may have been the real reason why the convicts stayed away and the soldiers beat their drums in church. Even the deaf Johnson heard that.

8 April 1794—Major Grose is pleased to represent me as 'a discontented and troublesome character'. He has not, however, signified in what respects or for what reasons I am so. However, since he has thus asserted the charge, I will, should this be true, endeavour to produce my reasons.

Soon after Governor Phillip left the colony, Major Grose gave out an order for divine service to be performed at six o'clock in the morning, which order, though for various reasons not meeting with my ideas, I strictly attended to.

One morning as I was going through the service, I was interrupted—first by the improper conduct of two soldiers, and soon after by the beat of a drum, when instantly the corps took their arms, got into their ranks, and marched away. I had then been barely three-quarters of an hour in the whole service, and was then about the middle of my discourse. Such strange and unprecedented conduct induced me to write to the major, and to make a serious complaint of such improper proceedings, which I believe was the first thing that gave offence. But, whether being thus interrupted in the discharge of my duty, I had not sufficient reason to make a complaint, or whether my conduct herein can be considered as any way criminal or improper, I submit, sir, to your consideration. I have consulted the canons of the Church of England, and to them I would refer you whether such conduct as has been shown upon this occasion is by any means justifiable or proper.

The next circumstance which I believe has given offence was my building my place of worship…Whether my conduct in what I have done deserves censure or merits condemnation (after having waited for five years and a half, and no prospect of any place being about to be built for this purpose), this also I do humbly submit, sir, to your impartial and candid consideration.

Some time after I had built the church, I made application for a sexton—an old man—to ring the bell, to keep the church clean, and to see that there was proper order and decency during the time of divine service. This request, though both reasonable and necessary, was denied me, though I then signified that this was the general custom throughout England, and, I may say, is common enough amongst all nations. The burying-ground is at a considerable distance from the camp; and when I have gone to bury a corpse it has sometimes happened that the grave has been to alter, and sometimes to make, on which account I have had to wait for half an hour, and sometimes longer, all this time exposed to heat or rain without any shelter or shade to cover me, and there being no-one appointed for the purpose of digging a grave.

THOMAS PALMER

Another America

The Reverend Thomas Palmer, son of 'Henry Fyshe of an ancient family', arrived in Sydney as a convict. One of the Scottish Martyrs, he was transported for supporting political reform. Despite his optimism in this letter, Palmer's farm proved unproductive and he turned to shipbuilding. His first enterprise was the construction of a small vessel, during which his only guide was the *Encyclopaedia Britannica*. In 1801 he sailed for England aboard the decrepit Spanish prize ship *El Plumier*, but died en route in Guam. His remains were taken to Boston by a religious sea captain and buried there in 1804.

15 December 1794—The reports you have had of this country are mostly false. The soil is capital; the climate delicious. I will take upon me to say that it will soon be the region of plenty, and wants only virtue and liberty to be another America. Nature possibly has done more for this than the last. I never saw a place where a man could so soon make a fortune, and that by the fairest means—agriculture…Transportation here will become a blessing. I heartily wish that all the paupers of Great Britain could make interest to be sent here.

To a philosophic mind it is a land of wonder and delight. To him it is a new creation: the beasts, the fish, the birds, the reptiles, the plants, the trees, the flowers, are all new—so beautiful and grotesque that no naturalist would believe the most faithful drawing, and it requires uncommon skill to class them...

PS—Send me, if you please, seed of the early York cabbage, onions, and the everlasting pea.

DAVID COLLINS

A Most Infamous Transaction

Judge-Advocate Collins' tales of woe continued through-out the 1790s. The trial of those accused of raping Mary Hartley revealed the depth of his ignorance of English law. The accused were perhaps the only people ever tried twice for the same crime in the history of Sydney. One wonders whether they were forgiven half their lashes because Collins was vaguely aware of his error.

15 April 1795—A criminal court was assembled for the trial of John Anderson and Joseph Marshall, settlers; and John Hyams, Joseph Dunstill, Richard Watson, and Morgan Bryan, convicts; for a rape committed on the body of one Mary Hartley, at the Hawkesbury. The court was obliged to acquit the prisoners, owing to glaring contradiction in the witnesses, no two of them, though several were examined, agreeing in the same point. But as such a crime could not be passed with impunity, they were recom-mitted, and on the 22nd tried for an assault, of which being very

clearly convicted, the two settlers and Morgan Bryan were sentenced to receive each five hundred lashes, and the others three hundred each; of which sentence they received one half, and were forgiven the remainder

This was a most infamous transaction; and, though the sufferer was of bad character, would have well warranted the infliction of capital punishment on one of the offenders, if the witnesses had not prevaricated in their testimony. They appeared to have cast off all the feelings of civilised humanity, adopting as closely as they could follow them the manners of the savage inhabitants of the country.

ELIZABETH MACARTHUR

Abate Your Scruples and Marry

Elizabeth and John Macarthur received a land grant at Parramatta in 1793, which they named Elizabeth Farm. Mrs Macarthur lived there for over forty years and, in later life, managed the extensive property. Elizabeth possessed unusual beauty and grace, and brought up her family at this outpost of empire with painstaking attention to education and manners. This letter, which possibly should have been dated 1798, is to Bridget Kingdon, a friend in England. It reveals a woman happy in her new home but missing the pleasures of female company. It shows with what profound success Elizabeth and her husband transplanted the model of a wealthy country estate to the other side of the world. Her preoccupations and advice in marriage are those of the age and worthy of Jane Austen herself.

1 September 1795—This country possesses numerous advantages to persons holding appointments under government. It seems the only part of the globe where quiet is to be expected. We enjoy here one of the finest climates in the world. The necessaries of life are abundant, and a fruitful soil affords us many luxuries. Nothing induces me to wish for a change but the difficulty of educating our children, and were it otherwise it would be unjust towards them to confine them to so narrow a society. My desire is that they may see a little more of the world, and better learn to appreciate this retirement.

Such as it is the little creatures all speak of going home to England with rapture—my dear Edward almost quitted me without a tear. They have early imbibed an idea that England is the seat of happiness and delight, that it contains all that can be gratifying to their senses, and that of course they are there to possess all they desire. It would be difficult to undeceive young people bred up in so secluded a situation if they had not an opportunity given them of convincing themselves.

But hereafter I shall much wonder if some of them make not this place the object of their choice. By the date of this letter you will see that we still reside on our farm at Parramatta—a native name signifying the head of a river, which it is.

The town extends one mile in length from the landing place, and is terminated by the Government House which is built on an eminence named Rose Hill. Our farm, which contains from four to five hundred acres, is bounded on three sides by water. This is particularly convenient. We have at this time, about one hundred and twenty acres in wheat all in a promising state. Our gardens with fruit and vegetables are extensive and produce abundantly. It is now spring, and the eye is delighted with a most beautiful variegated landscape—almonds, apricots, pear and apple trees are in full bloom. The native shrubs are also in flower, and the whole country gives a grateful perfume.

There is a very good carriage road new made from hence to Sydney, which by land is distant about fourteen miles; and another from this to the river Hawkesbury, which is about twenty miles from hence in a direct line across the country. Parramatta is a central position between both. I have once visited the Hawkesbury and made the journey on horseback. The road is through an uninterrupted wood, with the exception of the village of Toongabbie, a farm of government, and one or two others which we distinguish by the name of greenlands, on account of the fine grass, and there being few trees compared with the other parts of the country, which is occasionally brushy and more or less covered with underwood.

The greater part of the country is like an English park, and the trees give to it the appearance of a wilderness or shrubbery, commonly attached to the habitations of people of fortune, filled with a variety of native plants placed in a wild irregular manner. I was at the Hawkesbury three days. It is a noble freshwater river, taking its rise in a precipitous range of mountains that it has hitherto been impossible to pass. Many attempts have been made although in vain.

I spent an entire day on this river, going in a boat to a beautiful spot, named by the late governor Richmond Hill, high and overlooking a great extent of country. On one side are those stupendous barriers to which I have alluded, rising as it were, immediately above your head; below the river itself, still and unruffled—out of sight is heard a waterfall whose distant murmurs add awfulness to the scene. I could have spent more time here, but we were not without apprehensions of being interrupted by the natives, as about that time they were very troublesome, and had killed many white people on the banks of the river. The soil in the valley of this river is most productive; and greatly superior to any that has been tilled in this country, which has induced numbers to settle there, but having no vessels, there is at present much difficulty in transporting the produce to Sydney.

Our stock of cattle is large, we have now fifty head, a dozen horses, and about a thousand sheep. You may conclude from this that we kill mutton, but hitherto we have not been so extravagant. Next year, Mr Macarthur tells me, we may begin. I have a very good dairy, and in general make a sufficiency of butter to supply the family, but it is at present so great an object to rear the calves that we are careful not to rob them of too much milk. We use our horses both for pleasure and profit—they alternately run in the chaise or cart.

Mr Macarthur has also set a plough at work, the first which has been used in this country, and it is drawn sometimes by oxen and at others by horses. The ground was before tilled with the hoe. These details, I am sensible, have no other interest than as far as they serve to shew the progressive state of this yet infant settlement...

We fatten and kill a great number of hogs in the year, which enables us to feed a large establishment of servants. These labourers are such as have been convicts, and whose time of transportation has expired. They then cease to be fed at the expense of government, and employ themselves as they please. Some endeavour to procure a passage home to England; some become settlers, and others hire themseves out for labour. They demand an enormous price, seldom less than four or five shillings a day. For such as have many in their employment it becomes necessary to keep on hand large supplies of such articles as are most needed by these people for shops there are none...

How is it my dearest friend that you are still single? Are you difficult to please, or has the war left you so few bachelors from amongst whom to choose? But suffer me to offer you a piece of advice—abate a few of your scruples and marry. I offer in myself an instance that it is not always, with all our wise foreseeings, those marriages which promise most or least happiness prove in their result such as our friends may predict. Few of mine I am certain when I married thought that either of us had taken a prudent step. I was considered indolent and inactive; Mr Macarthur too proud and haughty for our humble fortune or expectations, and yet you see how bountifully providence has dealt with us.

At this time I can truly say no two people on earth can be happier than we are. In Mr Macarthur's society I experience the tenderest affection of a husband who is instructive and cheerful as a companion. He is an indulgent father, beloved as a master, and universally respected for the integrity of his character. Judge then my friend if I ought not to consider myself a happy woman.

I have hitherto in all my letters to my friends forborne to mention Mr Macarthur's name lest it might appear to me too ostentatious. Whenever you marry, look out for good sense in a husband. You would never be happy with a person inferior to yourself in point of understanding. So much my early recollection of you and of your character bids me say.

DAVID COLLINS

A Specimen of English Manners

Bennelong departed for England with Governor Phillip in December 1792. He set out again for Sydney at the start of 1795 in the company of the incoming governor, John Hunter, who recorded that homesickness had 'much broken his spirit'. Nonetheless, on his return Bennelong seems to have taken English manners to heart. He was to find, however, that this transformation set up a firm barrier between himself and his people. Which culture, he must have asked himself, was he happiest in? To compound his difficulties he discovered that during his years of celibacy in England his wife Goroobarroo-boollo had taken up with a man called Caruey. By early 1796 things had taken a turn for the worse.

Bennelong was not the only native to divert the attention of the judge-advocate that summer. If Black Caesar had done even half of what he claimed on his various escapades he would have been the toast of the colony. His boast that he had done away with the Aboriginal freedom fighter Pemulwy was soon to be disproved in the most alarming way.

November 1795—We heard nothing of the natives at the river; all was quiet there. About this settlement their attention had been for some time engrossed by Bennelong, who arrived with the governor. On his first appearance, he conducted himself with a polished familiarity towards his sisters and other relations; but to his acquaintance he was distant, and quite the man of consequence. He declared, in a tone and with an air that seemed to expect compliance, that he should no longer suffer them to fight and cut each other's throats, as they had done; that he should introduce peace among them, and make them love each other. He expressed his wish that when they visited him at Government House they would contrive to be somewhat more cleanly in their persons, and less coarse in their manners; and he seemed absolutely offended at some little indelicacies which he observed in his sister Carrangarrang, who came in such haste from Botany Bay, with a little nephew on her back, to visit him, that she left all her habiliments behind her.

Bennelong had certainly not been an inattentive observer of the manners of the people among whom he had lived; he conducted himself with the greatest propriety at table, particularly in the observance of those attentions which are chiefly requisite in the presence of women. His dress appeared to be an object of no small concern with him; and everyone who knew him before he left the country, and who saw him now, pronounced without hesitation that Bennelong had not any desire to renounce the habits and comforts of the civilised life which he appeared so readily and so successfully to adopt.

His inquiries were directed, immediately on his arrival, after his wife Goroobarrooboollo; and her he found with Caruey. On producing a very fashionable rose-coloured petticoat and jacket made of a coarse stuff, accompanied with a gypsy bonnet of the same colour, she deserted her lover, and followed her former husband. In a few days, however, to the surprise of everyone, we saw the lady walking unencumbered with clothing of any kind, and Bennelong was missing.

Caruey was sought for, and we heard that he had been severely beaten by Bennelong at Rose Bay, who retained so much of our customs that he made use of his fists instead of the weapons of his country, to the great annoyance of Caruey who would have preferred meeting his rival fairly in the field armed with the spear and the club. Caruey being the much younger man, the lady, every inch a woman, followed her inclination, and Bennelong was compelled to yield her without any further opposition. He seemed to have been satisfied with the beating he had given Caruey and hinted that, resting for the present without a wife, he should look about him and at some future period make a better choice.

His absences from the governor's house now became frequent, and little attended to. When he went out he usually left his clothes behind, resuming them carefully on his return before he made his visit to the governor.

December 1795—A report from the river was current about this time that the natives had assembled in a large body, and attacked a few settlers who had chosen farms low down the river, and without the reach of protection from the other settlers, stripping them of every article they could find in their huts. An armed party was directly sent out who, coming up with them, killed four men and one woman, badly wounded a child, and took four men prisoners. It might have been supposed that these punishments, following the enormities so immediately, would have taught the natives to keep at a greater distance; but nothing seemed to deter them from prosecuting the revenge they had vowed against the settlers for the injuries they had received at their hands.

A savage of a darker hue, and full as far removed from civilisation, black Caesar, once more fled from honest labour to the woods, there to subsist by robbing the settlers. It was however reported that he had done one meritorious action, killing Pemulwy, who had just before wounded Collins (the native) so dangerously that his recovery was a matter of very great doubt with the surgeons at our hospital, whose assistance Collins had requested as soon as he was brought into town by his friends. A barbed spear had been driven into his loins close by the vertebrae of the back, and was so completely fixed that all the efforts of the surgeons to remove it with their instruments were ineffectual. Finding, after a day or two, that it could not be displaced by art, Collins left the hospital determined to trust to nature.[*]

He was much esteemed by every white man who knew him, as well on account of his personal bravery, of which we had witnessed many distinguishing proofs, as on account of a gentleness of manners which strongly marked his disposition, and shaded off the harsher lines that his uncivilised life now and then forced into the foreground...

---

[*] And he did not trust in vain. We saw him from time to time for several weeks walking about with the spear unmoved, even after suppuration had taken place; but at last heard that his wife, or one of his male friends, had fixed their teeth in the wood and drawn it out; after which he recovered, and was able again to go into the field. His wife Warreweer shewed by an uncommon attention her great attachment to him.

March 1796—About this time Bennelong, who occasionally shook off the habits of civilised life and went for a few days into the woods with his sisters and other friends, sent in word that he had had a contest with his bosom friend Colbee, in which he had been so much the sufferer that until his wounds were healed he could not with any pleasure to himself appear at the governor's table. This notification was accompanied with the request that his clothes, which he had left behind him when he went away, might be sent him, together with some victuals, of which he was much in want.

On his coming among us again, he appeared with a wound on his mouth, which had divided the upper lip and broke two of the teeth of that jaw. His features, never very pleasing, now seemed out of all proportion, and his pronunciation was much altered. Finding himself badly received among the females (although improved by his travels the little attentions that are supposed to have their weight with the sex) and not being able to endure a life of celibacy, which had been his condition from the day of his departure from this country until nearly the present hour, he made an attack upon his friend's favourite, Booreea, in which he was not only unsuccessful, but was punished for his breach of friendship, as above related, by Colbee, who sarcastically asked him if he meant that kind of conduct to be 'a specimen of English manners'.

JOHN HUNTER

The Expense of Spirit

John Hunter arrived in Sydney Cove as captain of the *Sirius* with the First Fleet, and spent four years in the colony. On his appointment as governor of New South Wales in 1795 he found that, during his absence from

Sydney, the Rum Corps had established a stranglehold
on the market for spirits. Various governors tried to curb
the trade but, until Macquarie took command in 1810, all
their efforts came to nought.

11 July 1796—Several orders have lately been given out wherein,
in consequence of the shameful excesses which had so often
appeared in the use of spirituous liquors, the unlimited sale of
that destructive article was strictly forbidden; and although, for
the convenience of the labouring people of the colony, the governor has directed that licences for the sale of spirits in moderation
should be given under the hand of the civil magistrates to such
number of good characters as might be thought sufficient in each
district, yet he is sorry to observe that the same disorder in every
part of the colony does still prevail, and the disputes, quarrels,
and a total inattention to industry are the fruits of this scandalous
conduct amongst the settlers in various parts of the colony.

The shocking consequences of the abominable practice of
drinking to excess is too recent to require any other observation
than merely reminding the people at large that two men have lost
their lives by that violence which is but too frequently the effect
of drunkenness. The governor has judged it necessary to come
to the resolution of depriving all those settlers whose conduct he
has had but too much cause to be displeased with of that
assistance which has been so long afforded them at the expense of
government, and of which they have made so very improper use,
and to leave them to the exertion of their own ability.

BENNELONG

I Am at Home Now

John Turnbull, who visited Sydney in 1801, recorded our only insight into what Bennelong thought of England. 'It is not unpleasing to listen to his relations of the wonders seen by him,' wrote Turnbull. 'One incident in particular he relates with all the satisfaction of a favourite story; that of being at the house of a very respectable gentleman, and surrounded by numberless visitors of curiosity, an old gentleman, unmoved amidst the general eagerness, took no further notice of him than…bestowing a single glance, and then helped himself bountifully to a pinch of snuff, and requested the company to pass the bottle, which for some time had been neglected. This apathy and inflexible gravity seems to have made more impression on…Bennelong than all the wonders and glitters of dress that he had seen that evening; and from the pleasure he takes in relating this incident, he no doubt considers the old gentleman as one of the wisest men in the company, or perhaps in England.'

After returning to Sydney, and five years before he told Turnbull this story, Bennelong wrote to his English friend Mr Phillips, Lord Sydney's steward, ruefully informing him of the 'murry' (great) happenings since his return, and of his need for new stockings. The letter is Bennelong's sole surviving literary effort.

29 August 1796—I am very well. I hope you are very well. I live at the governor's. I have every day dinner there. I have not my wife; another black man took her away. We have had murry doings; he spear'd me in the back, but I better now; his name is now Caruey. All my friends alive and well. Not me go to England no more. I am at home now.

I hope Sir you send me anything you please Sir. Hope all are well in England. I hope Mrs Phillips very well. You nurse me Madam when I sick. You very good Madam; thank you Madam, and hope you remember me Madam, not forget. I know you very well Madam. Madam I want stockings, thank you Madam; send me two pairs stockings; you very good Madam. Thank you Madam. Sir, you give my duty to Lord Sydney. Thank you very good my Lord, very good; hope you well all family very well. Sir, send me you please some handkerchiefs for pocket. You please sir send me some shoes; two pairs you please Sir.

DAVID COLLINS

An Object of Much Terror

Ever since the founding of the settlement the rock stack known as Pinchgut served as a place of punishment. Incorrigibles were sent there to subsist on bread and water. Just what the Eora thought of this use of their 'favourite resort' is not recorded. They were clearly horrified, however, when the Europeans began hanging bodies in chains upon the spot.

November 1796—A criminal court was held on the 23rd, and continued sitting, by adjournment, until the 29th, when sentence of death was passed upon eight prisoners who were capitally convicted; one, of the wilful murder of the man whose body had been found on the north shore the 16th of last month, and seven of robbing the public storehouses at Sydney and the settlement at the Hawkesbury. Two others were found guilty of manslaughter.

Of these miserable people five were executed pursuant to the sentence of the court. At Sydney, Francis Morgan, for wilful murder, with Martin McEwen (a soldier) and John Lawler (a convict), for robbing the public stores. Matthew McNally and Thomas Doyle, convicts, suffered at Parramatta, on the following day, for the same offence.

Having thus satisfied the public justice of the country, the governor extended the hand of mercy to the three others who had been capitally convicted of the same crime, viz. John McDouall (another soldier), Thomas Inville and Michael Doland (convicts), by granting them a conditional pardon.

It was much to be lamented that these people were not to be deterred by any example from the practice of robbing the public stores, which had of late been more frequent than heretofore, and for which there could not be admitted the shadow of an excuse; as the whole of the inhabitants of every description were at this very time on a full and liberal allowance of provisions and clothing, neither of which were in any scarcity in the settlement. But the cause was to be found in the too great indulgence in the use of spirituous liquors which had obtained among them for a considerable time past...

The court having ordered that Francis Morgan should be hung in chains upon the small island which is situated in the middle of the harbour, and named by the natives Mattewanye, a gibbet was accordingly erected, and he was hung there, exhibiting an object of much greater terror to the natives than to the white people, many of whom were more inclined to make a jest of it; but to the natives his appearance was so frightful—his clothes shaking in the wind, and the creaking of his irons, added to their superstitious ideas of ghosts (for these children of ignorance imagined that, like a ghost, this man might have the power of taking hold of them by the throat), all rendering him such an alarming object to them—that they never trusted themselves near him, nor the spot on which he hung; which, until this time, had ever been with them a favourite place of resort.

JOHN HUNTER

Every Species of Infamy

Governor Hunter seems to have lived in terror of an
uprising led by the Irish political prisoners. His 'strong
log prison' in Sydney did not see much service, for it
was burned to the ground about two years after it was
completed. Nor did his windmill stand for its allotted
two centuries. His guards, however, continued to
plunder the government stores.

12 November 1796—We are now erecting, in each of the towns of
Sydney and Parramatta, a strong log prison, for the security of
turbulent and disobedient persons. These are works which have
been wanted from the beginning, but on account of the relaxed
discipline which private speculation and traffic has occasioned,
is more so now than it ever was, more particularly since it has
been found necessary to send to this country such horrid characters as the people called Irish Defenders, who, I confess, my Lord,
I wish had been either sent to the coast of Africa, or some place as
fit for them.

We are also erecting upon the high ground over Sydney a
strong substantial and well-built windmill with a stone tower,
which will last for two hundred years...

To prevent as far as it is possible the repeated robberies which
are so continually committing amongst us, I am now arranging
the inhabitants of this town of Sydney, which is a mere sink of
every species of infamy, into divisions, and shall have the different
houses numbered and a register kept of the people inhabiting
each. We shall have watchmen chosen from amongst the inhabitants to guard during the night their respective divisions, and a

constable will also be chosen who shall have proper instructions...Our gaols, my Lord, I am sorry to say, are at this time
quite full, many for robberies, a number for different and shocking murders, and some for plundering the public provision stores.
I am concerned to add that with the latter it appears some of the
sentinels on duty have been concerned, the very men who have
the care of our most valuable stores.

DAVID COLLINS

Man of the Earth

Until 1797 the Aboriginal resistance to the European
invasion had been fitful. As it became clear, however,
that the English would continue to alienate their land, an
organised resistance began. It was led by Pemulwy—his
name means 'man of the earth' in Eora—who in 1790
had killed the colony's 'game keeper'. The resistance was
to harry the outlying European settlements for years.

March 1797—While the governor was endeavouring to guard
against the injuries that might be done by these people, the
settlers found themselves obliged to assemble for the purpose of
repelling the attacks made upon them by the natives. The people
at the northern farms had been repeatedly plundered of their
provisions and clothing by a large body of savages, who had also
recently killed a man and a woman. Exasperated at such cruel
and wanton conduct, they armed themselves and, after pursuing
them a whole night, at sunrise in the morning came up with a
party of more than a hundred, who fled immediately on discovering that their pursuers were armed, leaving behind them a

quantity of Indian corn, some musket balls, and other things of which the soldiers had been plundered. They continued to follow, and traced them as far as the outskirts of Parramatta.

Being fatigued with their march, they entered the town, and in about an hour after were followed by a large body of natives, headed by Pemulwy, a riotous and troublesome savage. These were known by the settlers to be the same who had so frequently annoyed them; and they intended, if possible, to seize upon Pemulwy; who, in a great rage, threatened to spear the first man that dared to approach him, and actually did throw a spear at one of the soldiers. The conflict was now begun; a musket was immediately levelled at the principal, which severely wounded him. Many spears were then thrown, and one man was hit in the arm; upon which the superior effect of our firearms was immediately shown them, and five were instantly killed.

However unpleasant it was to the governor that the lives of so many of these people should have been taken, no other course could possibly be pursued; for it was their custom, when they found themselves more numerous and better armed than the white people, to demand with insolence whatever they wanted; and, if refused, to have recourse to murder. This check, it was hoped, would have a good effect; and Pemulwy, who had received seven buckshot in his head and different parts of his body, was taken extremely ill to the hospital. This man was first known in the settlement by the murder of John McEntire in the year 1790; since which he had been a most active enemy to the settlers, plundering them of their property, and endangering their personal safety...

April—Towards the latter end of the month, the governor, accompanied by some gentlemen of the settlement, set off from Parramatta on an excursion, in which he meant to obtain some knowledge of the ground between Duck River and George's River, with respect both to its quality and quantity. This tract was walked over, and much excellent land was found well provided with fresh water in chains of large deep ponds. On this ground some of the marine soldiers, who have been enlisted for three years in the New South Wales Corps, having completed their service, were desirous of being settled.

This party, on their arrival at the banks of George's River, whither a boat had been previously sent with some provisions and a tent, found that at low water it was as fresh as that in the Hawkesbury, where the settlement stood.

Having proceeded down the river, they stopped at a point near Botany Bay, where they met with several parties of natives, among whom was Pemulwy who, having perfectly recovered from his wounds, had escaped from the hospital with an iron about his leg. He saw and spoke with one of the gentlemen of the party; inquiring of him whether the governor was angry, and seemed pleased at being told that he was not; notwithstanding which, there could be but little doubt that his savage brutal disposition would manifest itself whenever excited by the appearance of an unarmed man.

JOHN HUNTER

Conflagrations of Astonishing Extent

By now the Eora had experienced a decade of European interference. The effects of disease, farms and settlements meant that they were no longer able to manage their land by burning it as they had done for millennia. Death-dealing bushfires, with their terrifying roar and unimaginable heat, were becoming a major problem.

10 June 1797—I am sorry, my Lord, to add to this letter that we have this last summer experienced the weather so excessively sultry and dry that from the very parched state of the earth every strong wind has occasioned conflagrations of astonishing extent, from some of which much public and much private property has been destroyed. Some of the settlers have been ruined by losing the whole produce of their harvest after it had been stacked and secured; others have lost not only their crops, but their houses, barns, and a part of their livestock, by the sudden manner in which the fire reached and spread over their grounds. Trains of gunpowder could scarcely have been more rapid in communicating destruction, such was the dried and very combustible state of every kind of vegetation, whether grass or tree.

The loss to government has been about 800 bushels of wheat, and we are now, for want of grass, obliged to feed some of our cattle with grain; but the expense through this necessity will be but small, as the young grass will soon be up. The people in general have been too careless in securing their crops when reaped against those vast and tremendous blazes to which this country in its present state is so liable in dry and hot summers. It is to be presumed that such experience will in future produce more care; and I shall not fail, in such seasons, to remind them in public orders of the necessity of greater attention to concerns of so much value. As we clear and lay open the country we shall get the better of such accidents; in the meantime their frequency this last summer has been very alarming, and their appearance truly dreadful.

I was called out at night lately at Parramatta, and informed that a vast fire was quickly approaching a field in which government had several stacks of wheat. All the men who could be found were ordered out. The field was near a mile out of town. I went thither myself. The night was dark, the wind high, and the fire, from its extent and the noise it made through lofty blazing woods, was truly terrible; we, however, gave it a direction which saved our grain, and we are busily employed in thrashing it out.

DAVID COLLINS

A Decade On

David Collins continued to shoulder his painful task of city historian. Convicts were still escaping, settlers killing Aborigines with impunity, forgers being hanged and perjurors having their ears nailed to the pillory. Christian charity was faring poorly, for Reverend Johnson found himself robbed by a childhood friend. Christmas was still given over to rioting and drunkenness, with a contestant in a drinking contest finished off by 'pernicious spirit'.

The colony's naturalists, however, delighted at the discovery of the platypus, while tribal fights continued in the streets of Sydney, when Colbee and Bennelong found themselves once again embroiled in conflict. The very last male initiation carried out by the Eora—the *Yoolahng Erah-ba-daihng*—also took place. And on the tenth anniversary of the city some Irish convicts attempted to walk to China.

October 1797—Two men were tried for having killed a native youth, well known in the settlement, but, it appearing to the court that he had been accidentally shot, they were acquitted. The natives certainly behaved ill, and often provoked the death which they met with; but there was not any necessity for wantonly destroying them, a circumstance which it was feared had but too often occurred. On the acquittal of these prisoners, they were assured by the governor that he was determined to make an example of the first person who should be convicted of having wantonly taken the life of a native.

Another prisoner, John Morris, was tried for the murder of Charles Martin, by violently kicking and beating him, so that he died the following day. He was found guilty of manslaughter, and sentenced to be burned in the hand and imprisoned for twelve months.

One man was found guilty of uttering a bill knowing it to be forged, and adjudged to suffer death; and two others, for theft, were ordered to be transported to Norfolk Island, one for the term of his life, and another for seven years.

It appearing on one of these trials that three of the witnesses had manifestly and wilfully committed the crime of perjury, they were brought to trial; and, being found guilty, were sentenced to stand in the pillory to which, as an additional punishment, their ears were to be nailed. Their sentence was put in execution before the public provision store, when the mob, either to display their aversion to the crime or, what might be more probable, to catch at anything that wore the form of amusement, pelted them with rotten eggs and dirt...

November—Towards the latter end of the month James Wilson, who had for some time taken up his abode in the woods...surrendered himself to the governor's clemency. He had been herding with the savages in different parts of the country, and was obliged to submit to have his shoulders and breast scarified after their manner, which he described to have been very painful in the operation. He made his appearance with no other covering than an apron formed of a kangaroo's skin, which he had sufficient sense of decency remaining to think was proper.

The governor, well knowing from his former habits that if he punished and sent him to hard labour, he would quickly rejoin his late companions, thought it more advisable to endeavour to make him useful even in the mode of living which he seemed to prefer; he therefore pardoned him, and proposed his attempting, with the assistance of his friends, to take some of the convicts who were at large in the woods; two of whom had, just before Wilson's appearance, stolen two mares, the property of private individuals, but which were allowed to be kept during the night in a stable belonging to government.

Wilson, among other articles of information, mentioned that he had been upwards of 100 miles in every direction round the settlement. In the course of his travelling he had noticed several animals which, from his description, had not been seen in any of the districts; and to the north-west of the head of the Hawkesbury he came upon a very extensive tract of open and well-watered country, where he had seen a bird of the pheasant species, and a quadruped, which he said was larger than a dog, having its hind parts thin, and bearing no proportion to the shoulders, which were strong and large.[†]

It is not improbable that Wilson invented these circumstances in the hope of obtaining some attention, and thereby averting the punishment which he expected, and well knew that he had long deserved.

If it be painful to the writer of these sheets to find little else than crimes and their consequences to record, how much more painful must it have been to have lived where they were daily committed…There can scarcely be recorded a stronger instance of human depravity than what the following circumstance, which happened in this month, exhibits. A convict, who had formerly been a school companion with the Rev. Mr Johnson, had been taken by that gentleman into his service, where he reposed in him the utmost confidence, and treated him with the kindest indulgence. He had not been long in his house before Mr Johnson was

[†] Possibly the lyrebird and wombat.

informed that his servant, having taken an impression of the key of his storeroom in clay, had procured one that would fit the lock.

He scarcely credited the information but, being urged to furnish him with an opportunity, he consented that a constable should be concealed in the house, on a Sunday, when all the family, this servant excepted, would be attending divine service. The arrangement succeeded but too well. Concluding that all was safe, he applied his key and, entering the room, was proceeding without any remorse to plunder it of such articles as he wanted when the constable, seeing his prey within his toils, started from his concealment, and seized him in the act of taking the property.

Thus was this wretched being without 'one compunctious visiting of nature,' detected in the act of injuring the man who, in the better day of his prosperity, had been the companion of his youth, and who had stretched out his hand to shelter him in the present hour of his adversity!...

Although the settlement had now been established within a month of ten years, yet little had been added to the stock of natural history which had been acquired in the first year or two of its infancy. The kangaroo, the dog, the opossum, the flying squirrel, the kangaroo rat, the spotted rat, the common rat, and the large fox-bat (if entitled to a place in this society) made up the whole catalogue of animals that were known at this time, with the exception which must now be made of an amphibious animal, of the mole species, one of which had been lately found on the banks of a lake near the Hawkesbury.

In size it was considerably larger than the land mole. The eyes were very small. The forelegs, which were shorter than the hind, were observed at the feet to be provided with four claws, and a membrane or web that spread considerably beyond them, while the feet of the hind legs were furnished, not only with this membrane or web, but with four long and sharp claws that projected as much beyond the web as the web projected beyond the claws of the fore feet.

The tail of this animal was thick, short and very fat; but the most extraordinary circumstance observed in its structure was its having, instead of the mouth of an animal, the upper and lower mandibles of a duck. By these it was enabled to supply itself with food, like that bird, in muddy places, or on the banks of the lakes in which its webbed feet enabled it to swim; while on shore its long and sharp claws were employed in burrowing; nature thus providing for it in its double or amphibious character. These little animals had been frequently noticed rising to the surface of the water, and blowing like the turtle.

The weather in November was, for the first and middle parts, very unsettled, blowing hard at times with much rain. On one day, there fell a shower of hail, the stones of which were each as big as a lark's egg...

December—A circumstance occurred about the beginning of this month that excited much interest in the town of Sydney and great commotion among the natives. Two of these people, both of them well known in the settlement—Colbee, the friend of Benne-long, and one of the Yeranibes—meeting in the town, while their bosoms were yet swelling on occasion of some former difference, attacked each other. Colbee had always been remarked for his activity, but Yeranibe had more youth than his adversary, and was reckoned a perfect match for him. On closing on each other, with their clubs, until which time Colbee had not gained any advantage over Yeranibe, the handle of Yeranibe's shield drew out, and it consequently fell from his grasp; while stooping to take it up, the other struck him on the head with a club, which staggered him, and followed his blow while he was in that defenceless situation.

Colbee knew that this would ensure him the appellation of *jee-run*, or coward, and that the friends of Yeranibe would as certainly take up his cause. As the consequences might be very serious if he should die of the blow, he thought it prudent to abscond for a while, and Yeranibe was taken care of by some of his white friends.

This happened on the 10th, and on the 16th he died. In this interval he was constantly attended by some of his male and female associates, particularly by his two friends, Collins (for Gnung-a-Gnung-a still went by the late judge-advocate's name) and Moroobra. On one of the nights when a most dismal song of lamentation had been sung over him, in which the women were the principal performers, his male friends, after listening for some time with great apparent attention, suddenly started up, and seizing their weapons went off in a most savage rage, determined on revenge. Knowing pretty well where to meet with Colbee, they beat him very severely, but would not kill him, reserving that gratification of their revenge until the fate of their companion should be decided. On the following night, Collins and Moroobra attacked a relation of Colbee's, Boorawanye, whom they beat about the head with such cruelty that his recovery was very doubtful. As their vengeance extends to all the family and relations of a culprit, what a misfortune it must be to be connected with a man of a choleric disposition!

Yeranibe was buried the day after his decease by the side of the public road, below the military barracks. He was placed by his friends upon a large piece of bark, and laid into a grave, which was formed by them after our manner (only not so deep), they seeming in this instance to be desirous of imitating our custom. Bennelong assisted at the ceremony, placing the head of the corpse, by which he stuck a beautiful waratah, and covering the body with the blanket on which he died. Being supplied with some spades, the earth was thrown in by the bystanders, during which, and indeed throughout the whole of the ceremony, the women howled and cried excessively; but this was the effect of the violent gusts of passion into which the men every moment threw themselves.

At this time many spears were thrown, and some blows were inflicted with clubs; but no serious mischief ensued. On the death of Colbee, all seemed determined; for the man whose life he had in so cowardly a manner taken away was much beloved by his countrymen.

With this design, a number of natives assembled a few days afterwards before the barracks, breathing revenge; at which time a young man, a relation to the object of their vengeance, received so many wounds, that he was nearly killed; and a lad, who was also related to him (Nanbaree, the same who formerly lived with Mr White, the principal surgeon), was to have been sacrificed; but he was saved for the present by the appearance of a soldier, who had been sent to the place with him for his protection; and it was thought that when the present tumult against his uncle (for Colbee was the brother of this boy's father) had subsided, nothing more would be thought of him.

Colbee, finding that he must either submit to the trial usual on such occasions, or live in the continual apprehension of being taken off by a midnight murder and a single hand, determined to come forward, and suffer the business to be decided one way or the other. Having signified his resolution, a day was appointed, and he repaired armed to the place of rendezvous. The rage and violence shown by the friends of the deceased were indescribable; and Colbee would certainly have expiated his offence with his life, but for the interference of several of the military, before whose barrack the affair took place.

Although active, and extremely *au fait* in the use of the shield, he was overpowered and, falling beneath their spears, would certainly have been killed on the spot, but several soldiers rushed in, and prevented their putting him to death where he lay; he himself, from the many severe wounds which he had received, being wholly incapable of making any resistance. His friends, the soldiers, lifted him from the ground, and between them bore him into the barracks.

Bennelong, the particular friend and companion of Colbee, was present at this meeting; but, it was supposed, without intending to take any part in it either way. The atrocity of his friend's conduct had been such that he could not openly espouse his quarrel; perhaps he had no stomach to the fight; and certainly, if he could avoid it, he would not, by appearing against him, add to the number of his enemies. He was armed, however, and unencumbered with clothing of any kind, and remained a silent spectator of the tumultuous scene, until the moment when the soldiers rushed in to save the life of Colbee.

His conduct here became inexplicable. On a sudden, he chose to be in a rage at something or other, and threw a spear among the soldiers, which dreadfully took effect on one of them, entering at his back and coming out at the belly, close to the navel. For this he would have instantly been killed on the spot had not Mr Smith, the provost-marshal, interfered and brought him away, boiling with the most savage rage; for he had received a blow on the head with the butt-end of a musket.

It became necessary to confine him during the night, as well to prevent the mischief with which he threatened the white people, as to save him from the anger of the military, and on the following morning he quitted the town.

This man, instead of making himself useful, or showing the least gratitude for the attentions which he received from everyone, had become a most insolent and troublesome savage. As it was impossible sometimes to avoid censuring him for his conduct, he had been known to walk about armed, and heard to declare it was for the express purpose of spearing the governor whenever he saw him. This last outrage of his had rendered him more hateful than any of his countrymen; and as the natives who had so constantly resided and received so many comforts in the settlement were now afraid to appear in the town, believing that, like themselves, we should punish all for the misconduct of one, it might rather be expected that Bennelong could not be far from meeting that punishment which he certainly provoked and merited.

During the time that Yeranibe was alive, the attendance of the natives who were then in the town was called to the performance of the ceremony named *Yoo-lahng Erah-ba-daihng*...The place of meeting at this time, in the middle harbour, and the various exhibitions which took place, were not observed to differ from those of the preceding years...

On the eve of Christmas day two young men, settlers on some land midway between Sydney and Parramatta, having been boasting of their respective abilities in drinking, regardless of the solemnity of the time, challenged each other to a trial of their skill; on which they were so deliberately bent that, to prevent their being interrupted, they retired to the skirts of a neighbouring wood, with a quantity of raw spirits which they had provided for the purpose. Their abilities, however, were not equal to their boasting; for one of them died on the spot, and the life of the other was fast ebbing when he was taken up. Had another hour elapsed, he too must have perished like his wretched companion...

January 1798—The Irish prisoners who had arrived in the last ships from that country had about this period become so turbulent and refractory, and so dissatisfied with their situation that, without the most rigid and severe treatment, it was impossible to derive from them any labour whatever. In addition to their natural vicious propensities, they conceived an opinion that there was a colony of white people, which had been discovered in this country, situated to the southwest of the settlement, and in which they were assured of finding all the comforts of life, without the necessity of labouring for them.

It was discovered that, in consequence of this extraordinary rumour, a plan had been formed by means of a correspondence carried on between these people, from one district to another, of escaping from the colony; which was to be put in execution so soon as they had completed a sufficient stock of provisions. The place of general rendezvous was fixed upon, and they were furnished with a paper of written instructions for their guidance to this fancied paradise, or to China; in addition to which, they had been supplied with the figure of a compass drawn upon paper.

STEPHEN HUTCHINSON

Some to Choose Wives

The indignity convict women suffered upon arriving in Sydney is revealed in this extract from a letter by Stephen Hutchinson, who may have travelled with ninety-four female convicts aboard the *Britannia*. The letter only exists as a copy in the handwriting of Sir Joseph Banks.

5 September 1798—As soon as we came to an anchor the decks were crowded with gentlemen settlers and men convicts, who came, some to choose servants and some to choose wives, as they please to call them. When those who were pitched upon were landed the others were taken in open boats up the river to a settlement called Parramatta. When they arrived there the gentlemen, after picking out those they wanted for different uses, gave the others their free will, to go with any man they chose.

Those who did not go with one man were sent to be hut-keepers, that is to take care of huts in which there are from two to ten men. There they are obliged to take care of the huts while the men are at labour. If a virtuous woman, as there may be among female convicts, should fall to that unfortunate lot, of being a hut-keeper, I leave you to judge how disagreeable it must be to her, but what must the unfortunate creatures do, when there is no settled house here for them? As soon as they are landed they must either go with a man who perhaps they never saw, be a hut-keeper or trust to the hospitality of a stranger.

Some to be sure get into places as servants but few places here are of great advantage, and the preference is generally given to buy a small house for oneself, and do the best a person can. For my part I think that is the best way too, but how can a woman, who perhaps has been confined for three or four years and leaves England without a penny, or even clothing, give at least nine or ten pounds for a small house? And if she could, a lonely woman is a poor thing in a country where there are so many villains.

It is true that government, if it is known, will not let a woman be ill-used, but yet I find it is very common for some of these villains to obtain an order to land a woman to live with him, and when he has had what he can get from her, and stripped her in a manner of what she had, he turns her out of doors and picks up with another.

John Hunter

Holy Smoke

The church that the long-suffering Richard Johnson erected at his own expense in 1793 was fated to have a short tenure upon this earth, for in 1798 it was set ablaze by some 'worthless and infamous person or persons'. Perhaps the perpetrators had been bored stiff by Johnson's interminable sermons.

3 October 1798—Whereas some worthless and infamous person or persons did on Monday last, between the hours of seven and eight in the evening, wilfully and maliciously set fire to the church and schoolhouse, by which it was completely consumed; and whereas the discovery of characters so extremely dangerous to the colony at large, as well as to its inhabitants individually, is of the utmost importance; notice is hereby given that if any person will come forward and give such information as shall serve to convict so horrid a character before a court of criminal judicature they shall receive a reward of £30. And if the informer shall happen to be a convict, such convict, in addition to the above reward, shall receive a full and absolute emancipation, and be recommended to the master of any ship in which he or she may desire to leave the colony.

RICHARD JOHNSON
Murder Most Horrid

Johnson was witness to much greater villainy than the razing of his church. The killing of the missionary Samuel High Clode, one of the earliest Europeans to attempt to convert the Eora to Christianity, caused even the most hardened to blanch. Clode was preparing to sail to England on the *Indispensable*, and decided to call in a debt before his departure. The house where he was slaughtered stood near the corner of George and Goulburn streets.

July 1799—A soldier of the name of Jones had for some time owed Mr Clode a sum of money. Mr Clode now thought it necessary to ask for it, and after some altercation Jones desired him to call on Tuesday the 2nd of July, in the afternoon, and he would settle with him.

My friend had dined with me on the Sunday and Monday preceding, and was likewise in the camp on the Tuesday; dined at Dr Harris's, surgeon to the corps, a gentleman who had from Mr Clode's first arrival been very kind and friendly towards him, providing him with a hut to live in, with plenty of vegetables, and giving him free access to his own barracks at all times.

About four o'clock he called upon us, sat a few minutes, and then took his leave for the night, promising to call the next morning, and to bring something for my little boy, who at that time was indisposed; but truly it may be said we know not what a day may bring forth; for the next morning, instead of seeing my friend, tidings were brought me that he was murdered; was found in a sawpit under water; his skull was fractured in different parts, and his throat cut from ear to ear.

Judge, sir, what was my surprise and horror upon receiving this information. A kind of stupor seized me; I could not believe it; it appeared as a dream; but recollecting myself I immediately went and acquainted his Excellency the governor with the melancholy news. The governor, with several other officers, went with me to the place, where we found everything as was related: a scene so shocking as I never shall forget, but too painful and distressing for me fully to relate.

It pleased God, however, that his horrid murder did not lie long concealed. Divine justice and vengeance soon pursued and overtook his cruel and bloodthirsty murderer. News of this shocking event soon spread in all directions: numbers of all descriptions of persons ran to the spot; Jones, the man before mentioned, among the rest, and was the first to lay the murder upon an innocent person who found my friend in this melancholy state; but this wretch's crime in the murder and his no less wicked intentions in throwing it upon another were both soon discovered.

Suspicions falling upon Jones, the path leading from the pit to his house was closely examined, and blood traced; besides some of the dear deceased's brains laid in different places, to the very door; and, making further search in the house, blood was discovered in different parts, particularly in a small skilling where, as afterwards appeared, my friend was dragged, after this horrid butcher had knocked him down. An axe was found with blood and brains upon it, though it had been previously washed; a knife and blanket were discovered in the same state; and, upon examining the person of Jones, blood was found upon one of his fingers; these and other circumstances fully confirmed the suspicion of his guilt.

Jones, his wife, and two other men who lived in Jones's house, were immediately apprehended, and the next day, Thursday, a criminal court was convened purposely to try them; when three, viz. Jones, his wife and Elbray were convicted upon the clearest evidence; and I fear the fourth, though acquitted, was a party in some way concerned. After their conviction, I officially visited these three horrid monsters who, for the purpose of obtaining a more full confession of this murder, and others it was conjectured that Jones had committed, were put in separate places. Jones continued hardened to the last, his wife little better; but Elbray, struck with remorse, which was occasioned by what I shall hereafter mention, made a full confession of the whole transaction, first to a sergeant in the corps and afterwards to myself, which I took down in writing and was to the following purport.

The scheme was first planned by Jones and his wife on the Sunday. Elbray was asked to assist in it, but at first refused; to gain him over, Jones gave him several drams of spirit, when at length, on the morning of Tuesday, he consented. Trotman, the other man that was tried but acquitted, was sent, with Jones's two children, to a settler's farm for turnips. Mr Clode was at that time in the town and, expecting him to return home before dinner, it was the intention of the other three to dispatch him before Trotman and the children returned; but Mr Clode not returning home as soon as was expected, this scheme failed.

About four o'clock, two other soldiers (for Jones and Trotman belonged to the corps) called in purposely to drink tea. At that time, Jones and Elbray were looking out for Mr Clode and seeing him come down the hill at a distance they went into the house, and Jones proposed that his wife, together with the two soldiers, Trotman, and the children, were to go to look at a piece of wood, which Jones was said to be cutting for the purpose of a canoe. This was agreed upon.

Mr Clode by this time was come to the door, was asked in, and a chair was set for him by the table to settle his accounts with Jones. The axe I have already mentioned was placed in the corner of the room; with this Elbray, coming behind him, was to knock him down; he took it up in his hand, but his heart failed him; he laid it down again and went out of doors, where he stayed a little while; returning in again, he heard the first blow given by Jones. This inhuman wretch repeated his blows so often that Elbray at last cried out, 'For God's sake, Jones, you have knocked him all to pieces.'

They then dragged him into the skilling, when Elbray came out again, Jones soon after him. Jones went into the skilling, and coming out a second time took up a large knife. Elbray asked him what he was going to do with it.

He replied, 'Damn him, he moves, he is not dead,' and taking the knife he went in again, and cut his throat from ear to ear, and then returned, both the knife and his hands reeking with blood. This he immediately washed, whilst Elbray scattered ashes over the room to conceal the blood upon the floor. The window shutters were put in, the tea-things set against the company returned; after tea, liquor was set upon the table; several songs were sung by Jones, his wife and others. About nine o'clock, Jones and Elbray went out, when they dragged their prey through a hole in the skilling, and taking him upon their shoulders carried him to the pit, threw him in, covered him over with green boughs, and then returned to their company, and kept up jovial mirth till after midnight.

The providence of God appears singularly in bringing this horrid murder to light. A man had been at work for several days upon the ground round this pit, and in the evening used to leave his hoe in the pit. Going to work the next morning, and looking for his hoe, he was surprised to see so many green boughs laid over the pit. Suspecting something was there planted, i.e., some property that had been stolen was concealed, he put in his hoe and removed the boughs, when he immediately saw the hand of a dead man.

He then called out to another man cutting firewood at a small distance. Three or four others came at the same time, Jones among the rest, and immediately charged the man that first discovered Mr Clode in this woeful plight with the murder, and wanted to tie his hands and take him into the camp a prisoner. Jones came into camp with others to bring tidings of the murder, expressed his concern for the murder of a man he so much loved and to whom he was indebted for his attention to him and family in times of sickness, and again endeavoured to throw the murder upon the man that first discovered Mr Clode in the pit.

From the tale he told, and other circumstances concurring, the man was committed to prison but, at the very time Jones was thus speaking, another man came up, myself and the governor and other gentlemen present, and said to Jones, 'Jones, you are the murderer, blood is traced from the pit directly to your house.'

He then began to protest his innocence, and to repeat what I have before related. His house, his body &c. were examined; he was taken to the pit, ordered to look at the body and to touch it.

He replied, 'Yes, I will and kiss him too, if you please, for I loved him as my brother.'

That this unfeeling wretch had reason to love Mr Clode, you may easily perceive by his wife's declaration to me, whilst under sentence. Speaking to her of this horrid business, and lamenting the unhappy end of a friend I so much esteemed, she replied, 'Oh! Sir, that dear man was the saving both of my life and the life of my husband. His attention was such to Trotman as I never saw in any other person in my life; three times a day he came to visit him, washing and cleansing his sores; and had it not been for his attention, he would surely have lost his hand!'

Who, my dear Sir, can hear such a declaration as this, but must shudder to think that such horrid monsters can exist!

By an order from the governor, the house in which the murder was committed was, on the Saturday, pulled down and burned to ashes. A temporary gallows was erected upon the same spot, and at twelve o'clock these three inhuman wretches were taken out and conveyed in a cart to the place where, having discharged my duty as chaplain, they were launched into eternity, to appear at the tribunal of a righteous and avenging God, and rather execrated than pitied by a numerous multitude of spectators. The bodies of the two men are hung in chains near the place; that of the woman given to the surgeons for dissection…

I promised to tell you what it was that occasioned Elbray to make a confession of the murder before. When the bell began to toll for the funeral of my friend, he asked what the bell was tolling for. The sergeant of the guard told him it was for the funeral of the person whom he and Jones had murdered. He was then taken out of the room when, seeing the corpse just taken from my hut, he asked who it was walking with Mr Johnstone before the corpse; he was told that it was the governor. He then hung down his head, went again into the guard room, burst into tears, desired one to read to him, and soon after made a full confession; which was in substance what I have above related.

JOSEPH HOLT

Flog Me Fair

Joseph Holt was a fast-talking Protestant farmer from County Wicklow, Ireland, who through a dispute with a neighbour became involved in the rising of the United Irishmen in 1798. 'General' Holt led a brilliant guerrilla campaign but as the revolt crystallised along sectarian lines he found himself at the head of an increasingly Catholic force. In November 1798 he surrendered on condition that he would be exiled without trial and on 11 January 1800 stepped ashore in Sydney Cove. Although a successful farmer, Holt was held in suspicion by the authorities who were in perpetual fear of an Irish uprising. In September 1800 he was denounced as a conspirator in a planned Irish revolt and ordered to attend the flogging he indelibly describes here. In 1806 Holt ran into further trouble when the authorities discovered his illegal still, and after having his pardon confirmed by Governor Macquarie in 1811 he returned to Ireland.

September 1800—We marched up to Toongabbie where all the government men was and this was the plan—to give them the opportunity of seeing the punishment inflicted on several. There was one man of the name of Maurice Fitzgerald. He was ordered to receive three hundred lashes. The place they flogged them— their arms pull round a large tree and their breasts squeezed against the tree so the men had no power to cringe or stir. Father Harold was ordered to lay his hand against the tree by the hand of the man that was flogging.

There was two floggers—Richard Rice and John Johnson, the Hangmen from Sydney. Rice was a left handed man and Johnson was right handed so they stood at each side, and I never saw two thrashers in a barn move their strokes more handier than those two man killers did. The moment they begun I turn my face round towards the other side and one of the constables came and desired me to turn and look on. I put my hand in my pocket and pull out my penknife and swore I rip him from the navel to the chin.

They all gather round me and would have ill used me but Mr Smyth came over and asked them who gave them any orders about me so they were oblige to walk off. I could compare them to a pack of hounds at the death of a hare, all yelping. I turned once about and as it happened I was to leeward of the floggers and I protest, though I was two perches from them, the flesh and skin blew in my face as they shook off of the cats.

Fitzgerald received his three hundred lashes. Doctor Mason— I never will forget him—he use to go to feel his pulse and he smiled and said, 'This man will tire you before he will fail. Go on.' It is against the law to flog a man past 50 lashes without a doctor and, during the time he was getting his punishment, he never gave as much as a word, only one and that was saying, 'Don't strike me on the neck. Flog me fair.'

When he was let down two of the constables went and took hold of him by the arms to help him in the cart, I was standing by. He said to them, 'Let my arms go', struck both of them with his elbows in the pit of the stomach and knock them both down and then step in the cart. I heard Doctor Mason say, 'That man had strength enough to bear two hundred more.'

Next was tied up was Paddy Galvin, a young boy about twenty years of age, he was ordered to get three hundred lashes. He got one hundred on the back and you could see his back bone between his shoulder blades. Then the doctor order him to get another hundred on his bottom. He got it and then his haunches was in such a jelly the doctor order him to be flog on the calves of his legs. He got one hundred there and as much as a whimper he never gave.

They asked him if he would tell where the pikes was hid. He said he did not know and if, he would not tell, 'You may as well hang me now,' he says, 'for you never will get my music from me.'

So they put him in the cart and sent him to hospital.

There was two more got one hundred each and they sung out from first to last. One of their names—Mick Fitzgerald, shoemaker by trade. Them three men was County Cork men...

When the flogging was over, Mr Smyth and I walked on to Parramatta and went in to the hotel kept by James Larra, a honest Jew. The table was soon furnished with a nice lamprey and some hung beef. We took dinner.

JOHN TURNBULL

White Hair, Black Eyes

Both François Péron and Alexandro Malaspina were impressed that Sydney's whores could fall pregnant. A life of vice, they believed, should cause sterility. 'Even those who have never been so before become pregnant,' Malaspina noted. 'Nothing is more common than children in the streets.' A decade or so later John Turnbull, who visited Sydney in 1801 and 1803, was also overwhelmed by these first Australians of European descent, and saw the prosperous future they promised for the city. In 1801 there were, he estimated, more currency lads and lasses, as Australian-born children were known, than convicts and they seemed all to have the same characteristics. The city's lawyers and tradesmen, Turnbull noted, were also of a type.

Sydney, according to the most accurate calculation I am enabled to make, has now a population of 2600 inhabitants. They may be classed under the following denominations:

Military and civil establishment, 450.

Convicts employed by the crown in the public works, bridges, batteries, and dockyards &c., 400.

Tailors, shoemakers, bakers, butchers, carpenters and masons, 250.

Fishermen, 20.

People employed in boats, getting wood for shipping, bringing grain from the Hawkesbury sealers in Bass's Straits, chiefly employed on the water, 350.

Petty traders or pedlars who gain a livelihood by trading, 40.

Women, 600.

Children, 450.

The space occupied by the town is about a mile from one extremity to the other. With the exception of the storehouses and other public buildings, eight out of ten of the houses are only one storey in height, and whether built at the first formation of the colony, or immediately afterwards, are for the most part composed of wattle and plaster, and some few, but few indeed, of brick and stone. The absolute want of lime, or any sufficient substitute, except that made from shells, is an invincible impediment against more substantial architecture.

Sydney, however, is in every respect well situated to become in progress of years a port of very active commerce. It already comprehends upwards of one-third of the whole population of New South Wales.

The effect of the climate has been rather overrated. It is chiefly visible in children born in the country of European parents, but it is not visible so much in any defect, as in a certain characteristic trait of countenance. These children differ nothing in size or stature from the common standard of Europe, but are invariably of one complexion, fair and with white hair. Out of eleven hundred children born in New South Wales there is scarcely a single exception to this national, as we may call it, distinction. Their eyes are usually black and very brilliant, their disposition quick and volatile, and their loquacity such as might render them a proverb.

Strange as it may appear, the multitude of law suits and litigations in this colony exceed all proportion to its population. There were not less than three hundred capiases, summons and executions, to be brought forward at the next sitting of the civil court, and the fees of office to the provost marshal were said to amount to nearly £300.

Indeed the lawyers and publicans are the most profitable trades in the colony. One of these kind gentlemen of the quill had the modesty to charge me £4 6s. for writing half a sheet of paper, and in answer to my remonstrance, replied that he lost money by me. This fellow was a convict. Another of a different trade, and a convict, demanded five shillings for some very trifling repairs of a lock; and being told by a colonist at hand that he had never charged him more than half the sum the fellow replied that the lock belonged to a ship, and that it was his rule of trade to charge a ship double. Many instances of the same kind might be enumerated, but the character of the people may as fully be inferred from these.

FRANÇOIS PÉRON

Sydney Town

As a youth Napoleon Bonaparte volunteered for service on the ill-fated La Perouse expedition. Had he been accepted the world might have been saved considerable vexation. Napoleon retained a life-long interest in

Australia and in 1800 sponsored the grandest expedition
ever to sail the austral seas. The Baudin expedition
arrived in Sydney in 1802, and its naturalist, François
Péron, was taken with what he saw as a model town.
Where others saw only lechery Péron perceived a colony
of fertile women.

April 1802—We were completely astonished at the flourishing
state in which we found this singular and distant establishment. The beauty of the port at first attracted our whole attention.
From an entrance, says Commodore Phillip (whose description is
not in the least exaggerated), of not more than two miles across,
Port Jackson gradually opens till it forms a spacious harbour,
with sufficient depth of water for the largest ships, and room
enough to contain, in perfect safety, all that could on any occasion
be collected. Even a thousand ships of the line might manoeuvre
here with ease. The bay takes a western direction, extends to the
distance of thirteen miles inland, and has at least a hundred little
creeks, formed by very narrow tongues of land, which afford
excellent shelter against winds, from any point of the compass.

Towards the middle of this magnificent port, and on its southern bank, in one of the principal creeks, rises Sydney Town, the
capital of the county of Cumberland, and of all the English
colonies in this part of the world. Seated at the base of two hills—
they are contiguous to each other—and having the advantage of a
rivulet which runs completely through it, this infant town affords
a view at once agreeable and picturesque.

To the right, and at the north point of Sydney Cove, you
perceive the signal battery, which is built upon a rock difficult of
access: six pieces of cannon, protected by a turf entrenchment,
cross their fire with that of another battery, which I shall presently
mention, and thus defend, in the most effectual manner, the

approach to the harbour and the town. Farther on appear the large buildings that form the hospital and which are capable of containing two or three hundred sick. Amongst these buildings there is one particularly worthy of notice, as all the parts of it were prepared in Europe and brought out in Commodore Phillip's squadron, so that, in a few days after its arrival, there was an hospital ready to receive such of the crews as were sick.

On the same side of the town, at the seashore, you observe a very fine magazine to which the largest ships can come up and discharge their cargoes. In the same direction are several private docks in which are built brigs and cutters, of different sizes, for the purpose of trading, either inland or beyond the colony. These vessels, which are from fifty to three hundred tons burthen, are built entirely with the native wood; even their masts are obtained from the forests of the colony...

It is at the spot called Hospital Creek that the ships of individuals unload their cargoes. Beyond the hospital, in the same line, is the prison, which has several dungeons capable of holding from an hundred and fifty to two hundred prisoners; it is surrounded by a high and strong wall and has a numerous guard on duty, both by day and night. A short distance from the prison is the storehouse, for the reception of wines, spirituous liquors, salt provisions, etc. In the front of it is the armoury, where the garrison is drawn up every morning, accompanied by a numerous and well-composed band, belonging to the New South Wales regiment. The whole western part of this spot is occupied by the house of the lieutenant-governor-general, behind which is a vast garden which is worth the attention both of the philosopher and the naturalist, on account of the great number of useful vegetables which are cultivated in it, and which have been procured from every part of the world by its present respectable possessor, Mr Paterson, a distinguished traveller, and member of the Royal Society of London.

Between the house and the magazine is the public school: here are educated, in those principles of religion, morality and virtue, those young females who are the hope of the rising colony but whose parents are either too degenerate or too poor to give them proper instruction. In the public school, however, under respectable matrons, they are taught, from their earliest years, all the duties of a good mother of a family. Such is one great advantage of the excellent colonial system established in those distant regions.

Behind the house of the lieutenant-governor-general, in a large magazine, are deposited all the dried pulse and corn belonging to the state. It is a sort of public granary, intended for the support of the troops and the people who receive their subsistence from the government. The barracks occupy a considerable square, and have in front several fieldpieces; the edifices, for the accommodation of the officers, form the lateral parts or ends of the building, and the powder magazine is in the middle. Near this, in a small private house, the principal civil and military officers assemble. It is a sort of coffee-house, maintained by subscription, in which there are several amusements, but particularly billiards, at which any person may play, free of expense.

Behind the armoury is a large square tower, which serves for an observatory to those English officers who study astronomy. At the base of this tower the foundation of a church has been laid of which the building, just mentioned, is intended to form the steeple; but a structure of this kind, requiring considerable time, labour, and expense, the governors have hitherto neglected to carry it into execution, preferring the formation of such establishments as are more immediately necessary for the preservation of the colony. While waiting, however, for the erection of a church, divine service is performed in one of the apartments of the great corn magazine. Two fine windmills terminate on this side the series of the principal public edifices...

A short distance to the southward of Sydney Town, to the left of the great road that leads to Parramatta, you observe the remains of the first gibbet that was erected on the continent of New Holland. The increase of habitations having caused it to be, as it were, surrounded, it has been succeeded by another that has been erected farther off, in the same direction, and near the village of Brickfield. This village, which consists of about two score of houses, contains several manufactories of tiles, earthenware, crockery, etc. Its site is agreeable, and the soil, less sterile than that of Sydney, is better adapted to the different kinds of cultivation that have been introduced into these distant regions.

The great road, just mentioned, passes through the middle of Brickfield; while a small rivulet intersects it in an opposite direction. Between this village and Sydney Town is the public burying-ground, which is already rendered an object of interest and curiosity by several striking monuments that have been erected in it; and the execution of which is much better than could reasonably have been expected from the state of the arts in so young a colony.

A crowd of objects, equally interesting, demanded our notice in every direction. In the port we saw, drawn up together, a number of vessels that had arrived from different parts of the world, and most of which were destined to perform new and difficult voyages. Some of them had come from the banks of the Thames or the Shannon to pursue whale-fishing on the frigid shores of New Zealand. Others, bound to China after depositing the freight which they had received from the English government for this colony, were preparing to sail for the mouth of the Yellow River; while some, laden with pit-coal, were about to convey that precious combustible to India, and the Cape of Good Hope. Several smaller vessels were on their way to Bass's Straits to receive skins, collected by a few individuals who had established themselves on the isles of those straits to catch the marine animals that resort to them.

Other ships, stronger built than those just alluded to and manned by more numerous and daring crews who were provided with all kinds of arms, were on the point of sailing for the western coast of America. Laden with various sorts of merchandise, these vessels were intended to carry on, by force of arms, a contraband trade on the Peruvian shores, which could not fail to prove extremely advantageous to the adventurers. Here they were preparing an expedition to carry on a skin trade with the people of the north-west shores of America; there all hands were engaged in sending off a fleet of provision ships to the Navigators', the Friendly, and the Society Islands, to procure for the colony a stock of salt provisions...[†]

The population of the colony was to us a new subject of astonishment and contemplation. Perhaps there never was a more worthy object of study presented to the philosopher—never was the influence of social institutions proved in a manner more striking and honourable to the distant country in question. Here we found united, like one family, those banditti who had so long been the terror of their mother country. Repelled from European society, and sent off to the extremity of the globe, placed from the very hour of their exile in a state between the certainty of chastisement and the hope of a better fate, incessantly subjected to an inspection as inflexible as it is active, they have been compelled to abandon their anti-social manners; and the majority of them, having expiated their crimes by a hard period of slavery, have been restored to the rank which they held amongst their fellow men. Obliged to interest themselves in the maintenance of order and justice, for the purpose of preserving the property which they have acquired, while they behold themselves in the situation of husbands and fathers, they have the most interesting and powerful motives for becoming good members of the community in which they exist.

[†] Samoa, Tonga and Tahiti respectively.

The same revolution, effected by the same means, has taken place amongst the women, and those who were wretched prostitutes have imperceptibly been brought to a regular mode of life and now form intelligent and laborious mothers of families. But it is not merely in the moral character of the women that these important alterations are discoverable, but also in their physical condition, the results of which are worthy the consideration both of the legislator and the philosopher. For example, everybody knows that the common women of great capitals, are in general unfruitful: at Petersburgh and Madrid, at Paris and London, pregnancy is a sort of phenomenon amongst persons of that description, though we are unable to assign any other cause, than a sort of insusceptibility of conception. The difficulty of researches, as to this subject, has prevented philosophers from determining how far this sterility ought to be attributed to the mode of life of such women, and to what degree it may be modified or altered by a change of condition and manners.

But both these problems are resolved, by what takes place in the singular establishment that we are describing. After residing a year or two at Port Jackson most of the English prostitutes become remarkably fruitful and what, in my opinion, clearly proves that the effect arises much less from the climate than from the change of manners amongst the women is that those prostitutes in the colony, who are permitted by the police to continue in their immoral way of life, remain barren the same as in Europe. Hence we may be permitted to deduce the important physiological result that an excess of sexual intercourse destroys the sensibility of the female organs to such a degree as to render them incapable of conception; while to restore the frame to its pristine activity nothing is necessary but to renounce those fatal excesses.

ROBERT HOBART

A Pint and a Prayer

As Home Office secretary responsible for the colonies Lord Hobart was reputed to have 'a better grasp of the local or colonial conditions…than did some of his predecessors'. Certainly his recommendation to Governor King to hand out 'a Sunday pint of grog' to deserving convicts probably did more to fill pews than anything else.

24 February 1803—In order to encourage the convicts to conduct themselves in an obedient and becoming manner, and with diligence in their respective avocations, I am induced to recommend to you to give on Sunday a pint of grog to each convict who shall have been reported by the superintendents and magistrates as having conducted himself in a regular and proper manner during the week, and who shall appear clean, and produce the whole of his clothing when mustered on the Sabbath day; and with a view of impressing more fully upon the minds of the convicts the absolute necessity of a strict observance of religious ceremonies, it is my positive and express direction that you do strictly enjoin every officer, both civil and military, to be constant and regular in attending divine service, and that orders be given to the troops who may not be upon duty to attend regularly in like manner.

A Bucket on the Brain

Australia's first newspaper, the *Sydney Gazette*, began publication on 5 March 1803. It was the voice of government in a despotic colony, and its editor, West Indian George 'Happy' Howe, was severely limited in the kind of material he could present. Politically neutral stories of snakebite were popular, as were tales of strange creatures hatched from hens' eggs. One old staple—the adventures of drunken matrons—got so frequent an airing that Howe was forced to devise ever more elaborate literary novelties to hold the public interest. This early example is among his finest.

19 March 1803—Last week an elderly matron who has seriously inclined herself to the influence of the spirit, actually conceiving that her faith was sufficient to sustain her, courageously tumbled into a well on the Rocks, and had nearly fallen a victim to her enthusiasm.

She remained in the water, the purity of whose element she had a natural aversion to, above three quarters of an hour, chin-deep, when fortunately a man, going to the well, let a bucket fall upon her head which, as it failed in its assault upon the pericraneum, proved instrumental in restoring her to the face of the earth.

No Law against It

Among the *Gazette*'s more serious tasks was to encourage the civic pride of the citizens of Sydney. The modern pedestrian will note that little has changed in Pitt Street, only now it's the government that's digging the holes.

12 June 1803—While every exertion is on foot to improve the colony, and consequently to benefit its inhabitants, yet some unthinking individuals, preferring their own private convenience to public advantage, seem only solicitous of opposing impediment to improvement.

Some of the principal streets in Sydney are rendered impassable after dark, save with the risk of breaking an arm or a leg, by numerous pits and hollows, which would seem purposely contrived for the annoyance of the passenger.

Having myself lately plunged into one of those occasional recesses, in Pitt's Row, which I was not prepared against, as the ground was perfectly level but a few hours before, I resolved to put a period if possible to this method of mining; and next day observing a man hard at work with a spade, at the very grave into which I had descended, I mildly asked him if he lived in the row. To which he bluntly answered, 'Yes.'

'Then why,' said I, 'do you dig so dangerous a hole into which some of your own family may tumble?'

'No fear of that,' was his reply, 'I live nine or ten door lower.'

At the bottom of the same row I accosted another who had just filled a barrow from the side of a cave that already extends itself nearly across the street. He wanted it to level his yard, and had come a great way for it—two substantial reasons why people should be in danger of dislocating their necks. Remonstrance was totally useless and, when I mentioned the impropriety of his thus wheeling away the public streets, he regarded me with ineffable disdain and informed me there was no law against it.

The Invisible Hand

When Joseph Luker, a police constable investigating the theft of a desk, was bashed to death, four men were charged, but only Joseph Samuels, a Jewish convict, was found guilty. He was sentenced to be hung with James Hardwicke, another convicted murderer. But the greatest public suspicion fell on Samuels' friend Isaac 'Hickey

Bull' Simmonds, who had managed to convince the court that the blood on his clothing came from his nose or a fish he was cleaning or a duck he had slaughtered. In the absence of DNA testing Samuels looked set to be launched into eternity, until fate intervened.

Sydney Gazette, 2 October 1803—At half past nine on Monday morning, the New South Wales Corps got under arms, and proceeded to the place of execution, to which Joseph Samuels and James Hardwicke were brought, in pursuance of the sentence passed upon them on the preceding Friday.

Both prisoners conducted themselves with becoming decency; and when the Reverend Mr Marsden had performed the duties of his function, and quitted Hardwicke, he turned to Samuels (who, being a Jew, was prepared by a person of his own profession) and, questioning him on the subject of the murder of Luker, he solemnly declared that during the interval of his confinement in the cell with Isaac Simmonds, nicknamed Hikey Bull, they in the Hebrew tongue exchanged an oath, by which they bound themselves to secrecy and silence in whatever they might then disclose.

Conjured by that God, before whom he was shortly to appear, not to advance anything in his latter moments that would endanger his salvation, he now repeated with an air of firmness what he had before declared; and, appearing deeply impressed with a becoming sense of his approaching end, appealed to Heaven to bear him testimony that Simmonds had, under the influence of the oath by which they were reciprocally bound, acknowledged to him that Luker had accidentally surprised him with the desk belonging to Mary Breeze; and that he, in consequence thereof, had 'knocked him down, and given him a topper for luck!' adding at the same time that if he had not been kept in the dark with respect to the concealment of the money that had been taken out of it, that catastrophe never would have happened; but, as it was, that he would hang 500 Christians to save himself.

Simmonds, who was purposely brought from George's Head to witness the awful end of the unhappy culprit, heard what he advanced and repeatedly endeavoured to check the declaration, which was delivered with mildness and composure, and which, as it appeared wholly untinctured with acrimony, gained credit among the spectators in whose breasts a sentiment of abhorrence was universally awakened.

Odium and suspicion were attached to Simmonds from the very day on which the dreadful crime was perpetrated, and every eye was fixed in doubt upon his countenance when he assiduously assisted to lower the mangled corpse into the grave. Although from the want of that full and sufficient evidence which the law requires he had escaped condemnation, yet he had been arraigned at the arbitrary tribunal of public opinion, and most of the spectators had pronounced judgment against him in their hearts. It is not to be wondered then that a testimony like the present, proceeding from the lips of a dying man, whose only probable concern it was to ease his burthened conscience in the hour of death, should at once remove all doubt, if such remained, and the feelings of the multitude burst forth into invective.

At about ten the criminals reascended the cart; and when about to be launched into eternity, a reprieve for James Hardwicke was received and announced by the provost-marshal.

Samuels devoted the last awful minute allowed him to the most earnest and fervent prayer; at length the signal was given, and the cart drove from under him; but by the concussion the suspending cord was separated about the centre, and the culprit fell to the ground, on which he remained motionless, with his face downwards. The cart returned, and the criminal was supported on each side until another rope was applied in lieu of the former. He was again launched off, but the line unrove, and continued to flap until the legs of the sufferer trailed along the ground, the body being only half suspended.

All that beheld were also moved at his protracted sufferings; nor did some hesitate to declare that the invisible hand of Providence was at work in the behalf of him who had revealed the circumstances above related. To every appearance lifeless, the body was now raised, and supported on men's shoulders, while the executioner prepared anew the work of death. The body was gently lowered but when left alone, again fell prostrate to the earth, this rope having also snapped short, close to the neck.

Compassion could no longer bear restraint; winged with humanity, the provost-marshal sped to his Excellency's presence, in which the success of his mission overcame him. A reprieve was announced—and if mercy be a fault, it is the dearest attribute of God, and surely in Heaven it may find extenuation!

Samuels, when the provost-marshal arrived with the tidings which diffused gladness throughout every heart, was incapable of participating in the general satisfaction. By what he had endured his reasonable faculties were totally impaired; and when his nerves recovered somewhat from their feebleness, he uttered many incoherences, and was alone ignorant of what had passed. Surgical assistance has since restored him; and may the grateful remembrance of these events direct his future course.

JOHN HARRIS

Your Unfortunate Memorialist

The extraordinary powers enjoyed by governors of New South Wales proved to be a form of tyranny to the author of this letter. John Harris, a Jew, was sentenced to death at the Old Bailey in 1783 for stealing eight silver spoons, but his sentence was commuted and he eventually reached Sydney Cove with the First Fleet. He was a member of the colony's first 'night watch' in 1789, but ultimately became an innkeeper in the Sydney area, supporting his convict wife and their three children. His troubles began when Governor King insisted he rejoin the police. The consequences of his refusal convinced Harris to join Thomas Palmer on the ill-fated *El Plumier*. Palmer died in Guam, but Harris made it back to England in 1803 where he wrote this letter to Lord Hobart. His plea apparently got no response, and Harris's ultimate fate is not recorded.

November 1803—Most respectfully and humbly sheweth: That your Lordship's unfortunate memorialist was transported from this country in the year 1787. That, in the year 1789, he was sent to Norfolk Island, where he was employed by Governor King (who was then commandant of the island) as an officer of the police. That your Lordship's memorialist discharged the duties of that office with zeal and fidelity for eight years. That he then received from his Excellency Governor Hunter an absolute and unconditional emancipation, bearing date the 13th of September, 1796. That the warrant of emancipation states, it was granted 'in consideration of the good conduct and services of J— H— as a principal of the nightwatch at Norfolk Island, and at the recommendation and request of Lieutenant Governor King'.

That, after your memorialist received his emancipation, as a reward of his integrity and diligent discharge of his duty, he settled at Port Jackson and became a licensed victualler, in the exercise of which trade he continued five years, and until his Excellency Governor King had begun to officiate as governor of the colony.

That, in a few months after Governor King's arrival, he sent for your memorialist and told him he should be immediately employed at the head of the police. That your Lordship's memorialist, having a large family to support, was unwilling to abandon a trade, the profits of which afforded him and his children a comfortable and decent subsistence, and therefore humbly requested that he might be excused from accepting the office the governor wished to place him in.

That in eight or nine days after your Lordship's memorialist had expressed his humble wish not to be engaged in the public service, he was suddenly taken into custody and brought before Governor King, who told your memorialist he should be immediately tried before a court of criminal judicature for purchasing the rations of the convicts for spirituous liquors.

That your memorialist, being entirely innocent of any such offence, denied the charge, and requested to be tried in any manner the governor might think proper. That Governor King, disregarding your memorialist's protestations of innocence, demanded the key of his cellar.

That the key was instantly given up, your Lordship's memorialist, well knowing that resistance was in vain, and Governor King, attended by several people, went to your memorialist's house, but finding several large casks of wine and spirits that could not be easily moved through the door, he directed one end of the house to be torn down; that all the wine and spirits belonging to your memorialist were then brought out into the streets, where every cask was staved and every bottle emptied; that the value of what was then destroyed was more at prime cost than £400, and comprised the whole of the hard-earned reward of many years' care, frugality and industry.

That Governor King then caused your Lordship's memorialist's bureau to be opened, and took from it his licence to sell wine and spirits.

That your memorialist was afterwards again brought before Governor King, who told him that he might take possession of his empty casks, and that he was discharged from his confinement.

That your Lordship's memorialist, when he returned to his house, found it in a great degree demolished, and all his property, the source of his own and children's support, destroyed.

That dreading worse persecutions, for worse were threatened, your memorialist fled in terror from the colony, taking with him his eldest child, and leaving two behind, who were too young to accompany him.

That your Lordship's memorialist has been since shipwrecked and made a prisoner of at the Spanish island of Guam, from whence he reached this country only a few days ago, in great penury and distress.

That your memorialist can appeal with confidence to Captain Hunter, the predecessor of Governor King, and to Captain McArthur and Mr Balmain, the late principal surgeon to the settlement, for their testimony of his honesty, industry, and propriety of conduct; and the two latter gentlemen can corroborate and confirm the truth of what your Lordship's memorialist has now humbly submitted.

Your Lordship's memorialist therefore humbly prays that in consideration of the distress and misery in which he and his family are most innocently involved, and of the great cruelty and oppression he has suffered, your Lordship will be pleased to bestow upon him such relief as your Lordship's humanity and regard to justice shall dictate. And your memorialist will be ever bound in gratitude to pray.

GEORGE CALEY

Peaches beyond Expectation

George Caley was employed by Sir Joseph Banks to work as a botanist in New South Wales and he was the first European to make a close study of the eucalyptus. At times grumpy and unpredictable, Caley wrote frequent letters and reports to Banks on the state of the colony: he was perceptive enough to see that the Eora and the British were now at war, and that the Irish convicts were planning an uprising. He could not anticipate, however, the dangers peach beverages might eventually pose.

December 1803—It is not uncommon to see people in a reputable situation to be without vegetables for some months in the year. Cabbages are more used than any other. Potatoes were very bad and stinking on my first coming here, but of late are much improved; and no doubt but if the seed was exchanged often, and by a proper attention, they would still improve. Pampions and watermelons are much thought of.† Onions do not bear good seed; this is obliged to be got from Norfolk Island. These are the chief vegetables in use. As for varieties, they are but in few gardens. Grapes do not answer, for they are subject to be blighted, even in all stages of growth. Apples seem to do well, and so do figs. But peaches are beyond expectation by succeeding so well, and no doubt but they will in a few years supply the colonists with a good beverage...

Houses in general are nothing more than simple wretched huts, particularly the farmers'. The walls are wattled, and plastered

† Pampions: a kind of grapefruit.

with clay, the roof thatched, the floor frequently nothing more than the bare ground. They generally consist of two rooms, and the furniture coincides with them. But of late the building of houses has much improved, particularly in the metropolis. The walls are boarded, and painted without and plastered within, the windows glazed and the roofs shingled. They are mostly only one storey, though it seems that upper ones are aimed at, as we have a few lately so built. There are some of stone walls. No doubt but if lime was as plentiful as stone, this would be the chiefest sort of building. At the commencement of the colony several brick houses were built, and the roofs tiled; but that method is now out of use. What is called weather-boarding is most preferred...

People are better clothed now than they were when I first landed, owing to the large investments that have been sent by government and brought by private traders...After having made a list of such articles as one wants, one must apply to the governor, who looks over the list. If it meets with his approbation, he signs it. Then one must go to the commissary for him to sign it. After that one goes to the stores, and perhaps may wait a long time before one gets served. I have heard people say that they have come from Hawkesbury and been obliged to stop three days before they could get their articles. Though the goods are vended retail, yet they are not exposed for sale the same as in a shop, but left in a large storehouse, with a sentinel placed at the foot of the stepladder, where the people oftentimes form a crowd in waiting, as only one person is but generally permitted to go up at once...

In some places the prisoners complain of being hard-worked. This appears to me to arise from their never knowing what hard work was...What I may here call a good workman can do his government task in half the time that a man works day labour in England. In short, by the manner of living, being badly clothed, and in general with scarcely a rag to cover them in the night, and

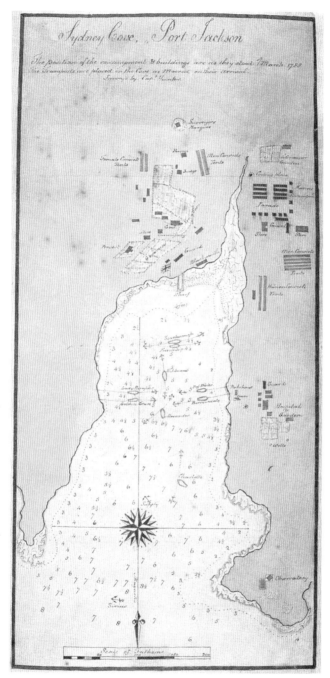

Just thirty-five days after the first convicts stepped ashore in Sydney Cove, Lieutenant William Bradley of the *Sirius* sketched the encampment. His map shows how the ships were moored, the depth of the cove, the position of the tents and the layout of the vegetable gardens, carefully planted at the height of summer.

This remarkably sensitive painting of Bennelong is attributed to the anonymous 'Port Jackson Painter'. The caption reads 'As painted when angry after Botany Bay Colebee was wounded'. Throughout much of Aboriginal Australia, painting the body with white ochre indicated martial intent. The bones fixed to Bennelong's hair are the jaws of bream.

Governor Arthur Phillip was a forty-eight-year-old retired naval officer when chosen to be governor of the proposed settlement at Botany Bay. Francis Wheatley's portrait, painted in 1786, was probably commissioned to celebrate Phillip's new posting.

Here William Bradley records the 'first interview with native women at Port Jackson'. His painting depicts a meeting between the Eora and his exploring party in Spring Cove on 30 January 1788: the first contact between two peoples separated for over 60,000 years.

A New South Wales native striking fish while his wife is employed fishing with hooks & lines in her canoe —

An Aboriginal couple fishing on the serene waters of Cadi, as the Eora knew Sydney Harbour, depicted in 1788 or shortly thereafter by the Port Jackson Painter. The Eora lived largely by fishing, often roasting their catch over a fire lit on a pad of clay in the canoe.

This view of Sydney, tentatively attributed to convict artist Thomas Watling, was painted around 1795. 'Everywhere,' the visiting Spanish navigator Alexandro Malaspina declared two years earlier, were 'the marks of oppression and disgust.' The Aborigines camped on The Rocks, the hastily lopped or ringbarked trees and the empty cove all attest to the raw nature of this most distant outpost of empire.

The most troublesome convicts in the colony were the Irish political prisoners. In 1804 a group labouring at Castle Hill, west of Sydney, rose in revolt. The uprising was crushed by Major Johnston and twenty-six soldiers of the New South Wales Corps. Johnston would later lead the only rebellion in Australian history to gain government by military force.

The French naturalist François Péron was 'completely astonished at the flourishing state' of the city he visited in the early 1800s. This view of Sydney was made by John Lancashire around 1805 and shows a far more extensive settlement: a bridge spans the Tank Stream, and boats are being built and repaired in the cove.

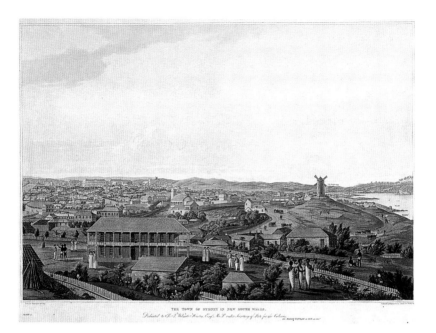

THE TOWN OF SYDNEY IN NEW SOUTH WALES.

James Taylor is responsible for this magnificent panorama of Sydney in 1821. Taken from a perspective near Brickfield Hill, it reveals a dramatically expanded and vital city. This was the place Rose de Freycinet admired but it terrified Hyacinthe de Bougainville. An unassimilated Eora presence remains evident.

By the 1840s Sydney had become what so many of its residents desired it to be—a thoroughly English port city, with all the filth and unplanned development of any major European settlement. Property agent Henry Allport depicted a bustling George Street in 1842. It doubtless appealed to prospective immigrants.

By the middle of the nineteenth century, stately mansions adorned the eastern ridge of Woolloomooloo, once a gathering place the Aborigines called Wallamola. George Peacock executed this painting of Sydney from that vantage point in 1849. It is a splendid view of a growing yet still somewhat bucolic city.

Harbourside picnics have always been an integral part of life in Sydney and this anonymous painting of 1855 is set in the area around Mrs Macquarie's Chair. Today the Opera House and Harbour Bridge are best viewed from this location, and crowds still flock to the spot.

Dawes Battery, Milsons Point, Green's yard & remains of the Dunbar.

Following the wrecking of the *Dunbar* off The Gap on the night of 20 August 1857, great rafts of flotsam drifted into Port Jackson. William Jevons photographed debris from the lost vessel at Green's Shipyard, Milsons Point, on 13 December. This is arguably Australia's first news photograph.

The discovery of gold brought enormous growth to Sydney. This photograph, taken by Alexander Brodie from the spire of St James Church around 1872, reveals the metropolis that Anthony Trollope fell in love with.

A little more than a century after Governor Phillip landed in Sydney Cove, an anonymous photographer snapped this image of Sydney's General Post Office. The building's clock tower stands over the now buried Tank Stream. Automobiles share a busy street with horse-drawn carts and pedestrians. It was only two lifetimes since the Eora had identified James Cook's ships as floating islands.

in winter they suffer much by cold, all of which must render them unfit for hard work...

Several executions have taken place for various crimes, but it is very common for to respite them at the gallows. But this does not appear to be a good way, for it causes the mind of the culprit to be in hopes to the last moment, and must tend to prevent a confession. I know an instance where two men were both found equally guilty of the crime, and both capitally convicted. At the place of execution a paper was put into the hands of each by the provost-marshal, and then returned to him again, who broke them open, and informed the one that he was to suffer and the other that he was respited! It was said that a lady on whom they had done the robbery wished for one of them to be reprieved, and the governor, being unwilling to show any partiality, he caused them to cast lots!...

The peace of the colony has been much disturbed at times. The Irish rebels have often caused great alarm, who were said to have made and concealed a deal of pikes, and that their intention was to take the colony by surprise. But all this seemed to be more talk than anything else, but in consequence necessary precautions were taken and a kind of a militia or association were embodied.

But the greatest alarm was seemingly to be apprehended from the natives, who plundered some of the settlers, robbed people upon the road, and spearing some few; and they threatened, as it was said, to set the growing wheat on fire. Strict orders were given forbidding all persons for harbouring or having any intercourse with them. At times nothing was heard of them; then all was silence. When they appeared again, then there was a hue and cry.

This sort of war lasted for about twelve months, at which time an order arrived from England respecting their behalf, and then the scene was reversed, for instead of shooting or killing them orders were given for no-one to molest them unless they were committing some depredation. The cause of this war began about some sheep which the stock-keepers said the natives had speared. Accordingly, war was declared without much deliberation and, the natives finding that we were bent upon hostility, it was not long before they revenged themselves by killing one of the stock-keepers. This affair ought and might have been settled at first, which would have prevented many of those depredations that were committed, and the inhabitants freed from that dread which incurred in their minds.

In some attempts that we made to take them by surprise, they completely duped us. I shall not hesitate to say that had they been bent for to do us as much injury as we would have done them, the matter would not have ended so well; for it was in their power for to have done us almost an irreparable injury by fire.

GEORGE SUTTOR

Desperate, Hardened and Depraved

In this letter to his patron Sir Joseph Banks, free settler George Suttor tells of the alarms and indignities suffered by himself and others during an uprising on the fringes of the settlement. The revolt originated among Irish convicts from the government farm at Castle Hill who planned a raid on the settlements of Hawkesbury, Parramatta and Sydney. In quashing it as they did, the authorities created a problem with a surge in bushrangers. Suttor also provides insights into the rift between convicts and free settlers that was to be a recurrent theme in Australian history.

> In later life Suttor was placed in charge of the lunatic
> asylum at Castle Hill, but he lost this post when accused
> of using lunatic labour on his farm at Baulkham Hills.

10 March 1804—I hope you will not be offended at this intrusion, but from the state of things in this colony I am induced to trouble you with this letter, giving an account of the wretched state of my family and a most alarming disturbance which happened on Sunday night, the 4th of March, 1804, when between one and two hundred convicts rushed out from government settlement at Castle Hill—which, indeed, had nothing to guard it but a few convict constables, the most of whom joined them.

Having seized the muskets there, the whole body came armed upon the poor settlers, plundered them of what guns and ammunition they had, threatened their lives if they made the least resistance. I had three muskets placed to my breast, and myself and wife narrowly escaped being shot. Overpowered thus by numbers, we were obliged to submit to their mercy. In this manner they continued to storm and plunder the settlers till, having possessed themselves of a hundred and eighty guns, swords, and pistols, they determined to take Parramatta, which was guarded by fifty soldiers. These they thought to overpower and get their arms.

Four hundred of them had by this time got together, and they expected in a little time to be fifteen hundred strong; but here, either from want of courage and a body of them not joining in time, they delayed their attack on Parramatta and retreated to Toongabbie Hill. They were led by two Irishmen, who had been soldiers. These and others of a like description were very busy drilling them and putting them in a military posture.

In the meantime a company of soldiers was marched up from Sydney. Even these they thought themselves strong enough to engage, but as the soldiers approached them they retreated towards the Hawkesbury, where they expected numbers to join them in their retreat. They were overtaken by a party of soldiers under Major Johnston. He rode up to them and endeavoured to bring them back to a sense of their duty, but in vain. Their cry was death or liberty, and a ship to take them Home. However, the major, by a successful manoeuvre, cut off their two leaders, and the soldiers began to fire upon them. They made but little resistance. Seventeen were killed. They began to fly in all directions till the night, which was excessively dark, put to an end to the pursuit.

Nothing can equal the horror and consternation of the country, the women and children running from farm to farm, but could find no place of safety. For three days we continued in this most wretched state of suspense, knowing we were surrounded by numbers of armed ruffians, as the fellows had at first surrounded all the passes into Parramatta. Many of them are now in the woods and, being armed, the settlers will be constantly exposed to them. Plunder they must for subsistence. Dreadful indeed must be the state of a country when such villains as these are let loose upon it. Every insult, every injury and every crime is to be expected from them that can be perpetrated by men so desperate, hardened and depraved.

Indeed, so many are the crimes that have been committed by them for the last twelve months that the bare recital is shocking to human nature—rapes, murders, robbery. Settlers' wives have been rushed in upon by seven or eight men, knocked down, treated in the most cruel manner, and ravished in sight of their family. No person in the colony is secure either in life or property, except the officers, civil and military...About a twelve-month since, twelve men left the above settlement, threatening the whole country, shot a man at a small distance from my farm. At another farm two of the scoundrels broke into the house, seized the women and ravished a young woman in sight of her mother. Since that, this worst of all crimes to society has several times been committed upon the defenceless and unprotected settlers. Indeed, the very name of settler is a term of derision.

A fault there must be somewhere, or these things would not happen. Where it originates I shall not presume to say; but surely it cannot be said that the country is in safety while the most abandoned, it is well known, have permission to range the country at large, and while so large a body of them that were kept to labour at a government settlement had no other guard over them but a few convict constables and overseers; and what confidence is to be placed in them the event has shown, and it must be confessed that the prisoners are the people most caressed in the colony. They live, in general, much better than the settlers, fill nearly all the places of trust in the colony below commissioned officers, to which they are always preferred before a free man.

George Johnston

Death or Liberty

The Castle Hill revolt of 1804 was quickly put down by Major George Johnston at Vinegar (Rouse) Hill, who recounts the event in this letter to a superior officer. After a forced march from Sydney at the head of twenty-six soldiers, he tricked the leaders of the uprising into surrendering, then cut their followers to pieces. Johnston's role in suppressing the uprising was to prove ironic, for just four years later he would head a coup against Governor Bligh and take command of the colony himself: the only rebel to take government by force in Australian history.

About half past one o'clock on Monday morning last, I took the command of the detachment marched from head-quarters by Lieutenant Davies, consisting of two officers, two sergeants, and fifty-two rank and file of the New South Wales Corps, and by his Excellency Governor King's orders, I proceeded immediately to Parramatta, where we arrived at the dawn of day.

I halted at the barracks at about twenty minutes to refresh my party, and then marched to Government House, and agreeable to his Excellency's orders divided my detachment, giving Lieutenant Davies the command of half, and taking Quartermaster Laycock and the other half, with one trooper with myself, having the governor's instructions to march in pursuit of the rebels along the Toongabbie Road.

I proceeded that way, and directed Lieutenant Davies to take the road towards Castle Hill. On my arrival at Toongabbie, I was informed the rebels, in number about four hundred, were on the summit of the hill. I immediately detached a corporal with four privates and about six inhabitants armed with muskets to take them in flank, whilst I proceeded with the rest up the hill, when I found the rebels had marched on for the Hawkesbury, and after a pursuit of about ten miles I got sight of them.

I immediately rode forward, attended by the trooper and Mr Dixon, the Roman Catholic priest, calling to them to halt, that I wished to speak to them. They desired that I would come into the middle of them, as their captains were there, which I refused, observing to them that I was within pistol shot and that it was in their power to kill me, and that their captains must have very little spirit if they would not come forward to speak to me, upon which two persons (C— and J—) advanced towards me as their leaders, to whom I represented the impropriety of their conduct and advised them to surrender, and that I would mention them in as favourable terms as possible to the governor.

C— replied they would have death or liberty.

Quartermaster Laycock with the detachment just then appearing in sight, I clapped my pistol to J—'s head, whilst the trooper did the same to C—'s, and drove them with their swords in their hands to the quartermaster and the detachment, whom I ordered to advance and charge the main body of the rebels when formed in a line.

The detachment immediately commenced a well-directed fire, which was but weakly returned, for the rebel line being soon broken they ran in all directions. We pursued them a considerable way and have no doubt but that many of them fell. We have found twelve killed, six wounded, and have taken twenty-six prisoners…Return of arms taken from the rebels: twenty-six muskets, one fowling piece, four bayonets on poles, one pitchfork, one pistol, eight reaping hooks, two swords.

A Prodigious Shark

As early as 1788 William Bradley wrote that 'the Harbour is full of sharks', and some were nasty customers indeed. The kind of shark present in Sydney Harbour varies with the seasons: winter brings the most deadly of all, the great whites, which prey on seals and cetaceans. When the sea temperature rises above 21 degrees Celsius the tropical species arrive, which include tiger and bull sharks. There has not been a shark fatality in Sydney Harbour for over half a century, but bull sharks have been blamed for several attacks in recent times. The unfortunate Aborigine mentioned in the following narrative was probably harried by a tiger.

Sydney Gazette, 23 October 1805—A few days ago some people who were at work in North Harbour were suddenly surprised by the shouts of terrible distress vociferated by a native, whom they observed to be paddling for the shore with every exertion of which the human frame can be conceived capable.

The author of his terrors was a prodigious shark which escorted him with voracious attention, and had once struck the little wretched vehicle that scarcely separated him from his apparently devoted prey. The poor fellow had fortunately been successful in collecting a little pile of fish, and these he one by one administered to the appetite of his pursuer, by which happy artifice he reached the shore at the very instant that his whole stock was expended.

He appeared thoroughly sensible of his obligation to the providence that had preserved him, and declared in amazement that ten yards must have sacrificed him.

Splendour and Magnificence

In March 1806, during the ten days of Muharram of the Muslim calendar, the crew of the *Sydney*, a sailing vessel then moored in Sydney Cove, treated the town to a spectacular festival. The 'festival of Hassan' is a re-enactment of the funerary parade of the burial of the Shi'ite leader Husain. It is unusual among Islamic festivals and probably incorporates pre-Islamic rites. The 'temple' that graced Back Row (now Phillip Street) was a reconstruction of Husain's coffin and the 'swords and bludgeons' Husain's arms. The portrayal of Husain's sufferings in battle and his death are meant to be highly realistic, and in this regard the *Gazette* acknowledged the festival a triumph. The Anglicisation of Sydney over the next few decades would banish such events from the city and a substantial Muslim population would not return until the late twentieth century.

*S*ydney *Gazette*, 23 March 1806—The Asiatic seamen of the Mahometan faith belonging to the *Sydney* have for several weeks past been making preparation for celebrating one of their chief festivals, that of their champion Hassan. These people have exerted every ingenuity in the formation of a temple composed of canework covered and beautifully decorated with paper stained by themselves, which will require one side of the shed in which it was constructed to be taken down before it can be exhibited in public.

Their customs on this occasion are very extravagant, and bear strong marks of unaccountable superstition. On Thursday evening they walked in procession from Mr Campbell's to their lodging house at the lower end of Back Row East, with torches, and each man armed with a sword or short bludgeon, with which they exhibited a sham battle royal, everyone indiscriminately battering his neighbour without dread of action or indictment.

This conflict at an end, the business took a quite contrary turn. They paraded round a fire, then housed, and ranging themselves in front of Hassan's temple, performed extravagancies wild and incredible amidst the odiferous fumigation of sandalwood and other perfumes. A couple singling themselves out as voluntary devotees, performed a thousand antics, many of which must have been accompanied with a lively sensation of pain. With instruments peculiarly constructed they seemed to pierce their cheeks, tongues and thighs, at the same time mechanically bellowing with pain, in which they never failed to keep time with three tamborines and the vocal accompaniment of the whole group.

They expressed not the slightest disapprobation of the spectators;

but one or two, who presumed by an impudent interference to insult their prejudices, were properly treated by other inhabitants who chanced also to be present, and compelled to leave the place.

The next day they were prevented by the rain from showing themselves in public, having only once caught an interval between the showers to display their champion's bow, bound round with red and blue bunting, and raised on a staff about twelve feet in length, to which they paid every mark of respect. From the best information we can obtain, next Friday or Saturday will conclude this festival in all the imitative pomp of eastern splendour and magnificence that the slender finances of a few individuals devoutly attached to their customs and religion will admit.

Several gentlemen at present in the colony who have witnessed the celebration of this festival in Asia declare it the most brilliant and interesting spectacle conceivable, the sums expended on it never amounting to less than from two to three hundred thousand rupees!

George Caley

Eradicate All the Peach Trees

Sydney was a thirsty city from the start, a fact which drove the authorities to despair. Despite his irascible nature George Caley reveals in this extract from a letter to Sir Joseph Banks that he was no prohibitionist: he simply preferred a better drop than peach cider.

7 July 1808—I have frequently taken the liberty to tell you of the ill effects caused by spirits not being allowed to be more

general in use. Whether you acquiesce with my opinions or not, I am at a loss to know. If you do not, I think I shall now convince you of the error. From the abundance of peaches that are now annually produced, a great quantity of cider is made. Though it may in a great respect be compared to hogwash, yet it is drunk with the same eagerness as if it was of a good quality; and I have witnessed it to produce as great a scene of intoxication as I ever did from foreign spirits. What is to be done now? Will it be good policy to eradicate all the peach trees?

Read All about It

So many robberies filled the pages of the *Gazette* that any opportunity to vary their reportage was eagerly grasped. 'Happy' Howe, who was to remain editor from the paper's inception until his death in 1821, was not entirely without his own spark of literary genius. Week after week, he kept the inhabitants of Sydney informed about much more than the governor's latest decree or the continuing skirmishes with the leading Eora warriors. Accounts of cannibals, advertisements for wives, the break-up of relationships and even lightning strikes were all grist to Howe's mill.

Sydney Gazette, 12 March 1809—On Sunday last James Hutchinson...was apprehended at a public house in Sydney, into which he had entered by squeezing through two iron bars at the back window of a bedroom, which were so close together as to oblige him to strip stark naked before he could make his entry good.

With scarce a feeble glimmering of light in the room, the mistress first perceived what she considered to be the faint shadow of a human likeness, which imagination she communicated to her husband in a very low whisper; and he, considering upon the other hand the vast improbability of any corporal substance being gifted with the power of compressing itself sufficiently to enter any aperture in the apartment, soon made his mind up that what she saw and was now to himself visible could be neither more or less than one of those ethereal visitors better known by the denomination of a ghost; nor did she hesitate a moment to fall into the conception, as it had long been mutually understood the house was *haunted*.

The discovery was perfectly sudorific: the teeth chattered; the sinews received an agitated motion; piety burst forth in ejaculations fervent, with every other circumstance of pure and unadulterated terror.

It happened also that the *Tales of the Genii*, and some very ancient and respectable histories of British goblins had frequently contributed to the evening's family recreation. This therefore was a favourable opportunity for the recollection to harrow up some of the most terrific visions with which those chimerical productions improve the taste and enlarge the understanding. Without the aid of so much useful reading, the sensation of terror could not have been half so perfect; but as it was, so rationally wound up, every hair stood individually erect like 'quills upon the fretful porcupine'.

It is generally understood that terror, which is one of the baser affections, does not operate upon every mind alike; in fact this also has been remarked with respect to the noblest passions of the human heart. This remark, so far as relates to terror, was here sufficiently exemplified: for while the husband decorously observed a profound silence, not willing that the apparition should even hear him draw his breath, the wife went off into a fit, and with her screams still more alarmed him than the ghost had done already. As there can be no hazard in stirring in things that are already at the worst, desperation sometimes has the effect of courage, and very frequently accomplishes more than deliberate bravery would have attempted—but, be it as it might, the consequences are all we have to look at. For he leaped as the ghost was about to retire, and caught in his arms the choice spirit abovementioned to whom may be attributed a more mischievous design in his nocturnal visit than could have entered the imagination of any real ghost that ever returned to tell the secrets of his dwelling.

★

Sydney Gazette, 3 September 1809—Some of the distant settlers have had recent occasion to complain of the conduct of the natives, a few among whom have manifested a disposition to mischievous acts. A man of the name of Tunks in company with another was attacked near Parramatta by three blacks, among whom was young Bundle and Tedbury, the son of Pemulwy, who was shot some years since on account of his murders, and the horrible barbarities he had exercised on many solitary travellers.

The son appears to have inherited the ferocity and vices of his father. Upon the above occasion he pointed his spear to the head and breast of Tunks, and repeatedly threatened to plunge the weapon into him; but, other persons fortunately appearing in sight, the assailants betook to the woods.

Several other such attacks have been made, but as Tedbury is stated to have always been of the party, which consisted but of two or three, it may be inferred that a spirit of malevolence is far from general; and under this belief, it may be hoped the settlers will not permit their servants or families to practise unnecessary severities which may irritate and provoke those, who are at present peaceably disposed, to join in the atrocities of a few miscreants, whom their own tribe, if not exasperated by ill treatment, would no doubt as they have frequently done before, betray into our hands, and avowedly assist in apprehending.

★

Sydney Gazette, 5 November 1809—By a recent arrival it is credibly reported that Thomas Ray, otherwise Ratty, who has been repeatedly advertised as an absentee under the head Police Notice, was some time since devoured by the natives at New Zealand, having effected his escape from hence, and afterwards deserted the vessel there to prevent his being returned hither, which the unfortunate man too late discovered must have been the inevitable consequence of his rashness.

★

Sydney Gazette, 12 November 1809—I am one of the oldest residents in this colony, and therefore beg to offer a few general remarks upon a subject, with observation for my guide, in which my feelings most seriously interest me; and this is, Sir, the very unaccountable indifference with which some of my old acquaintances have renounced deserving women, with whom they passed whole years in social habits, and to whose care and industry they have in many cases been principally indebted for the little they were in possession of at the very moment of their separation.

One of this unhappy class of females occupies a little wretched hovel in my neighbourhood, and passes most of her time in lamenting the misfortune of having placed a generous confidence in a man who, after an eleven years association, had inhumanly renounced her at a period of life which leaves her hopeless of ever more enjoying the sweets of comfort. This poor woman's industry I had frequently been an eye-witness of; she had lived a sparing life, and was attached to the interests of the man she dwelt with, whose wants she constantly endeavoured to anticipate.

At their first outset in this part of the world they met on equal terms, for if one had little the other had no more; but, after a patient struggle against the poverty of their condition, the dawn of better fortune opened gradually upon their prospects, and perseverance strengthened hourly their mutual expectations.

At length the sun of friendship ceased to shine upon the fortunes of this poor Penelope; for the hero of my story, who had just attained the age of fifty-one, became enamoured of a little creature of *thirteen*, and in the fever of his passion at once resolved to throw his life and fortune at her feet! The treaty for a time was secretly conducted; but shame was vanquished by all-conquering love, and the young lady introduced eventually—to take possession of the dwelling.

That the supplanted fair became a prey to grief I scarcely need inform you; her very presence soon became a reproach to the Adonis, not to be endured. Her sobs, her sighs, her tears and lamentations were offensive also to her happy rival, and yet, to quit for ever the place to which her prudence and economy had given the air of comfort was far from tolerable, but contumely and insult were still less to be supported.

In so deplorable a dilemma, resolution could alone befriend her, for she had lost the only friendship that she valued. The time of her departure drawing near, she craved some small supply to her immediate wants, and yet this pittance was denied her. When the separating moment came, the remembrance of the past unkindly darted into her imagination, and in a transport of affliction she caught him by the hand, and bathed it with her tears. Then, with a glance of kind forgiveness, bade adieu! invoking blessings as she went upon the injurer, whose guilt permitted no reply...

Now, then, I must inform you, that this discarded miserable is in extreme want; while the author of her wretchedness supports his little favourite in a very handsome style. The poor soul has so constantly indulged her griefs as to impair her intellects, and now, unable to contribute much to her own support, lives mostly upon the little charitable donations of her poor neighbours. She has at all times, however, a strong recollection of the man that has so barbarously used her, and ever bursts into tears upon the mention of his name.

★

Sydney Gazette, 10 December 1809—Matrimonial Overture— Wanted, an agreeable lady to approach the holy altar in communion with the lonely advertiser, whose circumstances in life are neither above want nor beneath extravagance. The lady's years, if past the climacteric, are requested not to exceed seventy-one or two, the advertiser being in the animating bloom of *eighty-five*: a season when the passions promise to endure *durante vitae.*

Although a foe to sordid notions, yet the advertiser, more inclined to Platonism than tempestuous love, considers it convenient to suggest that a little wealth will not diminish the lustre of the lady's charms, since, time immemorial, few matrimonial contracts have been entered into in which the golden deity hath not been more candidly consulted than the god of love, whose arrows wound no more.

Unwilling to put modesty to the blush by requiring a personal interview prior to the conclusion of the treaty, the interference of a friend will be accepted; and, unsight, unseen, if the circumstances of the fair one answer contract, and she have no objection to a rural retirement among the overhanging shades of Bardo-Narrang, a line left at the *Gazette* office will find attention from the ever constant.

★

Sydney Gazette, 17 December 1809—Answer to the Matrimonial Overture of last week—If the Narcissus of Bardo-Narrang will be kind enough to leave his portrait for inspection at any convenient place, the advertiser will take the earliest occasion to wait upon the shadow, and immediately determine on the degree of estimation in which she is to hold the represented substance; and being desirous that sincerity should strictly be adhered to, she trusts the one may be a true copy of the other.

Without vanity, the advertiser begs to assure the gentleman, whoever he may be, that should matters be brought to a happy issue, he will undoubtedly find himself as eligibly matched as he could wish. His age, so far from opposing any obstacle to the union, is a chief inducement to this communication, as the advertiser has for eight-and-twenty years at least held in contempt the present generation of admirers, who either go to market for a lady's fortune without regard to her person; or if pecuniary considerations be in a few romantic instances lain aside, that then consult a woman's age and stature with as much precision as a Smithfield jockey bargaining about a horse, instead of deliberately imagining that he was making choice of a partner upon whom, more than upon the whole combination of events in life beside, depends the smoothness or roughness of the journey.

In point of wealth the advertiser is no boaster; her condition in this respect bringing to mind the case of a once distinguished character who having occasion for very heavy bail, brought forward a poor simpleton of a Jew to swear himself intrinsically worth ten thousand pounds. The gentleman's great modesty and politeness in declining any personal interview previous to the conclusion of the treaty is an exemplary proof of a disinterested passion perfectly suited to the celestial spot of his retirement; and as an additional charm to eighty-five, when the passions promise to endure *durante vitae,* the advertiser begs to suggest, that should a dissonance of temper mingle acids with connubial sweets, all little jarrings between seventy-two and eighty-five are likely to be soon obliviated in the silent tomb.

The advertiser is vain enough, however, to imagine, that she may answer contract; and unsight, unseen, has no objection to an immediate negotiation, as at seventy-two there is no time to be lost.

Chloe

★

Sydney Gazette, 7 January 1810—The thunderstorm that set in between four and five yesterday afternoon was accompanied with very vivid lightning, the effects of which were sensibly felt by many, some of whom have had as sensibly to feel their obligation to the divine protection.

The *Gazette* office was struck in several places at different intervals. Many of the printing materials being formed of iron, the causes of attraction were no doubt the stronger, and the effects were truly awful. In the two lower rooms were eleven persons, six of whom were children, and all were affected in a greater or less degree, but none seriously injured. By the first shock, a young man, an assistant, felt a violent concussion on the head, which bowed him to the ground, but which he at the moment attributed to the fall of some weighty substance overhead.

He immediately left the place on which he stood, however, and in retreating into the adjoining room was opposed in his passage by a crash occasioned by the bursting in of a back door, the whole wood and brickwork connected with which was rent to atoms, some of the shattered materials being driven inwards, and others outwards to the distance of thirty feet from the door.

The publisher, happening at the time to be revising a proof impression of this paper, was thrown backwards with his feet, unconscious to what cause to attribute the disaster so instantaneously impaired was his recollection. On rising, he found himself enveloped in smoke as he then imagined, but more probably in the dust of lime and mortar scattered from the brickwork.

Those who were less affected than himself declare that the electric matter had the appearance of a ball, which rebounded to and fro with a velocity peculiar to itself. On subsequent examination it appears to have entered the house at different parts, the inner brickwork of the chimney being in many places fractured, one of the rafters of the roof and a board in the upper floor splintered, and the brickwork of many parts both within and without the house visibly impaired by the same awful and terrific cause.

LACHLAN MACQUARIE

Sin City

Lachlan Macquarie arrived in Sydney on 1 January 1810 and governed the colony for twelve years. His improvements were many: he issued the first coinage and established the first bank; under his encouragement agriculture and public works flourished. The Hyde Park Barracks was completed by the end of 1810 and shortly afterwards the 'Rum Hospital' was erected—its construction paid for by granting a limited monopoly to import spirits to principal surgeon D'Arcy Wentworth and two others.

Despite his great works, Macquarie was to make enemies in the colony, especially over his determination to see former convicts returned to society. Many free settlers, among them the Reverend Samuel Marsden, who had been in Sydney since 1794, were horrified by the idea. By 1818, Marsden had fallen out so badly with the governor that he was called to Government House and denounced as a secret enemy. Marsden had his revenge, however, for the mistrust he whipped up in London over Macquarie's governorship resulted in J. T. Bigge being sent to New South Wales to investigate matters. Bigge was a bigot when it came to ex-convicts, and his report was, Macquarie said, 'false, vindictive and malicious'. To the end of his life, in 1824, Macquarie felt that the report had ruined his reputation.

In early 1810, however, Macquarie was determined to fulfil the brief given him by Viscount Castlereagh, secretary of state for the colonies, of improving the morals of Sydney, encouraging marriage, providing education and curbing the use of spirituous liquors. He wasted no time, closing grog shops and brothels, arresting absconders from church and instituting the first gun laws. He shaped the city we know today, giving its streets the names they are still known by. His prediction that 'my name will not readily be forgotten' has been amply fulfilled.

Sydney Gazette, 17 February 1810—The very great and unnecessary number of licensed houses for retailing wines and spirituous liquors that have hitherto been allowed to exist in the town of Sydney, and adjacent districts, cannot fail of being productive of the most mischievous and baneful effects on the morals and industry of the lower part of the community, and must inevitably lead to a profligacy of manners, dissipation and idleness.

In view, therefore, to check these evils, as well as in the hope of its awaking sentiments of morality, and a spirit of industry amongst the lower orders of the people, his Excellency the governor has deemed it his indispensable duty to make a reduction of the number of the licensed houses for retailing spirits &c., and no more than the following numbers in the town and adjacent districts will be hereafter allowed on any account whatsoever;

namely, twenty houses in the town of Sydney; one at the Half-way House on the road between Sydney and Parramatta; three in the town of Parramatta; one at the Half-way House between Sydney and Hawkesbury; and six at Hawkesbury and adjacent districts...

Any person, therefore, retailing or attempting to retail wines or spirituous liquors without a license, after the promulgation of this order, will be fined in the sum of twenty pounds sterling, besides forfeiting the whole stock of wines or liquors found in their possession—half of which wines and liquors to go to the informer, and the other half to the crown.

Sydney Gazette, 24 February—His Excellency cannot forbear to make known his indignation towards those persons who, in defiance of all law and decency, scandalously keep open, during the night, the most licentious and disorderly houses, for the reception of the abandoned of both sexes, and to the great encouragement of dissolute and disorderly habits; and he publicly avows his resolution to give strict orders to the officers of the police, to report to him the proprietors of all such houses, and to punish such offenders to the utmost extent allowed by law.

Sydney Gazette, 19 March—The total disregard with which many of the lower classes of the inhabitants of this town treat the Sabbath day, and their notorious and shameful profanation of it even during the time of divine worship, compel his Excellency the governor, however reluctantly, to have recourse to coercive measures to put a stop to this growing evil.

In pursuance of this intention his Excellency directs that regular patrols of constables shall be established in the different quarters of the town during the time of divine service in the morning and evening of every Sunday, for the purpose of taking up and committing to gaol all vagrants, and such other idle persons as may be found walking about the town during the time of divine worship who cannot give a satisfactory account of themselves.

Sydney Gazette, 7 April—Whereas a most unwarrantable and dangerous practice hath existed for some time past, and appears to be daily increasing, of certain persons carrying guns and shooting in the immediate neighbourhood of the town of Sydney, and close upon his Excellency the governor's Domain, in violation of decency, and at the risk of individuals passing on their private concerns. Notice is hereby given, that all persons who may be found to offend in this way in future will be deprived of their guns, and otherwise dealt with, as the law in such cases directs.

Sydney Gazette, 6 October—His Excellency the governor, being extremely desirous to do everything in his power that can in the least degree contribute to the ornament and regularity of the town of Sydney, as well as to the convenience, accommodation and safety of the inhabitants thereof, has already, in prosecution of these views, divided the town into five separate districts, and has given directions for the erecting immediately a proper watch-house in each district, for the protection of the inhabitants from night robberies, and for the more effectually securing the peace and tranquillity of the town, and apprehending all disorderly and ill-disposed persons committing nightly depredations. In further prosecution of these views, his Excellency also intends to establish a well-regulated and strict system of police in the town, as soon as the watchhouses are completely finished.

As a necessary preparatory step to the proposed arrangements, his Excellency deems it expedient to give regular and permanent names to all the streets and ways leading through the town, and to order posts and finger-boards, with the names of the streets painted on them, to be erected in conspicuous parts of the different streets where they cross each other, as well as at their respective terminations. These posts and finger-boards are accordingly to be immediately put up, and the streets are henceforth to be known and called only by the new names now given them…

It being intended to remove all those old buildings and enclosures now on that space of ground which is bounded by the government Domain on the east, by the judge-advocate's, secretary's, chaplain's, and commissary's houses on the south, by the spring of water and stream on the west, and by the houses of Mr Lord, Mr Thompson, and Mr Reibey on the north, and to throw the same into an open area, the said area or space of ground, has been named Macquarie Place, and it is henceforth to be so denominated.

The present marketplace being very badly and inconveniently situated, it is his Excellency's intention to remove the market very soon to a more commodious and centrical situation for the inhabitants of the town in general. The place thus intended to remove the market to is that piece of open ground (part of which was lately used by Messrs Blaxland as a stockyard &c.) bounded by George Street on the east, York Street on the west, Market Street on the north, and the burying ground on the south; and is henceforth to be called Market Square.

For the further accommodation and convenience of the inhabitants in general, and particularly of those persons bringing corn or other grain, goods or other merchandise, in vessels or boats from the Hawkesbury &c. to the market, it is intended to erect a wharf immediately at Cockle Bay, contiguous to the new marketplace; and from thence there will be a good road or street made to communicate directly with the said market square; and which, when completed, is to be called Market Wharf.

The whole of the open ground yet unoccupied in the vicinity of the town of Sydney, hitherto known and alternately called by the names of 'the common', 'exercising ground', 'cricket ground', and 'race course', bounded by the government Domain on the north, the town of Sydney on the west, the brickfields on the south, and Mr Palmer's premises on the east, being intended in future for the recreation and amusement of the inhabitants of the town, and as a field of exercise for the troops, the governor has thought proper to name the ground thus described Hyde Park, by which name it is henceforth to be called and denominated...

New names of streets	Old names of streets
1. George Street	High Street, Spring Row or Sergeant Major's Row
2. Prince Street	Windmill Row
3. York Street	Barrack Street
4. Clarence Street	Middle Soldiers' Row
5. Kent Street	Back Soldiers' Row
6. Cumberland Street	(No Name)
7. Sussex Street	(No Name)
8. Cambridge Street	(No Name)
9. Pitt Street	Pitt's Row
10. Castlereagh Street	Chapel Row
11. Phillip Street	Back Row East
12. Hunter Street	Bell Street

Death of a Champion

Bennelong was estimated to be forty-nine when he passed away on 3 January 1813. The official report of his death in the *Sydney Gazette* reveals a man confident in his own culture who was, from the first, unwilling to bend to the will of another. He remained the brilliant, mercurial and distinctly 'other' kind of being that Tench had met and admired some twenty-five years earlier.

9 January 1813—Bennelong died on Sunday morning last at Kissing Point. Of this veteran champion of the native tribe little favourable can be said. His voyage to and benevolent treatment in Great Britain produced no change whatever in his manners and inclinations, which were naturally barbarous and ferocious.

The principal officers of government had for many years endeavoured, by the kindest of usage, to wean him from his original habits and draw him into a relish for civilised life; but every effort was in vain exerted and for the last few years he has been but little noticed. His propensity to drunkenness was inordinate; and when in that state he was insolent, menacing and overbearing. In fact, he was a thorough savage, not to be warped from the form and character that nature gave him by all the efforts that mankind could use.

ALEKSEY ROSSIYSKY

The Russians Are Coming

The first Russian vessel to anchor in Port Jackson arrived in 1807, and there were subsequent visits in 1814 and 1820. The Russian visitors made important observations of the colony and of the Aborigines who dwelt on its fringes. Here we meet Aleksey Rossiysky, the navigator of the *Suvorov*, as he observes Eora combat. He writes of the pleasure some colonists took in witnessing these battles. Upon going out to check the chronometers the following morning, however, he was to discover another aspect of Aboriginal life.

August 1814—On the 20th, I learned that there was that day to be a fight amongst the natives, at a place designated for that purpose. The event struck me as so interesting that I certainly did not wish to miss it: I resolved even to neglect the checking of chronometers that day. Having first obtained the captain's permission to do so, I got ready at 9 a.m. and went to the spot in question with Mr de Silvier and Krasil'nikov, the supercargo's assistant.

On our arrival, there was nobody about; but after a little time a large crowd began to gather (for the English have a particular love of fights of every sort). At 11 a.m., we saw some thirty armed and running natives, all quite naked. Each had with him three spears, a shield, and a bludgeon, all these articles being made of an exceedingly hard wood which the English call ironwood. At length, another twenty or so men ran up and, at a signal given by one of their number, they divided into several parties. Then a dreadful racket was raised on all sides and, in an instant, from two opposite quarters, spears flew.

The spears of these natives are four, eight, and ten feet long. The ten-foot spears are of three joined parts, two being of ordinary wood, the third of ironwood. The tip is sharpened and little jags are made. These spears are cast by hand indeed, but only by means of a hook which is attached to the tip, to produce greater force. The shields are made of the bark of the ironwood tree, and are oval and slightly convex; a small handle is attached to their back. They are usually about two and a half feet in length, one and a half feet in breadth, and an inch or so thick, and are daubed with various red and white figures.

These natives can protect themselves from flying spears, with their shields or simply by dodging, with extraordinary skill. But meanwhile, almost imperceptibly, more and more natives had been gathering from all directions, until at length they numbered about a hundred.

With every hour, the fighting became more stubborn. Finally, when all their spears had been hurled, the combatants started in with their bludgeons, from which they likewise defended their bodies with amazing dexterity, now covering themselves with their shields, now retreating, advancing, turning aside. These bludgeons are called *sagays*: lower down the shaft is slender, but it thickens out steadily towards the end, which is tipped with the very hardest wood. The bludgeons are three or three and a half feet long.

Woe betide those who are not nimble at this juncture! All at once, the bludgeon goes to the head and a man is half killed by a single blow. One can scarcely imagine with what desperation and what ferocity the natives fall upon each other, now striking, now repulsing. If a man falls, his strength gone, other men instantly club him almost to death, striking at his temple with a bestial joy. The clash of shields, flying fragments of spear, the wild cries of the victors, the pitiable wail of the wounded, bloodied faces, broken limbs: I confess that only the English could admire all this. But the battle lasted for more than two hours and ended only when many had grown weak. I remained a few minutes longer at the scene of conflict to gaze at the wounded combatants. I looked and was horrified: blood flowed in streams, here from a head, there from a chest or shoulder. One individual had had an eye put out; from the forehead of another there protruded the tip of a spear. In short, almost all the natives were wounded in the most awful fashion.

Any sensitive man would shudder at such bestial conflicts; but the English, so far from averting the natives from them, attempt further to stir the natives up against each other. The sight of one's fellows' sufferings has been made a spectacle of entertainment.

The following morning, Mr de Silvier and I went to check the chronometers on Bennelong's Point, and there we met with a curious incident. We had only made a few preliminary readings when we caught sight of five natives, including a woman. They were approaching us. Having our astronomical instruments with us, we were rather nervous lest the natives disturb them; but then we calmed down, thinking that the natives had not spotted us. To the contrary, they came straight to us and sat close by on the grass, repeating many times words that they had learned from the English: 'How do you do?' and 'Very well'.

They looked at the sextant, chronometer, and artificial horizon with astonishment. The woman was the most inquisitive of all the five, and examined the horizon so minutely that she saw her own reflection in the mercury and was startled. However, she examined it anew, and this time she shouted in a very loud voice: at which, all the others rushed right up to the mercury holder. How this amazed them, and how wonderfully they contorted their bodies, was a sight to behold. But the woman was incessantly asking me now, by signs and words, to raise the mercury holder. I did so, having first poured the mercury out into a specially made phial. Seeing nothing in the holder this time, the natives were saddened; but their curiosity burned yet brighter.

Whilst I had been pouring out the mercury, and Mr de Silvier removing our sextant from them, one native had discovered the chronometer and was showing its moving second hand to his fellows, in amazement. All then drew close to the instrument and, no matter how hard I tried to keep them off, they stubbornly insisted that I show it to them—to such a point, indeed, that they began seriously to alarm me by indicating their weapons. So, to satisfy them, I was forced to take off my own watch, which also had a second hand, and to show them its inside.

Their wonder at the sight of the pendulum, which shone in their eyes, was indescribable. They handed the watch round delightedly, and I failed to observe how ultimately one of their number took up a twig and thrust it between the wheels, which made the watch stop. This so irritated me that I took the watch back and started to drive them away; but Mr de Silvier advised me to be more circumspect since they were five and we—only two. After remaining a few minutes longer, the natives laughed loudly and went off.

Having parted from us, they next proceeded to lay a fire and gather mussels on the shore. When they had roasted these on the fire, they began to eat and said hardly a word for an hour. Then they started to talk among themselves, softly at first, but then extremely noisily—about what, we could not say. We surmised that they were boasting about the fight of the day before, for they were continually pointing to their weapons or wounds, and it seemed that each man was trying to convince the rest that he was braver than they.

JACQUES ARAGO

A Gesture So Expressive

A botanic artist, Jacques Arago accompanied Louis de Freycinet's expedition to the Pacific. They set out in the *Uranie* from Toulon on 17 September 1817 and by November 1819 were approaching Port Jackson when they encountered a squall. They finally anchored at Sydney Cove on 19 November 1819. At first, like many visitors, Arago was transported with rapture by the beauty of the settlement. He was also fascinated by the Aborigines, and even followed one poor couple into the bushes to see what they were up to. French curiosity about Eora sexual practices had been intense: back in 1802 artists from the Baudin expedition had taken to drawing the 'voluptuous' positions favoured by the Aborigines.

Arago was to discover much more than he might have imagined when, following his lovers, he stumbled into an Aboriginal maternity ward.

November 1819—It is seven o'clock in the morning. We are still plying to windward, and I am afraid we shall not see Port Jackson today. How vexatious!

But the wind suddenly ceases; we have a chopping sea, as after a violent storm; flashes of white lightning furrow the cloud that flies rapidly over the mountains, already enveloped in dark night. This vast mass of vesicular vapour separates from the earth and remains motionless at a small elevation; other copper-coloured clouds fall on it, they become tornadoes, collect, and change their shapes and hues. The eye perceives balls of fire, sheaves, phantoms. You wish to point out an object; it is gone. Rapid fires rend them, the thunder sullenly growls: you would say that all the elements in confusion were warring against each other in the air. The ship is motionless and prudently awaits the issue of the turmoil it witnesses. The sails are brailed up. Presently the sea boils around it: it is agitated, it rises, it bellows and we, tossed about by it, are driven twenty or thirty leagues from that land at which we had flattered ourselves with arriving some days sooner...

I will not give you a description of the town, which I have just gone through. I am enchanted and I had rather give my admiration some respite. Magnificent hotels, majestic mansions, houses of extraordinary taste and elegance, fountains ornamented with sculptures worthy the chisel of our best artists, spacious and airy apartments, rich furniture, horses, carriages, and one-horse chaises of the greatest elegance, immense storehouses—would you expect to find all these four thousand leagues from Europe? I assure you, my friend, I fancied myself transported into one of our handsomest cities.

The English garden that embellishes the government house particularly fixed my attention. I spent two hours there in one evening and, beneath a Norfolk pine, whose horizontal and graceful branches agreeably sheltered me from the heat of the sun, I sat down to meditate on my native land. The shrill cry of the yellow-crested white cockatoo occasionally struck my ear and, while I pursued with my eye and could stroke with my hand the silky plumage and rounded bodies of several black swans that stalked sedately through the walks, my attention was distracted by the irregular noise of the swift kangaroo which, resting on its tail and long hind feet, leaped over hedges and bushes without any object in view.

Everything was new to me, trees and animals; and I cannot express to you the magic charm I felt as my memory dwelt on the dearest objects of my own country from which everything in nature told me I was far away.

A single instant had produced this metamorphosis, a single step had caused these new emotions. In the town I beheld Europe, for European hands had raised it: here nature was not altered and not a form, scarcely a leaf, resembled the productions of our countries. I was alone with myself, I was a stranger to everything...

I cannot comprehend how the government of Sydney, so sage in its regulations, so just and severe in its policy, can permit savages from the interior to reside in the capital. For the purpose of concealing from women and young girls the disgusting spectacle of hideous nakedness, it ought to confine to a separate quarter all those wretches who wear no kind of clothing or, by a regulation strictly enforced, oblige the savages to conceal at least certain parts with the skin of a kangaroo, or some other covering...

The manners of these poor creatures, their habits and customs, furnish the curious inquirer with a number of interesting particulars. When we think of the poverty of their country, and the scanty resources they find in the waters of the ocean and rivers, and when we calculate the small advantages they can derive from their weapons, we need not be surprised at the small number of individuals that travellers have found in these vast solitudes.

The wandering and precarious life they are forced to lead, and the very frequent recurrence of a total want of food, sufficiently account for their feeble constitutions. A body lean, and far from robust, supports a head void of expression, or rather characterised by brutal ferociousness. They have in general small eyes, a very flat nose, a mouth of monstrous width, enormous feet and hands, excessively slender legs and arms, and very white teeth.

Most of them want the two front teeth of the upper jaw; and I have seen a young girl of fourteen or fifteen undergo this painful operation with astonishing fortitude. She rested her head against a wall, while a woman much older than herself, whom I took to be her mother from the likeness between them, applied to the two teeth she wished to be removed a bit of wood of the thickness of a quill, and struck it with a large stone. The young girl did not utter a single cry, or make the least wry face, though the operation was twice repeated. As I was very desirous of knowing whether this custom were generally adopted by all girls, and whether there were any period at which this sacrifice was enjoined them, I endeavoured by my gestures to make the old woman understand me, and asked why she had thus removed these two teeth.

She answered me by a gesture so expressive, adopted in all the islands of the South Sea, that I no longer doubted but the young girl was about to be married; and I was still more convinced of this when I saw a savage painted with a thousand stripes come up, throw a kangaroo skin over the shoulders of his intended, spit repeatedly in her face, and trace on her body stripes of all colours with ochre and gums. I confess this fashion of dressing, and the attention paid to it by her gallant adorer, so raised my curiosity, that I followed the happy couple as far as the wood that surrounds the governor's garden. The two spouses made their appearance a few minutes after, and I observed on the face of the husband some traces of the stripes that I had seen on that of the woman.

Alas! how brief is the duration of gallantry among these men, barbarous as they are, though so near the state of nature! On his return from this excursion, the husband threw on his wife's shoulders a little bag containing some provision for which he was indebted to the generosity of the English; ordered her to walk a little faster; and even assisted her with a few kicks that made her advance more speedily than she wished. Indignant at the brutality of this man, I followed him, well disposed to put a stop to his ill-treatment, when chance again made me witness of a scene that I cannot refrain from relating to you.

By the side of the river, and near the house of Mr Piper, my two savages descended a hill that brought them near the shore, where was a small creek, in which were five or six little canoes; I ran after them, as if I were engaged in the chase, and soon heard loud cries, or rather fearful yells. I hesitated for a moment, but at length determined to advance cautiously.

A score of savages were dancing, leaping, brandishing their spears, and clapping their hands against each other or some part of the body, round a woman hideously ugly, who was crouching on some kangaroo skins. As soon as I made my appearance, he whom I took for the chief of the party knew me, came to me, and pressed me to advance. He spoke to his companions, who soon came eagerly round me, offering me their hands. The cries of the woman put a stop to their entreaties; they resumed their posts; and howled their best.

At length the woman was delivered, uttering a few deep sighs, and the hurly-burly was at its height...What was my astonishment at seeing the poor creature with difficulty rise up, carry in her arms the little infant just born, enter a canoe, and dip the child several times into the water! After this ablution, and a few more grimaces and gambols by the two persons who appeared most interested about the woman, I approached in my turn, and gave the poor mother my handkerchief and cravat, which she accepted without the least sign of acknowledgment, to cover the newborn babe.

Rose de Freycinet

Saluting the Chef

At just nineteen Rose Pinon had fallen deeply in love with a dashing French naval captain, Louis-Claude de Saulles de Freycinet. The pair were married on 6 June 1814. Three years later, her husband was preparing to embark on a perilous globe-circling journey of scientific exploration. An educated woman, Rose would have known that the great explorer Matthew Flinders had set out on an expedition to Australia in 1797 but on his return voyage was held captive on Mauritius for six years. He did not see his wife until 1810, having endured an absence of thirteen years. Flinders died from the stress of his voyage just six weeks after Rose was married.

She could not contemplate such a separation, so at half-past midnight on 16 September 1817 she smuggled herself aboard the *Uranie*, dressed as a cabin boy. For two years she wandered the remote islands of the world in her husband's company, keeping a diary of what she saw. While exploring the Samoas, Louis named a small island for his intrepid wife.

For three weeks after the *Uranie* entered Port Jackson Rose was too ill to maintain her journal, but on 28 November she took up the quill again. She was hosted for some of the time in Sydney by Judge Barron Field and his young wife Jane, who took her on the obligatory visit to the lighthouse on South Head. Judge Field, incidentally, wrote the first poems to be published in Australia in book form. Wordsworth and Coleridge were reputed to be big fans of his poem 'Kangaroo'. A Sydney contemporary, however, described his head as 'a barren field indeed'. Whether he was referring to the quality of the judge's poetry or his receding hairline is unknown.

Soon after her expedition Rose recorded an incident

which informs us that the temperaments of French chefs have not changed over the years.

The *Uranie* was wrecked in the Falkland Islands in 1820 and the de Freycinets returned to France in November of that year. Time would prove that Rose's decision to stay by her husband's side was wise, for their marriage was brief: Rose died of cholera in 1832.

December 1819—I went with M. and Mme Field to visit the lighthouse. Mme Macquarie had promised to take me, but a serious illness confined the governor to bed and prevented him from travelling to Sydney. Mme Field lent us her carriage; M. Field, his wife and young Macquarie travelled on horseback. The road struck me as extraordinary both on account of the care with which it was maintained, and because of the difficulties which had to be overcome to make it less steep, as the lighthouse is built on top of quite a high mountain. The sides of the road are surrounded by wild vegetation just two miles out of town, this area being less fertile than Parramatta. The view from the mountaintop is splendid. The building which houses the lighthouse is made of stone and contains several rooms. The lighthouse itself was brought out from England.

M. Field had organised quite a substantial meal and, while it was being prepared, we went for a walk to enjoy one of the beautiful panoramas of the harbour. We climbed down a hill along a gentle slope which led us to a small fishing bay. There, we noticed a tree so large and whose shade was so dense and so extensive that a table could be laid out underneath it with twenty place settings and be as sheltered as if it were under a roof.[†] Feeling hungry and hot, we returned to the lighthouse. After resting there awhile, we headed back to the town...

[†] Massive figs, including perhaps the one that caught Rose's eye, still shelter picnickers at Watson's Bay.

Deprived, after a long voyage, of many items which are necessary for an official function, we resolved nevertheless to organise a dinner on board for all the people from whom we had received such hospitality. It was a very modest affair but we counted on the fact that our guests would understand our difficult situation. The deck was cleared of everything that crowded it, including the top mast. This provided two separate reception areas, decorated with flags and garlands of foliage and flowers. Regimental music was played throughout the meal.

A young crewman, who was a good artist, designed two watercolour portraits on transparent material—one representing the King of England, the other the King of France. They remained out of sight until the moment when Louis proposed a toast to King George, which was accompanied by a twenty-one-gun salute. The portrait of Louis XVIII was unveiled when the governor drank a further toast to his health. There was more noise and uproar than you could possibly imagine.

Nor could you imagine the distress of our chef who, fifteen minutes before serving dinner, sent me word that all was lost and ruined. The deck space set aside for the kitchen was so limited that the poor man had encroached on a cannon, placing a plank on it and thus making a table on which he had placed all the prepared dishes. When the order came to prepare for the salute during the dessert, gunners had removed a little too abruptly all the monuments raised to the glory of our chef, their arrangement being thus rather disrupted. Imagine the anger of that haughty man who, a few days earlier, had refused to be taught by an English cook how to make puddings because he claimed that a French cook had nothing to learn from English cooks...

I saw Mme Field on numerous occasions. She was extremely courteous towards me and a fortnight ago sent me the first ripe apricot of the season. I had not tasted one since leaving France! We spent the last few days together and we dined at her house frequently. She has a charming disposition, is very well educated and has a good knowledge of French literature. Her appearance is equally agreeable; she is very pretty, with a ravishing ankle, or so Louis noticed. I must say that I spent some delightful moments in her company.

On the day we were due to return on board, I went to have lunch with her and felt a pang of anguish when it was time to bid her farewell. She gave me a little cornelian ring on which was written 'Remember'. I did not need this inscription to remember all her friendly and kind deeds towards me.

We returned on board on 24 December but only set sail on the 25th, on Christmas morning, after the Abbé had said Mass. All the English sailors were unhappy to see us leave on a Friday because they claimed it was unlucky!

My sadness on leaving this land where I had been so well received was diminished only by the thought that, from that moment on, we would be heading back to France.

The wind was fresh and we quickly drew away from the coastline. The next day, we were far out at sea when we noticed the presence of ten convicts who had stowed away. To avoid further delays, and because the season was already advanced, Louis decided to keep them on board and employ them in various functions.

James O'Connell

A Botany Bay Greeting

James O'Connell was an Irish sailor and actor who claimed to have arrived in Sydney in 1820 and to have lived there for five years. No clear record of the vessel he said he sailed on, however, can be found. This might lead one to doubt his story, but it is clear that O'Connell was familiar with Sydney society. His description of Bunga-ree, the Aborigine who circumnavigated Australia with Matthew Flinders in 1801–3, is detailed, though he omits to mention Bungaree's double-jointed arm, the result of a break that failed to heal.

O'Connell had a wonderful ear for language and his renditions of 'flash talk' (as convict slang was called) are impressive. Flash talk served as a sort of code language, and the unforgiving Captain Rossi probably found it as incomprehensible as today's reader.

L and ho! from the fore-top-gallant yard, land ho! on deck, and land ho! the hearts of two hundred women responded...

It was four or five days after making the land before we could fetch the harbour. The first joy at the sight of land had changed, on the part of the women, to impatience, and from impatience to a sort of careless, half despair, which did not a whit abate at sight of the rocky heads of Sydney Cove. When the headland was doubled, and the romantic situations of gentlemen's country seats, and then the settlement at Sydney, was spread before them, hope and expectation were awake again, and there was nothing in their deportment to remind the observer that they were unwilling emigrants.

The pilot boarded us outside the Heads. The next visitor was a much more interesting and august personage—no less than King Bungaree, of flash memory, by descent, ratified by permission of HBM's government, chief of the Sydney Cove blacks, boarding officer, and official welcomer and usher of newcomers to Botany Bay.

He paddled alongside of us in a whaleboat, for his safety in which, all riddled as it was, he had the sufficient guarantee that the boat 'carried Caesar'. His Bungaree Majesty's coat was of approved texture and quality, inasmuch as it had served a long apprenticeship to an English corporal, before falling into his hands. Upon his neck was suspended the order and insignia of his nobility—a plate which might have been gold, but was brass, bearing the inscription, 'BUNGAREE, KING OF SYDNEY COVE'.

Bungaree, like the ancient Pharaoh of the Egyptians, is the hereditary title of the royal family. His Majesty's pantaloons were of similar extraction with his coat; and as for shoes or sandals, it was sacrilege to suppose that the royal feet of the House of Bungaree need such plebeian defences. His head was surmounted with a cocked hat of magnificent dimensions, in which waved, and swam, and flaunted in air, a martial plume; the dependent feather's feathers of which kissed his sable cheeks, giving and receiving lustre. The brightness of darkness of his face, who shall describe? And who in fitting colours paint the glory of his suite, the tribe of Bungaree? The fair representatives of St Giles, Wapping, St Catherine's Lane, Ratcliffe High Way, Winnifield Bay, and St George's Fields, entertaining high ideas of royalty, stood all abashed at the magnificence of the monarch, of whose fame the gossip of a five months' passage had possessed them.

In silver tones, their queries and comments rose in exquisite confusion, as they crowded round his Majesty of Port Jackson. 'The rum cove of this vile is up to lushing max, like a Billingsgate fishmonger.' 'The cove's kicksies is rayther seedy.' 'His kelp and his tug, stewed down, would fill the doctor's coppers with soup'—with thousands of other observations, more various than edifying.

King Bungaree, who is indeed better entitled to his rank than the English to his land, deigned no notice of the gadding women, but proceeded aft, to announce himself to the officers, and demand of them, in addition to the 'max', which he had received of course, the customary tribute. Even royalty must submit to disagreeables, and King Bungaree was ordered away, upon the arrival on board of Dr Bowman, quarantine physician and F. A. Healey, Esq., superintendent.

Vessels which have sickness on board are ordered to the quarantine ground; those which, as was our case, have no apparent sickness, other than the usual effects of a long passage, ride out a half quarantine outside the usual range of anchorage. People are not allowed to come on board, but all communication is by no means cut off, as boats are continually alongside, selling fresh provisions, bread &c. to the convicts...The conversations of the passengers with the boats alongside are peculiar, and have a character which no greetings away from New South Wales can resemble.

'Lord lov'ee, Sal! is that you? And how long are ye lagged for?'

'Only for seven years.'

An Irish girl among our passengers was hailed by her mother, who had preceded her to this land of promise about two years. 'Och, Mary!' cried the parent, 'is it here I see you? And how long are ye lagged for?'

'Only eighty-four months, mother.'

'Och, my child, avourneen machree! It's glad I am that you're not lagged for seven years. I tould ye at home that the mornin' snake 'ud bring the avenin' boult upon your fate. An' where did ye lave Jemmy, my son?'

'He's hanged, mother, the assize before they lagged me. An thin we brought him to St Giles', an a beauthiful corpse he made, ounly he had the black stroke roun his neck.'

As many as can make themselves heard are singing out at once. 'Where is one-eyed Suke of St Giles'?'

'Oh, she's aboard for a seven yearser.'

'Oh well, she needn't grunt—it's a long run she had before the pigs brought her to the scratch.'

'Did you see Tom Brown in Newgate?'

'Ay, he stood his patter last assizes, and has got a bellowser...'[†]

No secret is attempted to be made of the cause of one's

[†] Bellowser: life sentence.

sojourn at Sydney. If two strangers meet in any situation where conversation seems necessary, almost the first question exchanged is, 'Are you free, or a transport?' The next may be, 'What were you lagged for, and for how long?' Freemen are sometimes foolish enough to take offence at a Botany Bay greeting. I was at first, but soon learned the folly of permitting any such sensitiveness to appear and, becoming acclimated, I ceased to feel it. It purchases no good by squeamishness to say, 'I am better than thou!'

Crime detected is misfortune; sentence and transportation are events, inconvenient, at first, it is true, but they lose much of their particular stigma in the atmosphere of Australia, and become mere circumstances, convenient for reference in fixing dates...

While I was at Sydney there was no regular theatre, but a large hall in a building in George's Street, belonging to Mr Levi, was used sometimes by amateurs. The upper storey was a flour mill, the sails—for it was carried by wind—being on a tower in the centre of the roof. Admission to the pit was a dollar and a half. Seats in the music gallery across one end of the hall were called box seats, and sold at two dollars. Queer scenes sometimes occurred there, the directions for which were not laid down in the prompt book.

One Palmer, a nice little fellow belonging to the prisoners' barracks, obtained leave of absence one play night, till nine o'clock. It was not known at the barracks what use he purposed to make of his time, and the officers were astonished when from the front they recognised in the voice which began the soliloquy, 'Now is the winter of our discontent,' the convict Palmer's.

'By Gar, I shall make it a one dam sauvage season!' growled Captain Rossi, astonished at seeing such an offence to his dignity. But there was no help for it—King Richard was on liberty. A warrant was made out, however, in readiness for the hunchback tyrant, should he overstay his time. Meanwhile, the play went on briskly. Richard stormed, wooed, murdered his way through, drawing down peal upon peal of applause, till at length came the tent scene. The index of Captain Rossi's watch began to near the point at which he so impatiently wished it. The bell commenced ringing—

> 'Do hear it, Richard! for it is a knell
> That summons thee to—'

the barracks! No, no; he is too busy in the tent scene with the ghosts of Buckingham, and Rivers, and Anne, and the young princes; but the noses of less airy torments are peeping in at the side scenes. Squirming, after the most approved spasmodic fashion, Richard bounds from his couch, comes down to the footlights on his bended knee, and tries the temper of his sword, à la Kean, by raising his weight upon it. But why are the plaudits of the house all at once changed to hisses and swinish grunts? Why is the tender language of the delicate pig, the manly base of the reverend father of pork, and the angry rock-ok-ok-ok of the matron swine, imitated in all sorts of voices by flash ventriloquists? Alas, to the question, 'Who's there?' no Shakespeare murdering amateur answered, 'Tis I, my lord, the early village cock,' but the pigs have nabbed the royal dreamer!

'Let him alone!' 'Don't stop the piece!' hisses, grunts, and all sorts of pig music were of no avail. Richard was hardly allowed to doff his stage habiliments, before he was walked to the barracks. Divers of the audience were also snaked out, as having trespassed by overstaying their time.

Nor did the amateur performances of the constables cease here. Between the play and the farce was a song, to be sung 'by a lady'. Captain Rossi's eyes dilated, when a bellowser, a flash blowen, entered, simpering and smiling to the audience, waited very engagingly till the prelude to the song was played, and then began to warble 'Home, Sweet Home!' Again the pigs ran upon the stage, and the cantatrice was not allowed to finish even the first stanza, before she was ingloriously dragged off, to remain in custody till the next morning, when Captain Rossi would dispose of her.

Upon the next day Rossi had his hands full of employment in which he delighted. The theatre offenders were summarily disposed of. 'You shall play Richard de tree times, hey? By Gar, so you shall vingt-et-un, twenty-one, twenty-eight days, by Gar! You shall ride de treadmill for one horse!' Mrs Chambers, the vocalist, was sent to the factory. 'Ha! miladi! you shall sing "Sweet Home", hey? So shall you wid you head shave-ee, by Gar! Home! hey! you shall find home in the factory tree, yes, twelve monts, by Gar!'

HYACINTHE DE BOUGAINVILLE

The Treadmill

Hyacinthe-Yves-Philippe-Potentien de Bougainville, the elder son of explorer Louis de Bougainville, accompanied Nicolas Baudin on his great expedition in 1800 when he was not yet eighteen years old. Baudin believed the young man was lazy and not cut out to be an officer. Nonetheless de Bougainville fought in the Napoleonic Wars and in 1821 was selected to command a new expedition around the world in the *Thétis* and *Espérance*. He arrived in Sydney in July 1825, a quarter of a century after his first visit, and found himself so busy on board his ship reading the journals of explorers such as Oxley, Evans, Hume and Hovell that he could scarcely drag himself ashore. When he did walk through the streets of Sydney—accompanied by the city's French-speaking captain of police, Francis Rossi—he discovered a terrifying world of crime and punishment.

July 1825—Sydney itself, although already of a considerable population which grows every day (perhaps too fast in the interests of the colony), can not really be compared with even our third-rate towns. Apart from the suburb of the Rocks, a confusing mass of little houses originally built on the tongue of rocky uneven land that separates Sydney Cove from Cockle Bay, the roads are wide and well aligned, and the façades of the buildings, adorned with a little garden or flower-bed and separated by a simple fence from the footpath, are agreeable enough to look at; but these houses, made of quarry stone or bricks, are almost all badly constructed and badly laid out. The roads are not paved or lit, and they were so unsafe at night during our stay that several people, amongst them the provisions officer of the *Espérance*, were attacked and robbed right in the middle of George Street, the biggest and busiest street in Sydney.

The surrounds of Sydney were even more dangerous at this time, when everyone complained about the lethargy of the police and the brazenness of the roving convicts, whose number, according to a name-roll I was shown, had risen to more than one hundred and fifty. Gathered inland in gangs, these men, whose way of life and itinerant existence has given them the name *bushrangers*, had become so dangerous, particularly on the other side of the Blue Mountains, that the governor had just organised a company of fifty dragoons especially to pursue them. And as the law forbids the armed forces to act against citizens unless directed by a magistrate, the officers of this corps had been temporarily invested with the necessary powers, and the soldiers given the commission of constable.

These comments were passed on to me by M. de Rossi, recently arrived from Ile de France, and in charge of the Sydney police force, which he was working hard to knock into shape. In order to control such a population, whose passion for and easy access to strong spirits (in some sectors of the town there are almost as many taverns as houses) makes it even more ungovernable, it is necessary to have a very firm hand in the form of active police surveillance. The powers of the magistrate are considerable, and the means of punishment at his disposal are formidable: life sentence to the coal mines, hard labour in irons, solitary confinement, the treadmill and flogging (an obligatory accompaniment to every British penal code). All these fates are a constant threat to the guilty...

I must say a few words about the treadmill, a penitentiary machine little known in France, as far as I am aware, and which was first thought of, I believe, in the United States. Since being imported from England to New South Wales, it has been investigated by a commission. Monsieur de la Touanne, our doctor Busseuil and I visited this machine in the company of the attorney-general Bannister, a member of the commission, and one of the leading citizens in the colony who paid us much attention.[†]

As the name implies, the treadmill is a particular kind of mill, moved by people treading on it. It is a large wheel whose horizontal blades are wide enough to allow a certain number of men to position themselves, each next to the other, on the outside. The condemned men are naked from the waist up, and the only clothing they wear is a short skirt like our bakers wear.[‡] Holding on to a wooden crossbar that is separate from the wheel and attached at the height of the chin, they climb without stopping from one blade to the next, in the same way as the men who set cranes in motion, except that the latter are inside the wheel and have no other support than it. This labour continues for forty minutes without a break; the men rest for twenty minutes, then they start up again, and so on for the whole day.

[†] Touanne served as artist on de Bougainville's expedition. Saxe Bannister arrived in Sydney to take up his post of attorney-general in April 1824.

[‡] Convicts in Brisbane, who worked the machine in coarse prison trousers, called it 'the cock-chafer'.

The aim of this punishment was to exploit the time recalcitrant convicts spent in their cells, which they seemed to treat as a place of relaxation. And it was difficult to imagine an activity more boring and tiring at the same time, by its monotony and the care necessary to apply to this task, in the fear of missing the blade and having your legs mutilated. This continual concentration must be even more unbearable because these wretches are forbidden to speak, sing or whistle, and they are constantly overseen by people who treat them the way our cart drivers treat their horses: if one of them, worn out by this work, refuses to perform, he receives twelve or more strokes of the lash in order to get him willingly to pull his weight.

I could only look at this spectacle for an instant, and I didn't dare stare at these unfortunate men reduced to such a pitiable state. According to Doctor Busseuil, chest and heart illnesses would eventually occur as a result of this punishment which has been used for a long time in English prisons, and to which several parliamentarians have raised strong objections. It has, however, been acknowledged, some say, that the punishment does not in fact affect their health, and that the men, weighed before and after several days of this labour, did not lose any of their stoutness; some of them had even gained weight.

The Sydney prison has two of these mills; the smaller, operated by twenty men positioned in two rows on opposite sides of the wheel, was the only one functioning; the other, newer machine, whose mechanism has been perfected, needs sixty men, and produces sixty to eighty bushels of unsifted flour a day.

PETER CUNNINGHAM

Objects of Paramount Importance

Peter Cunningham, surgeon, journeyed five times to New South Wales aboard convict transports between 1819 and 1828. He was a man of exceptional ability and of the 747 convicts who were transported under his charge he lost only three. In 1825 he acquired land on the upper Hunter River north of Sydney, but in 1830 a drought forced him to abandon his farm and return to England. Cunningham was a prolific writer on matters as diverse as astronomy, physiology and social life in New South Wales, but his greatest talent must surely have been that of diplomacy, for even in the tiny divided society, which he shrewdly analysed in 1827 he appears to have left no enemies.

Although all you see are English faces, and you hear no other language but English spoken, yet you soon become aware you are in a country very different from England, by the number of parrots and other birds of strange note and plumage which you observe hanging at so many doors, and cagefuls of which you will soon see exposed for sale as you proceed...

Agreeable amusements are still much wanted to relieve the dull monotony of a town like Sydney, forming the capital of a small territory, and cut off, in a manner, from all communication with the other parts of the civilised world, excepting by the casual arrival of a vessel about once a month, bringing broken and garbled accounts of occurrences probably some six months old. Partly on account of this tediousness and uncertainty in receiving intelligence, together with the impossibility of any but a very few ever having access to the English prints, to keep unbroken the chain of connection that links them to home, the affairs of the mother country soon become objects comparatively of no interest to the great body of the colonists; while colonial news, colonial politics, and conversational discussions about the private affairs and personal good qualities or failings of individuals and families, engross here the whole of the public attention.

In all small communities, where people know too much of each other's private affairs, and where consequently idle gossipings and retailings of personal scandal creep in to fill the blanks occasioned by the flagging of other subjects, some such innocent recreation as theatricals, balls and evening parties (chiming in now and then to serve for topics of pleasant discussion, and divert the mind from objects only serving to engender bad feeling), are of manifest utility...

Dressiness and gaiety of appearance are much affected among our sprightly females; and every London fashion most devoutly 'bowed the knee to'. The moment a lady blooming fresh from England is known to be tripping along a Sydney street, you will see our prying fair, singly or in groups, popping eagerly out their pretty 'repositories for curls', to take note of the cut of her gown, the figure of her bonnet, and the pattern and colour of the scarf or shawl she displays upon her shoulders, that they may forthwith post off to put themselves in the 'dear fashion' too.

Instead, however, of sighing after China crepes and India muslins, like the English beauties, our Sydney belles languish after nothing but what comes with the name of 'London' stamped upon it: the products of the Eastern loom being here too common, too cheap and too durable for them to bedizen themselves out with...

Gentlemen foreigners of all nations may be met with now in our Sydney streets, tempted by the fineness of our country and climate to take up their permanent abode among us. French,

Spaniards, Italians, Germans (Americans I had almost added, but kindred feelings proclaim the impossibility of ever classing them as such), all add to the variety of language current among us; while even the subjects of his celestial Majesty cannot resist the fascination of the name of Australia; and several ingenious and industrious individuals of that distant region now flourish as members of our community. Over a snug cottage at Parramatta, for example, may be seen the sign of 'John Shan (or some such spelt name), carpenter, and dealer in groceries, teas &c.' with his tidy English wife and group of Anglo-Chinese descendants around him.

In the streets of Sydney, too, may often be seen groups of natives from various of the numerous South Sea islands, with which we trade, in all their eccentricities of costume. A considerable portion of Otaheiteans and New Zealanders are employed as sailors in the vessels that frequent our port; and in the evening, as you stroll along the picturesque shores of our harbour, you may be often melted with the wild melody of an Otaheitean love song from one ship, and have your blood frozen by the horrific whoop of the New Zealand war dance from another, the shrill piercing notes of which thrill through you with a sensation as if these cannibals were pouncing with brandished war-clubs upon you to glut their appetites with the tempting picnic fate had thus placed in their way...

Our society is divided into circles as in England; but, from the peculiarity of its constitution, still farther differences naturally exist, which have at various times received colonial baptisms. We have, as I said before, first, the sterling and currency, or English and colonial born, the latter bearing also the name of corn stalks (Indian corn) from the way in which they shoot up. This is the first grand division. Next, we have the legitimates, or cross-breds—namely, such as have legal reasons for visiting this colony; and the illegitimates, or such as are free from that stigma. The pure merinos are a variety of the latter species, who pride them-selves on being of the purest blood in the colony.

We have likewise our titled characters, who bear 'their blushing honours thick upon them' in the decorations of P. B. and C. B. which profusely adorn their persons; and untitled, who, like myself, have neither 'mark nor character' impressed upon our outward man. The titled are official characters employed under the govern-ment, in street-mending, brick-making, and suchlike—the titular letters not portending that they belong to any such illustrious order as the Bath, but merely that they claim the prisoner's barracks or the carter's barracks for their respective domiciles.

Convicts of but recent migration are facetiously known by the name of canaries, by reason of the yellow plumage in which they are fledged at the period of landing; but when fairly domiciliated, they are more respectfully spoken of under the loyal designation of government-men, the term convict being erased by a sort of general tacit compact from our botany dictionary, as a word too ticklish to be pronounced in these sensitive latitudes...

The grand division, however, of the free classes here, without reference to colonial technicalities, is into that of emigrants, who have come out free from England, and emancipists, who have arrived here as convicts, and have either been pardoned or completed their term of servitude. It is between portions of these two classes that there has been so much bickering. One sub-division of the emigrant class alluded to is termed the exclusionist party, from their strict exclusion of the emancipists from their society; while again, a subdivision of emancipists is denominated the confusionist party, from their endeavouring to embroil society, as the others say. As in all small communities, private feuds, backbiting and scandal exist to a great extent in our circles (or rather have existed, for improvement in this respect seems to be gaining ground), but those thoroughly initiated into the prevailing habits soon learn to hear without believing these things, and to repeat them merely for talking's sake, so that the repetitions may go on *ad infinitum* with scarce an atom of credit being attached thereto, even by the retailers.

Etiquette is, if possible, more studied among our fashionable circles than in those of London itself. If a lady makes a call, she must not attempt a repetition of it until it has been returned, on pain of being voted ignorant of due form. Morning visits, too, are made in the afternoon; afternoon calls near the hour the bats come abroad; while cards are ceremoniously left, and rules of precedence so punctiliously insisted on by some of our ultras, that the peace of the colony was placed in imminent jeopardy only a few years back by the opening of a ball before the leading lady of the town made her appearance—the hurricane being fortunately smoothed down at its outset by the facetious master of the ceremonies assuring the indignant fair that it was nothing more than the experiment of a few couples to try the spring of the new floor, and that they were still waiting her arrival to commence...

The pride and dignified hauteur of some of our ultra aristocracy far eclipse those of the nobility in England. An excellent Yorkshire friend of mine, in command of a merchant ship, unaware of the distance and punctilio observed here, very innocently stepped up to one of our 'eminent lawyers', to whom he had been casually introduced but a few days previous, to ask some trifling question, which he prefaced with 'Good morning, Mr —.'

The man of the law, however, recoiled as if a toad had tumbled in his path, and ejaculated with a stern frown, 'Upon my life, I don't know you, sir.' This proved a subject of much merriment afterwards to my friend, who would receive my usual 'How dy'e do's,' when we met, with a disdainful toss of the head, and 'Upon my life, I don't know you, sir!'

ROGER THERRY

A Thrill of Horror

An Irish Catholic, Sir Roger Therry arrived in Sydney in 1829 as commissioner of the court of requests (small debts), with the right of private practice. Like Peter Cunninghan he was startled by the countless caged rosellas hanging in the doorways of the city's retailers.

Therry's legal practice flourished and he came to be regarded as one of the most distinguished barristers in the colony. Sympathy for the convicts is evident in his writings, as is his interest in education. One does not think of early nineteenth-century Sydney as being well endowed with jewellery shops but, as Therry explains, their presence was a natural consequence of the state of the colony. Like many new to Sydney, he found it difficult to reconcile the city's pleasant appearance with the medieval torture it inflicted on some of its inhabitants.

4 November 1829—In the evening of the day of our arrival I paid a visit to the town of Sydney…The cages with parrots and cockatoos that hung from every shop door formed the first feature that reminded me I was no longer in England. A more significant intimation, however, was afforded on entering a few shops.

In one, the English accent came trippingly off the tongue; in another you needed no assurance that the proprietor had spent his early days amongst the 'banks and braes of bonnie Doon'; and the next told plainly that the infancy of the owner had been cradled in Moore's 'first flower of the earth and first gem of the sea'. The several tribes of Israel too, even at that early period, in proportion to the rest of the inhabitants, were numerously represented. Indeed, from the variety of strange sounds and divers tongues that met the ear, Sydney at the time might be not untruly described as a city of Babel on a small scale.

George Street—the principal in the town—was brilliant with jewellers' shops, and I soon ascertained that Sydney had been remarkable, even at an earlier period, for the same phenomenon— for it could seem no less to one unacquainted with the reason. The display of splendour was, after all, but a very natural result of the convict element in the town. The receivers of stolen plate and articles of bijouterie in England had chosen Sydney as a safe depot for the disposal of such articles, as agents for such a purpose might at that time easily be found there.

A lady, the wife of an officer, wore a valuable gold comb, which was snatched out of her hair on coming out of the opera one night in London. The thief escaped, and no trace of the stolen article was found in England. Two years afterwards—about 1825—the lady joined her husband in Sydney. On the first day she walked out she was attracted by the display of brilliant articles in the shop of a well-known jeweller of that period. The first article that caught her eye, prominently displayed, was the identical stolen comb.

She communicated the fact to her husband, and they visited the shop. Terms were proposed, either that the name of the consignor of the property or the property itself should be given up. The shopkeeper did not hesitate for a moment. He gave up the comb rather than disclose the name of the party who sent it to him, probably aware that, on the disclosure of how and where he obtained it, all the other articles in his shop similarly obtained might be subjected to a compulsory surrender...

Commodious verandahed cottages, around which English roses clustered, with large gardens, were scattered through the town. There was scarcely a house without a flower-plat in front. A band of one of the regiments, around which a well-dressed group had gathered, was playing in the barrack yard, and every object that presented itself favoured the impression that one had come amongst a gay and prosperous community. Nothing met the stranger's eye to convey the notion that he was in the capital of a penal colony. Thus far, the first impression of Sydney on a summer evening's visit was pleasant and full of agreeable promise. The convicts, at an early hour of the evening, were shut up in their barracks, which accounted for their disappearance from the streets on the occasion of my first visit.

When, however, day dawned in Sydney, the delusion of the evening was dispelled. Early in the morning the gates of the convict prison were thrown open, and several hundred convicts were marched out in regimental file and distributed amongst the several public works in and about the town. As they passed along—the chains clanking at their heels—the patchwork dress of coarse grey and yellow cloth marked with the government brand in which they were paraded—the downcast countenances—and the whole appearance of the men, exhibited a truly painful picture.

Nor was it much improved throughout the day, as one met bands of them in detachments of twenty yoked to wagons laden with gravel and stone, which they wheeled through the streets; in this and in other respects they performed all the functions of labour usually discharged by beasts of burden at home.

These were painful scenes, but to the pain they caused was soon added a thrill of horror, by a scene that I witnessed a day or two subsequently. The Sydney hospital, well situated, was in a line with the prisoners' barracks, and at a short distance from them (about 300 yards). In an enclosed yard of these barracks, shut out from the public road by a very high brick wall, flogging was administered. A band of from ten to twenty were daily at one period marched into this yard to be flogged.

As I passed along the road about eleven o'clock in the morning there issued out of the prisoners' barracks a party consisting of four men, who bore on their shoulders (two supporting the head and two the feet) a miserable convict, writhing in an agony of pain—his voice piercing the air with terrific screams. Astonished at the sight, I inquired what this meant, and was told it was 'only a prisoner who had been flogged, and who was on his way to the hospital!' It often took the sufferer a week or ten days after one of these lacerations before he was sufficiently recovered to resume his labour; and I soon learned that what I had seen was at that period an ordinary occurrence.

CHARLES VON HÜGEL

Moping in the Cabin

Baron Charles Alexander von Hügel arrived in Port Jackson on St Valentine's Day 1834, a disconsolate man, quite unprepared for the unruly scene, superintended by Billy Blue, that confronted him when he finally found the nerve to disembark. His fiancée had broken their engagement and married another, and the heartbroken baron sought solace in travelling the world. Despite this jaded account, his visit was to prove of great importance, for von Hügel was a botanist and here was fertile ground indeed for his researches. He would send a vast collection of objects that included 32,000 natural history specimens back to Austria. Many common Australian plants received their scientific name as a result of his efforts, and his gardens became famous throughout Europe for their collections of fashionable 'New Holland plants'.

Although von Hügel cut a striking figure in his Austrian army uniform, his quest for marital bliss was not an easy one. In 1847, aged fifty-two, he finally

became engaged to Elizabeth Farquharson, but because
she was a Protestant the baron had to wait on a papal
dispensation to marry. This arrived at last in 1851,
leaving the pair time to rear two sons and a daughter
before the great botanist passed away in 1870.

Friday 14 February 1834—At first light Captain Lambert
began to raise the anchor and to bring the ship further up the
bay. I stayed quietly in the cabin, without even looking out
through the gun-ports. If anyone had told me in the days of my
youth, or at any time in Europe, that I would one day come to
Port Jackson, and that here, instead of rushing out on deck full of
curiosity, I would sit moping in the cabin, I would most certainly
have disbelieved him. But, by degrees, the extraordinary becomes
ordinary and humdrum...

The town runs for one and a half miles due south along the
depression between Dawes Point and Bennelong Point, including
the whole of the rocky hill behind Dawes Point, as far as the next
deep bay called Darling Harbour. At the present time some very
solid houses are being built on this side. The view of the town
from the spot between Bennelong Point and Pinchgut Island
where ships drop anchor (except when they anchor in Sydney
Cove to load and unload) is quite extraordinary. The foreground
is taken up with a small fortress, Macquarie Fort, which looks as
if it had been copied from some French illustration, with a trouba-
dour swooning in ecstasy in front...Wohlfahrt the confectioner
might well turn out a model like this out of stiffened icing-sugar
to grace a dessert table. It is no more than a *papier mâché* building
in every respect.

To the left from here, you look across the Domain garden and
the botanical garden, which up till very recently might have been
better described as a kitchen garden, to a hill called Woolloomooloo, on which stand several considerable country houses,

looking as though they had just arrived from England and had been set up here for sale as an experiment. This hill is absolutely treeless. To the left of the houses, you can see the rise. Woolloomooloo hill terminates towards the inlet beyond, continuing on towards South Head, near the end of which stands the lighthouse. To the right of Woolloomooloo, on the highest point of the hill, stand several colossal windmills, and these are without any doubt the most picturesque feature of the whole panorama.

Beyond the Domain, on the hill connecting with Woolloomooloo, stand several houses and public buildings rising in terraces. Of these the hospital, the Catholic church (which has just been completed) and the new prison are the most conspicuous. This is on the left-hand side and directly beyond the Domain. The horse stables, which resemble a fortress, are beyond Fort Macquarie and difficult to see from here.

To the right of the fort referred to above, you can see the government garden proper, in which pines and oaks have ousted Australian native plants. Wide stretches of lawn alternate with large groups of trees and flowerbeds, but the whole garden is neglected although it has been laid out with some taste. It covers a large area, in which the insignificant single-storey residence is quite lost. The garden stretches down to the water, from which it is separated by a wall and a footpath. A goodly number of Norfolk Island pines have been planted in the garden, but they are of such a spindly hothouse habit that they give pleasure to no one. The soil is not deep enough for them.

Beyond the government garden and a few government buildings, the town proper begins, with buildings stacked up one behind the other in the greatest disorder. This is particularly the case in the so-called Rocks area, extending from the centre of the town to Dawes Point. Halfway up the hill on that side stands a small fort called Dawes Battery, a puerile edifice built for show, a companion piece to Fort Macquarie. A dozen cannon are mounted here, to return ships' salutes and to fire the royal salute on ceremonial occasions.

The whole scene resembles a big European town, the more so as, at first sight, it seems incredible firstly that such a confused townscape, in which the buildings have been built pell mell without either plan or directive, could have come into being within living memory; and secondly that it never occurred to the governor to lay the town out on a more regular plan. I am not in favour of absolutely regular street plans when they run counter to the natural contours of the site and therefore to the convenience of the inhabitants, but in Sydney the exact opposite is the case.

Sydney Cove, between Bennelong Point and Dawes Point, is 1500 feet wide and runs backs 2500 feet. Here lay between thirty and forty three-masters. With their flags flying, they presented a very lively scene. A large number of boats were plying about; some skimming lightly over the smooth surface, others labouring with slow strokes of the oars to propel a heavy lading; wherries, gigs and jolly-boats were criss-crossing in all directions. At the various wharves and quays of the major merchants there were ships lying at berth, and the sailors were singing out of tune as they worked with block and tackle to load and unload heavy chests and bales. It was a scene of cheerful bustle and activity, and the visitor could see at once that he was in one of the commercial outposts founded at the ends of the earth by the mistress of the seas. While I was making these observations, the *Alligator* had fired its salute, which was returned by the battery. These salutes cost the British government a goodly sum every year and are, in actual fact, a bit of nonsense. But in this town there is good reason to give the inhabitants clear proof of the effectiveness of heavy artillery from time to time...

It was ten o'clock when Captain Lambert and I stepped ashore in the dockyard and trod the soil of New South Wales for the first time. Captain Nicholson, who is the port captain here,

escorted us from the ship to this point. After laboriously climbing
a series of dilapidated, sunken steps, the new arrival enters an
irregularly shaped yard, sloping diagonally uphill and distinguished by some wretched little buildings almost in ruins—the
office—and a dirty pavement full of loose stones. Passing through
a dilapidated gate, one finds oneself all at once in the main street,
George Street, and in the middle of town.

But the human scene which presents itself to the visitor is not
impressive or calculated to afford him any pleasure: a few drunk
and noisy Aborigines, surrounded by a noisy throng of common
people, more or less affected by spirits. One and all are dressed in
somewhat tattered, drab holland garments, so dirty that the...
original colour can only be guessed at. They themselves are
unwashed and unkempt, and such is the group that first meets
the visitor's eyes.

Not far away, sitting on a stone or standing in the middle of
the street, he will come upon a black man with a pack on his
back, shouting something crazy in a loud voice at every passer-by.
Meanwhile, some street-lounger has come up and asked the
stranger whether he needs a guide. On asking him who the joke-
ster is, the visitor is told that this is the 'Old Commodore', whom
Governor Macquarie appointed port captain. The visitor gazes
at the guide in astonishment, wondering whether he has struck a
second clown and repeats the question. He is told that he had
heard aright, and that the black man is a West Indian called Billy
Blue who has been in Sydney for many years, is a favourite with
the townsfolk and has a jest for everyone. I had no wish to put his
wit to the test, but in passing I heard samples of it in phrases such
as: 'Not a word about the pig!' or 'Who is that long-legged
beauty, your honour? I won't say anything to your lady!'—which
reduces the public to tears of laughter.

Further along George Street, you come upon large numbers of
more or less carefully attired young females of the first class,

riding around on an old nag, until we reach those others at the end of their career who stagger out of a gin shop, take a few steps and then sprawl full-length. This class of persons has been greatly augmented by the latest imports which were intended to bring industrious young girls into the colony…Many of these are very pretty, but I would not recommend any stranger to look too deeply into their eyes. Not that the danger of being carried away is particularly great, or that some jealous lover might pose a threat. But because it requires the utmost concentration to steer a safe course along the street, which even in summer is always dirty in front of the gin shops and butchers' stalls, full of stones in some places and dotted with occasional rubbish heaps.

CHARLES DARWIN
A Second Creation?

Charles Darwin sailed into Port Jackson over four years after leaving England on his voyage round the globe. Emotionally and physically exhausted by the journey, he had just enough time during his seventeen-day Australian visit to cross the Blue Mountains and travel to Bathurst. On the whole he did not like what he saw, either in Sydney or his next port of call, Hobart. 'Nothing,' he wrote, 'but rather severe necessity should compel me to emigrate.' Perhaps he realised that this antipodean horror of chain-gangs and convicts was the necessary price that a nation paid to make a genteel English country life possible.

Darwin's biological researches in Australia were limited, but it was here that a critical insight occurred to him. Upon watching a platypus gambol in a creek and after observing a lion ant (the larva of a lacewing-like creature) he allowed—just for a moment—the thought that Australia's fauna is so different that 'two distinct creators must have been at work'. This questioning of the existence of the supreme creator was a vital step on the road to his theory of evolution.

12 January 1836—Early in the morning, a light air carried us towards the entrance of Port Jackson. Instead of beholding a verdant country scattered over with fine houses: a straight line of yellowish cliff brought to our minds the coast of Patagonia. A solitary lighthouse, built of white stone, alone told us we were near a great and populous city. Having entered the harbour, it appeared fine and spacious; but the level country, showing on the cliff-formed shores bare and horizontal strata of sandstone, was covered by woods of thin scrubby trees that bespoke useless sterility. Proceeding further inland, the country improved; beautiful villas and nice cottages were here and there scattered along the beach. In the distance stone houses, two and three storeys high, and windmills, standing on the edge of a bank, pointed out to us the neighbourhood of the capital of Australia.

At last we anchored within Sydney Cove. We found the little basin occupied by many large ships, and surrounded by warehouses. In the evening I walked through the town, and returned full of admiration at the whole scene. It is a most magnificent testimony to the power of the British nation. Here, in a less promising country, scores of years have effected many times more than the same number of centuries have done in South America. My first feeling was to congratulate myself that I was born an Englishman. Upon seeing more of the town afterwards, perhaps my admiration fell a little; but yet it is a fine town; the streets are regular, broad, clean and kept in excellent order; the houses are of a good size and the shops well furnished.

It may be faithfully compared to the large suburbs, which stretch out from London and a few other great towns in England; but not even near London or Birmingham is there an appearance of such rapid growth. The number of large houses just finished and others building was truly surprising; nevertheless, everyone complained of the high rents and difficulty in procuring a house. In the streets, gigs, phaetons and carriages with livery servants were driving about; and of the latter, many were extremely well equipped. Coming from South America, where in the towns every man of property is known, no one thing surprised me more than not being able to ascertain readily to whom this or that carriage belonged.

Many of the older residents say that formerly they knew every face in the colony, but now that in a morning's ride it is a chance if they know one. Sydney has a population of 23,000, and is rapidly increasing: it must contain much wealth. It appears that a man of business can hardly fail to make a large fortune. I saw on all sides fine houses—one built from the profits of steam-vessels—another from building, and so on. An auctioneer, who was a convict, it is said, intends to return home, and will take with him £100,000. Another has an income so large that scarcely anybody ventures to guess at it— the least sum assigned being 15,000 a year. But the two crowning facts are—first, that the public revenue has increased £60,000 during this last year; and secondly, that less than an acre of land within the town of Sydney sold for £8000 sterling...

I hired a man and two horses to take me to Bathurst, a village about 120 miles in the interior, and the centre of a great pastoral district. By this means I hoped to get a general idea of the appearance of the country...The extreme uniformity of the vegetation is the most remarkable feature in the landscape of the greater part of New South Wales. Everywhere we have an open woodland, the ground being partially covered with a very thin pasture. The trees nearly all belong to one family; and mostly have the surface of their leaves placed in a vertical instead of as in Europe a nearly horizontal position; the foliage is scanty, and of a peculiar, pale green tint, without any gloss...

In the dusk of the evening I took a stroll along a chain of ponds, which in this dry country represented the course of a river, and had the good fortune to see several of the famous platypus, or *Ornithorhyncus paradoxus*. They were diving and playing about the surface of the water, but showed so little of their bodies that they might easily have been taken for water-rats...it is a most extraordinary animal; the stuffed specimens do not at all give a good idea of the recent appearance of its head and beak, the latter becoming hard and contracted.

A little time before this I had been lying on a sunny bank, and was reflecting on the strange character of the animals of this country as compared with the rest of the world. An unbeliever in everything beyond his own reason might exclaim, 'Two distinct creators must have been at work; their object, however, has been the same, and certainly the end in each case is complete.' While thus thinking, I observed the hollow conical pitfall of the lion-ant: first a fly fell down the treacherous slope and immediately disappeared; then came a large but unwary ant; its struggles to escape being very violent, those curious little jets of sand, described by Kirby as being flirted by the insect's tail, were promptly directed against the expected victim. But the ant enjoyed a better fate than the fly, and escaped the fatal jaws which lay concealed at the base of the conical hollow. There can be no doubt but that this predacious larva belongs to the same genus with the European kind, though to a different species.

Now what would the sceptic say to this? Would any two workmen ever hit upon so beautiful, so simple, and yet so artificial a contrivance? It cannot be thought so: one Hand has surely worked throughout the universe.

★

On the whole, from what I heard, more than from what I saw, I was disappointed in the state of society. The whole community is rancorously divided into parties on almost every subject. Among those, who from their station in life ought to be the best, many live in such open profligacy that respectable people cannot associate with them. There is much jealousy between the children of the rich emancipist and the free settlers; the former being pleased to consider honest men as interlopers. The whole population, poor and rich, are bent on acquiring wealth; amongst the higher orders wool and sheep-grazing form the constant subject of conversation. The very low ebb of literature is strongly marked by the emptiness of the booksellers' shops, for they are inferior even to those in the smaller country towns of England.

There are many serious drawbacks to the comforts of families; the chief of which, perhaps, is being surrounded by convict servants. How thoroughly odious to every feeling to be waited on by a man who the day before, perhaps, was flogged, from your representation, for some trifling misdemeanour. The female servants are of course much worse; hence children learn the vilest expressions, and it is fortunate if not equally vile ideas...

On the whole, as a place of punishment the object is scarcely gained; as a real system of reform it has failed, as perhaps would every other plan: but as a means of making men outwardly honest—of converting vagabonds most useless in one hemisphere into active citizens of another, and thus giving birth to a new and splendid country—a grand centre of civilisation—it has succeeded to a degree perhaps unparalleled in history.

JAMES MUDIE

So Agreeable a Retreat

In 1822 James Mudie, a cashiered lieutenant of the marines who was facing insolvency, was offered a free passage to New South Wales, to begin life anew. He was given a land grant on the Hunter River and there he became rich and tyrannical. He hated convicts, perhaps fearful that his own free passage to Botany Bay would draw invidious comparisons. Flogging for minor offences was de rigueur at Castle Forbes, as his pile was known, and in 1833 six convicts rebelled as a result of their treatment. Three were hung, but their testimony brought about an inquiry, and an account of Mudie's treatment of convicts was published in the *Sydney Gazette*.

Disgusted with the colony, Mudie went back to London in 1836 and published *The Felonry of New South Wales* the following year, from which this extract is taken. It is perhaps the bitterest attack ever launched on the emancipists. Though he was hardly a Botany Bay Swift, Mudie's satire occasionally bites.

Four years later he returned to Sydney, where he was horsewhipped in the street and forced again to leave for London. It was a fitting denouement for a cruel and twisted man, who perceived even the 'factory' at Parramatta, where female convicts were housed and punished, as some sort of holiday home.

The author has ventured to coin the word felonry, as the appellative of an order or class of persons in New South Wales—an order which happily exists in no other country in the world. The major part of the inhabitants of the colony are felons now undergoing, or felons who have already undergone, their sentences. They occupy not only the station of the peasantry and labourers in other civilised communities, but many—very many—of them are also, as respects their wealth or their pursuits, in the condition of gentry, or of dealers, manufacturers, merchants and lawyers or other members of the liberal professions.

Hitherto there was no single term that could be employed to designate these various descriptions of persons, who now bear the denominations of 'convicts' and 'ticket-of-leave-men'; as also, 'emancipists' (as they are absurdly enough called), who again are subdivided into 'conditionally pardoned convicts', 'fully pardoned convicts', and 'expirees', or transported felons whose sentences have expired; together with 'runaway convicts', sub-divided into 'absentees' (a name foolish for its mildness), and 'bushrangers'...

If the male convicts are depraved and profligate, the female convicts are even still more so...and even arrive in the colony with pretensions to religious character and pious attainments; but on their being assigned as servants, and dispersed amongst the settlers, they almost invariably show themselves to be the most vicious and abandoned of their sex.

The assignment of the female convicts, like that of the males, usually takes place eight or ten days after their arrival in Sydney; and, when the applicants have been supplied, the remaining females (if any) are forwarded to what is called the factory, at Parramatta...

The factory cannot properly be regarded as a place of punishment. The females are well fed, having, in addition to abun-dance of animal food, flour, bread, and vegetables, the indulgence of tea and sugar. They are not put to any labour; and though they are certainly and necessarily cut off from external intercourse, they have the range of an extensive garden, in which they are permitted to walk...the females pass their time in sufficient merriment, relating to each other their former histories—their amours and debaucheries—the thefts in which they have been concerned—and the crimes for which they respectively received sentence of transportation!

So agreeable a retreat, indeed, is the factory, that it is quite a common thing for female assigned servants to demand of their masters and mistresses to send them there, and flatly, and with fearful oaths, to disobey orders, for the purpose of securing the accomplishment of their wish!

In the factory, too, there is a good chance of getting married; for the convict swains scattered amongst the settlers, when they obtain the consent of their masters, or choose, when they become free, to enter into the connubial state, usually apply for permission to go to the factory in quest of a fair helpmate, with the full knowledge that it is more likely to be for worse than for better that they make their election.

On the arrival of one of these at the abode of the recluses, the unmarried frail ones are drawn up in line for the inspection of the amorous and adventurous votary, who, fixing his eye on a vestal to his taste, with his finger beckons her to step forth from the rank. If, after a short conference, they are mutually agreeable, the two are married in due time and form. If, on the contrary, either the Macheath or the Polly prove distasteful to the other, the resolute amateur continues his inspection along the line, till he hits upon a Lucy more complying, or more suitable to his mind!

Not that either party is likely to be very fastidious on such occasions.

A young fellow who had just become free, and had got himself established on thirty acres of land, with a few pigs &c., set off for the factory in search of a wife.

On his way, he had to pass the estate of the writer of this work. In conversation with the wife of the porter at the gate, he mentioned the object of his journey. The porter's wife advised him to pay his addresses to one of her master's convict female

servants, whom she recommended as being both sober and industrious, whereby he would at once gain a good wife, and spare
himself an additional journey of a hundred and forty miles.

At the request of this Celebs of Australia, the damsel was sent
for, and the bargain struck on the instant, provided the necessary
consent of the lady's assignee master could be obtained, which
she herself undertook to solicit.

Entering the breakfast room of her master with an unusually
engaging aspect, and having made her obeisance in her best style,
the following dialogue ensued:

Marianne—I wish to ask you a favour, your honour.

His Honour—Why, Marianne, you have no great reason to
expect particular indulgence; but what is it?

Marianne (curtsying and looking still more interesting)—I
hope your honour will allow me to get married.

His Honour—Married! To whom?

Marianne (rather embarrassed)—To a young man, your
honour.

His Honour—To a young man! What is he?

Marianne (her embarrassment increasing)—I really don't
know!

His Honour—What is his name?

Marianne—I can't tell.

His Honour—Where does he live?

Marianne—I don't know, your honour.

His Honour—You don't know his name, nor what he is, nor
where he lives! Pray how long have you known him?

Marianne (her confusion by no means over)—Really, to tell
your honour the truth, I never saw him till just now. Mrs Parsons
sent for me to speak to him; and so—we agreed to be married, if
your honour will give us leave. It's a good chance for me. Do,
your honour, give me leave!

His Honour—Love at first sight, eh! Send the young man here.

Exit Marianne.

Enter Celebs.

His Honour—Well, young man, I am told you wish to marry Marianne, one of my convict servants.

Celebs (grinning)—That's as you please, your honour.

His Honour—As I please. Why, have you observed the situation the young woman is in? (Marianne being 'in the way ladies wish to be who love their lords'.)

Celebs (grinning broadly)—Why, your honour, as to that, you know, in a country like this, where women are scarce, a man shouldn't be too 'greedy'! I'm told the young woman's very sober—and that's the main chance with me. If I go to the factory, why—your honour knows I might get one in the same way without knowing it—and that, you know, might be cause of words hereafter—and she might be a drunken vagabond besides! As to the piccaninny, if it should happen to be a boy, you know, your honour, it will soon be useful, and do to look after the pigs.

The author having afterwards satisfied himself as to the man's condition, and as to his being free, gave his consent to the match; and the enamoured pair were of course united in the holy bond of matrimony.

LOUISA ANN MEREDITH

The Detestable Snuffle

After a Regency childhood, Louisa Ann Meredith burst upon the English literary scene as a brilliant poet, illustrator and writer of prose. Her first book, a collection of illustrated poems, was published in 1832 when Louisa was just twenty-three. Four years later she and her husband were bound for Australia, where they settled on the east coast of Tasmania. Despite her longing for the society she had enjoyed in England, Louisa's literary career flourished in the colonies. She published several books and in 1884 was granted a pension by the Tasmanian government in recognition of her achievements. It was a slender sinecure, however, for she died in relative poverty in the Melbourne suburb of Fitzroy in 1895, having outlived her husband by fifteen years. Here we see Louisa in happier times, pronouncing judgment in 1844 on the belles of Sydney society in terms which would have delighted James Mudie.

Sydney boasts her Hyde Park but a park utterly destitute of trees seems rather an anomaly. It is merely a large piece of brown ground fenced in, where is a well of good water, from which most of the houses are supplied by means of water-carts...

The circulating libraries are very poor affairs, but, I fear, quite sufficient for the demand, reading not being a favourite pursuit. The gentlemen are too busy, or find a cigar more agreeable than a book; and the ladies, to quote the remark of a witty friend, 'pay more attention to the adornment of their heads without than within'.

That there are many most happy exceptions to this rule, I gladly acknowledge; but in the majority of instances, a comparison between the intellect and conversation of Englishwomen and those of an equal grade here would be highly unfavourable to the latter. An apathetic indifference seems the besetting fault; an utter absence of interest or inquiry beyond the merest gossip—the cut of a new sleeve, or the guests at a late party. 'Do you play?' and 'Do you draw?' are invariable queries to a new lady-arrival. 'Do you dance?' is thought superfluous, for everybody dances; but not a question is heard relative to English literature or art; far less a remark on any political event, of however important a nature—not a syllable that betrays thought, unless some very inquiring belle ask, 'if you have seen the Queen, and whether she is pretty?' But all are dressed in the latest known fashion, and in the best materials, though not always with that tasteful attention to the accordance or contrast of colour which an elegant English-woman would observe.

The natives (not the Aborigines, but the 'currency', as they are termed, in distinction from the 'sterling', or British-born residents) are often very good-looking when young; but precocity of growth and premature decay are unfortunately characteristic of the greater portion. The children are mostly pale and slight, though healthy, with very light hair and eyes—at least such is their general appearance, with of course many exceptions.

They grow up tall; the girls often very pretty and delicate-looking whilst young (although very often disfigured by bad teeth); but I have seen women of twenty-five or thirty, whose age I should have guessed to be fifty at least. They marry very young, and the consequent 'olive branches' are extremely numerous. The boys grow up long and often lanky, seldom showing the strong athletic build so common at home, or, if they do, it is spoiled by round shoulders and a narrow chest and, what puzzles me exceedingly to account for, a very large proportion of both male and female natives snuffle dreadfully: just the same nasal twang as many Americans have. In some cases English parents have come out here with English-born children; these all speak clearly and well, and continue to do so, whilst those born after the parents arrive in the colony have the detestable snuffle. This is an enigma which passes my sagacity to solve.

Of course a large proportion of the population are emancipists (convicts who have served their allotted years of transportation) and their families or descendants, and a strong line of demarcation is in most instances observed between them and the free emigrants and settlers. Wealth, all-powerful though it be—and many of these emancipists are the richest men in the colony—cannot wholly overcome the prejudice against them, though policy, in some instances, greatly modifies it. Their want of education is an effectual barrier to many, and these so wrap themselves in the love of wealth, and the palpable, though misplaced importance it gives, that their descendants will probably improve but little on the parental model.

You may often see a man of immense property, whose wife and daughters dress in the extreme of fashion and finery, rolling home in his gay carriage from his daily avocations, with face, hands and apparel as dirty and slovenly as any common mechanic. And the son of a similar character has been seen with a dozen costly rings on his coarse fingers, and chains and shirt-pins, glistening with gems, buying yet more expensive jewellery, yet without sock or stocking to his feet; the shoes, to which his spurs were attached, leaving a debatable ground between them and his trousers! Spurs and shoes are, I imagine, a fashion peculiar to this stamp of exquisites, but among them very popular.

Many instances occur of individuals of this class returning to, or perhaps for the first time visiting England, with the purpose of remaining there to enjoy their accumulated wealth and, after a short trial, coming back to the colony, heartily disgusted with the result of their experiment. Here, as 'small tritons of the minnows', they are noted by their riches and courted for them; but at Home, shorn of their beams by the thousands of greater lights than their own, and always subject to unpleasant prejudices and reflections touching Botany Bay, and other like associations, they find their dreams of grandeur and importance woefully disappointed, and gladly hasten with all speed from the scenes of mortified vanity.

One of these adventurous worthies made the voyage to England, landed and remained in London a very brief space—not more, I believe, than one or two weeks—when, fully satisfied, he took ship and set forth back again. On arriving in Sydney, his friends inquired his opinions of England—Did he not admire the magnificent buildings and streets in London? 'Oh! very well; but nothing like George Street!' At all events, the extraordinary perfection and beauty of the English horses must have delighted him? 'No, not at all; nothing to be compared with Mr Cox's breed.'

JOSEPH SMITH

Kill Them or Work Them

During his life as a convict in the first years of settlement, Joseph 'Smashem' Smith had experiences burned into his memory that would never leave him. Smith was a handsome man with a 'military sort of face'. When he gave this interview to the philanthropist Caroline Chisholm in 1845 in the Hunter River district, he was dressed in a red flannel shirt with a black bandanna tied sailor-fashion, exposing his neck, and a pair of fustian trousers. Out of courtesy to the great reformer he added a blue coat with gilt buttons, but being uncomfortable in so formal a dress soon took it off again. At the conclusion of the interview he presented Mrs Chisholm with a souvenir. It was a loaded pistol that he pulled from his belt, saying 'you may depend on it!'

3 October 1845—I arrived in the colony fifty-six years since. It was Governor Phillip's time and I was fourteen years old; there were only eight houses in the colony then. I know that myself and eighteen others laid in a hollow tree for seventeen weeks, and cooked out of a kettle with a wooden bottom; we used to stick it in a hole in the ground, and make a fire round it.

I was seven years in service (bond), and then started working for a living wherever I could get it. There was plenty of hardship then. I have often taken grass and pounded it, and made soup from a native dog. I would eat anything then. For seventeen weeks I had only five ounces of flour a day. We never got a full ration except when the ship was in harbour. The motto was, 'Kill them or work them, their provision will be in store.'

Many a time have I been yoked like a bullock with twenty or thirty others to drag along timber. About eight hundred died in six months at a place called Toongabbie, or Constitution Hill. I knew a man so weak, he was almost thrown into the grave, when he said, 'Don't cover me up; I'm not dead. For God's sake don't cover me up!' The overseer answered, 'Damn your eyes, you'll die tonight, and we shall have the trouble to come back again!' The man recovered; his name is James Glasshouse, and he is now alive at Richmond.

They used to have a large hole for the dead. Once a day men were sent down to collect the corpses of prisoners and throw them in without any ceremony or service. The native dogs used to come down at night and fight and howl in packs, gnawing the poor dead bodies.

The governor would order the lash at the rate of five hundred, six hundred, to eight hundred; and if the men could have stood it they would have had more. I knew a man hung there and then for stealing a few biscuits, and another for stealing a duck frock. A man was condemned—no time—take him to the tree, and hang him. The overseers were allowed to flog the men in the fields. Often have men been taken from the gang, had fifty, and sent back to work.

Any man would have committed murder for a month's provisions. I would have committed three for a week's provisions! I was chained seven weeks on my back for being out getting greens, wild herbs. The Rev. —— used to come it tightly to force some confession. Men were obliged to tell lies to prevent their bowels from being cut out by the lash.

Old —— (an overseer) killed three men in a fortnight at the saw by overwork. We used to be taken in large parties to raise a tree. When the body of the tree was raised, he (Old ——) would call some of the men away—then more. The men were bent double—they could not bear it—they fell—the tree on one or two, killed on the spot. 'Take him away; put him in the ground!' There was no more about it.

J. C. BYRNE

Seeing Things

J. C. Byrne spent a dozen years wandering the outposts of the empire between 1835 and 1847, and bound his experiences up in grand Victorian fashion into two large volumes. Such traveller's tales depended on sensation to hold their readers' interest, and we must remain grateful, as Byrne was, to the man at the telegraph station for his brilliant explanation of what Byrne saw.

A strange phenomena, never witnessed in England, is often seen in New South Wales—the visual deception caused by the mirage. Barren, sandy, desert plains and valleys appear at times to be covered with water; all as far as the eye can reach, seems but one vast lake. Yet, strong as is the illusion, in reality, not one drop of water exists around. It is liquid air, 'the mirage'.

The writer was once standing in the neighbourhood of the lighthouse on Port Jackson's head, at midday. The sun was shining brightly, but a misty haze pervaded the atmosphere, and seemed to rest in density on the bosom of the ocean as he cast his eyes across the waves of the Pacific, while they slept in calmness and quiet. When he raised his eyes from the waters, there, elevated into the heavens, seemed suspended two ships under sail, with yards, masts, sails, hull, all beautifully displayed and developed. Astonishment was the first feeling; but a single inquiry of the man at the telegraph station produced a satisfactory explanation.

What he had seen was nothing but the reflection on the heavens of two ships, far out at sea. It was a visual deception, caused by the purity of the atmosphere, and was frequently witnessed. It was probable that the two ships, apparently in sight, were not less than one hundred miles out at sea, and far beyond the reach of human eye. Curiosity prompted the writer to put this to the test; he remained in the vicinity till towards the evening; a breeze sprung up, and exposed to view the bosom of the ocean, dissipating the mists that hung thereon: but not a sail was in sight—the blue waters alone were to be seen, unrelieved by a single object else.

GEORGE BENNETT

The Whaling Wall

William Sheridan Wall was employed in 1840 as a 'collector and preserver' at the Australian Museum, Sydney. He succeeded that 'rascally bird-stuffer' and convict John Roach, whose fall from employment was caused by one of the strangest thefts ever attempted in the thief colony: that of a foetal dugong sent to the museum from Moreton Bay. What Roach wanted with this bizarre trophy remains unknown. In 1844 Wall undertook an expedition to the Murrumbidgee River. It was an ill-fated sortie down the future Hume Highway (which even then had a weekly coach service) which yielded little except discomfort to the collector.

Wall's skills as a preserver were to be tested to the limit five years later when, at the beginning of summer, the putrid carcass of a twelve-metre whale was towed into Sydney Harbour and Wall decided that its skeleton would make an excellent exhibit for the museum. The diverting tale of Wall's whale is told by George Bennett, naturalist, and a trustee of the Australian Museum, Sydney. Sadly, Wall's new species turned out to be nothing but a common cachalot or sperm whale but its remains still form part of the museum's collection.

It was announced in the *Sydney Morning Herald* of 5 December 1849 that a dead sperm whale had been found floating upon the water at sea by the schooner *Thistle* and towed into the harbour of Port Jackson. It was suggested to the committee by Mr W. S. Wall, curator of the Australian Museum, that the skeleton would form a valuable addition to the osteological collection, if it could be procured. This proposition appeared full of difficulties, both from the gigantic size of the creature, as well as from the labour that would be required to clean and prepare the bones of an animal so oily and rapidly putrefying during this, the hot season of the year.

At the request of some of the committee, Mr Wall visited the schooner, which was at anchor in Neutral Bay, with the carcass of the whale alongside, which they were cutting up for the oil. Having introduced himself to Mr Williamson, the master of the vessel, he explained the object of his visit, when he gave him permission to take the whole of the bones. As soon, therefore, as all the blubber had been removed from the whale (that is, the portions of it required for 'trying down' for the oil), the carcass was given up to Mr Wall, who then commenced the arduous and disagreeable task of preparing the bones for the skeleton.

There was considerable difficulty in obtaining men willing to undertake so unpleasant and, as they considered, unhealthy an employment, during the heat of summer. On the following day, however, four sailors were hired who had been in the whale-fishery. After engaging them on their own terms, he found that, owing to previous employment, they would not be able to commence their work for four days. This was to be regretted, as decomposition takes place rapidly in the hot month of December in Australia, but as these were the only men willing to undertake it he was compelled to submit.

In the meantime the curator received a notice from the water-police magistrate to remove the putrefying carcass from Neutral Bay, as it was a nuisance to the residents in the vicinity. The removal of the whale to a secluded bay in the harbour being accomplished, it was secured by a strong cable to a projecting point of rock. It was now discovered that a portion of the tail, consisting of ten bones of the caudal vertebrae, was deficient: this was of importance for a complete skeleton and, after many inquiries, it was ascertained that the missing part had been sent to Sydney with the blubber. The exact place was not found for some time, as the schooner had sailed from Sydney but, after much anxious search, it was discovered lying on a wharf in Sussex Street. This was fortunate, for on the return of the men from dinner, in half an hour, it had been ordered that the whale's tail, the object of so much anxiety and search, was to be sunk in the harbour to get rid of the disagreeable effluvium arising from it.

The tail being recovered, all difficulties appeared at an end, when the head of the monster was missing from the rock on which it had been deposited, separate from the body. The curator had now to seek for this important portion of his truant whale, which perplexed him exceedingly by flying away in portions—although of some tons' weight each—in a very troublesome manner. At last the head was found in an inlet at Neutral Bay. This valuable portion of the animal was only saved by chance; for the head, having been left near the residence of the collector of customs, to whom its smell became disagreeable, the coxswain of the Custom House boat was ordered to tow it out of the harbour. Fortunately I was in the boat on that day, and seeing the enormous head on the rocks he informed me of the order he had received; but on my expressing a desire to preserve the skeleton for the museum, he said it should be secured in some part of the bay where it would be no annoyance. On the following day he told me he had lashed it to a rock in one of the bays in the harbour; adding that 'he had left two blue sharks helping to dissect it beautifully'.

This information respecting the head was conveyed to the disconsolate curator, who was delighted at the discovery of his missing treasure. The head was still doomed to more troubles: the sharks had performed on their part a beneficial operation but the huge jaws, lying out of the water, had attracted some of those creatures (mischievous all over the world) called 'small boys', who were caught labouring hard at the lower jaw, endeavouring to extract the teeth; fortunately they were discovered before any material damage had been effected.

The men engaged, having now commenced cleaning the bones, began with the lower jaw, from its being a great attraction to depredators for the sake of the teeth. When this was completed, it was removed to the museum without the loss of a tooth. The preparation of the skeleton was proceeding with as much expedition as possible, and was nearly completed when one of the fins was missing, which, if not recovered, would have necessitated the replacement of it by artificial means, rendering the skeleton incomplete.

The disagreeable task of cleaning the huge bones of this animal, in a highly putrid state, occupied four days. It may be observed that when the men were about to tow the viscera to sea they were, fortunately, previously examined, when two separate bones were discovered, forming the *os hyoides*. From the quantity of oil still remaining in the bones, and the offensive smell emanating from them, they could not be removed, but were placed on one of the small islands in the harbour, where they remained for two months, under treatment with lime and other preparations, until they were properly bleached, when they were deposited in the museum.

Every part of the skeleton was now complete excepting one fin. One morning the curator was informed that a strange fish was lying upon the rocks near the baths, at Woolloomooloo Bay. This, fortunately, was the lost fin, and was the more interesting from being the right one, the bones of which are considerably larger than the left, and more perfect. It was subsequently ascertained that the fin had been removed, for the oil, by the crew of a coasting vessel, while windbound in the bay but, a fair wind springing up, it was cut adrift and must have floated to the spot where it was found.

All obstacles being at length overcome, the skeleton was articulated in a masterly manner and became an object of great attraction to the public. The only parts deficient were two little, loose pelvic bones which, not being articulated to the rest, were likely to escape notice. But the curator now heard that another whale had been cast ashore on an open sandy beach between Port Hacking and Botany Bay. Although in an advanced stage of decomposition, and in spite of the danger from the heavy seas which rolled upon the beach and dashed over the whale, he succeeded in getting into the carcass of the animal and, after repeated attempts, having been washed out several times by the heavy surf, in procuring the pelvic bones, which are found suspended in the soft parts.

The skeleton, when set up, was 33 feet 6 inches in its entire length; the length of the head from the snout to the occiput was 9 feet 6 inches. Although a complete skeleton of a sperm whale is rare in museums, the value of this specimen was much increased when it was found, on examination of its osteological structure, to be a new species. It has been named *Catodon Australis*; and a valuable account of it was published in Sydney by the distinguished naturalist, Mr W. S. McLeay.

GODFREY CHARLES MUNDY

My Eyes, He's a Whopper!

Lieutenant Godfrey Charles Mundy arrived in Sydney in 1846 to begin a five-year stint as deputy adjutant-general of the military forces in Australia. Like many mid-nineteenth-century visitors he complained of the plagues of goats and dogs in the streets: 'I once saw a powerful mastiff seize a horse by the throat...and pull it to the ground,' he recorded. Mundy was also forcibly struck by how English the colony had become, with its 'barefaced, smug-looking' tenements 'blameably ill-suited to a semi-tropical climate'. It was, he felt, more exclusively English than either Liverpool or London, a sensation heightened when he heard the drums and fifes of the 99th Regiment rattling away Mrs Waylett's pretty old song of 'I'd Be a Butterfly', an old air 'abandoned by the London butcher-boys a quarter of a century ago'.

William Wall's putrefying whale lured flotillas of sharks into Sydney Harbour, with the most unfortunate consequences. When a portion of the whale (possibly its gizzards, which had been towed out to sea by Wall's assistants) floated into Botany Bay, Mundy decided upon revenge.

If there is one luxury greater than another in a hot climate, one exercise more healthy than another, it is bathing. Until late in the year 1849 it might be enjoyed to perfection at Sydney; for there is a bathing cottage at Government House, a large hulk moored and fitted as a public bathing-house in Woolloomooloo Bay, and every villa near the harbour possesses a like convenience. A shady bank of the Domain called the Fig-tree is the favourite bathing-place of the populace. Although large sharks had more than once been caught far up the harbour, no accident was ever heard of, and bathers swam about the coves without fear and with impunity.

It was in November of that year, I think, that a dead whale was floated by some accident within Port Jackson, and was picked up and 'tried out' by some speculating fisherman. A troop of sharks must have followed the dead fish and, having disposed of his carcass, remained foraging near the shores round Sydney. One day a large Newfoundland dog, swimming for the amusement of his master near the battery, was seized by a shark, and only regained the shore to die. The newspapers warned bathers; but no caution was observed until, early in December, a poor man swimming near the Fig-tree was attacked by a huge shark so near the bathing-place that another person repeatedly struck the fish with a boat-hook, thereby forcing it to release its victim. The unfortunate man was so dreadfully torn that he bled to death a few minutes afterwards. Not many days later I saw a foolhardy fellow swimming about in the very same place with a straw hat on his head and a cigar in his mouth!

Soon after the destruction of the man in Woolloomooloo Bay some fishermen reported that, a part of the dead whale having been carried by the tide into Botany Bay, a detachment of sharks had followed it there. An expedition against these tigers of the deep was organised while the desire of vengeance was still vivid, and I accepted an invitation to join it.

We were four amateurs, with an old experienced fisherman, and a stout youth, his son. We met at the Sir Joseph Banks Hotel on the shore of the bay, and proceeded at high tide to a spot usually frequented by sharks, and by other fish of different kinds, in a good staunch little boat furnished with sail and oars. There was plenty of tackle both for larger and smaller game: shark hooks, as big and strong as those on which butchers hang up a sheep or calf for flaying, with stout chain lines to resist their teeth, and a graduated scale of others suited to the capacity of jaw of schnapper, flathead, bream &c., and adapted to their habits, whether of grovelling at the bottom like the latter fish, or hunting in mid-water for his food like the former.

Besides the implements for securing our finny foes, there lay across the thwarts a small magazine of weapons for dispatching them when hooked—iron lances, with handles of stout ash, and long and strong iron gaffs or landing hooks. Anchoring the boat in about thirty feet water, the first operation was the baiting of the spot with burnt fish, and with the eggs of sharks. Lines were then thrown in as far as possible from the boat, the hooks for sharks being baited at first with pieces of starfish and, afterwards, when some of these had been caught, with huge hunks of shark's flesh. The latter seemed peculiarly tempting to the sharks themselves— the huge pot-hook to which it was attached, together with a yard or two of dog-chain, being swallowed as an accompaniment too trifling to mention—much less to damp appetite.

When one of the sportsmen feels a tug at his line, and judges by its energy that he has a shark for his customer, all other lines are, if possible, hauled aboard, in order that there may be no confusion and ravelling. If the fish be strong, heavy, and active, no little care is requisite to save your tackle from breakage and your quarry from escape. He who has hooked the fish holds tight—like grim death—on his victim, and if you watch his face you will see powerful indications of excitement, mental and muscular. His teeth are set, his colour is heightened, the perspiration starts on his brow, while something like an oath slips through his lips as the cord strained to the utmost cuts into the skin of his empurpled fingers. He invokes aid, and with his feet jammed against stretcher, thwart or gunwale, gradually shortens his hold. Meanwhile the others, seizing lance and gaff-hook, 'stand by' to assist the overtasked line, as the monster, darting hither and thither in silvery lightnings beneath the translucent wave, is drawn nearer and nearer to the surface.

'My eyes, he's a whopper!' cries the excited young boatman.

'He's off!' shouts another, as the shark makes a desperate plunge under the boat, and the line, dragged through the hands of the holder, is again suddenly slackened.

'He's all right, never fear—belay your line a bit, sir, and look here,' says the old fisherman.

And sure enough there was the huge fish clearly visible about ten feet under the keel of the boat, and from stem to stern about the same length as herself.

'Now, sir, let's have him up.'

And the instant the line was taut the shark shot upwards—his broad snout showing above the surface close to the boat. Then comes a scene of activity and animation indeed. The fish, executing a series of summersets and spinnings, gets the line into a hundred twists, and if once he succeed in bringing it across his jaws above the chain links—adieu to both fish and tackle. But, in the midst of a shower bath splashed up by the broad tail of the shark, both lance and gaff are hard at work. He is speared through and through, his giant struggles throwing waves of bloody water over the gunwales of the little boat. The gaffs are hooked through his tough skin or within his jaws—for he has no gills to lay hold on. A shower of blows from axe, stretcher or tiller falls on his devoted head and, if not considered too large, heavy or dangerous, he is lugged manfully into the centre of the boat, and, threshing right and left with his tail to the last, is soon dispatched. A smart blow a few inches above the snout is more instantly fatal than the deepest stab.

The 'school-shark' is dealt with as above. But if the 'grey-nurse,' or old solitary shark be hooked, the cable is cut or the grapnel hauled on board, and he is allowed to tow the boat as he darts away with the line. The tables, however, are soon turned upon him; and after being *played*, as this cruel operation in fishing is blandly styled, for a while until some portion of his vast strength is exhausted, the line is drawn over a roller in the stern of the boat, the oars are set to work and, towed instead of towing, the shark is drawn into some shallow cove near the shore, where his bodily powers avail him less than in deeper water; and after a fierce resistance and some little risk to his assailants, he falls a victim to their attacks.

Man has an innate horror of a shark, as he has of a snake; and he—who has frequented tropical climates, felt the absolute necessity of bathing, had his diurnal plunge embittered by the haunting idea of the vicinity of one of these sea pests, and has occasionally been harrowed by accidents arising from their voracity—feels this antipathy with double force. There is, therefore, a species of delightful fury, a savage excitement experienced by the shark-hunter, that has no affinity with the philosophy of Old Isaac's gentle art. He revels in the animated indulgence of that cruelty which is inherent in the 'child of wrath'; and the stings of conscience are blunted by the conviction that it is an act of justice, of retribution, of duty he is engaged in, not one of wanton barbarity.

These were precisely my own sensations when, drenched to the skin with showers of saltwater, scorched to blisters by the burning sun, excoriated as to my hands, covered with blood and oil and dirt, and breathless with exertion, I contemplated the corpse of my first shark.

Tiger hunting is a more princely pastime; boar hunting in Bengal Proper the finest sport in the world; fox hunting an Englishman's birthright. The chase of the moose is excellent for young men strong enough to drag a pair of snowshoes five-feet long upon their toes; and Mr Gordon Cumming tells you how man may follow the bent of his organ of destructiveness on the gigantic beasts of South Africa. Shark fishing is merely the best sport to be had in New South Wales, and affords a wholesome stimulation to the torpid action of life in Sydney.

The humane or utilitarian reader will be glad to hear that the shark is not utterly useless after death. The professional fishermen extract a considerable quantity of excellent oil from the liver; and the fins, cut off, cured and packed, become an article of trade with China—whose people, for reasons best known to themselves, delight in gelatinous food.

The most hideous to behold of the shark tribe is the wobe-gong, or woe-begone as the fishermen call it. Tiger shark is another of the names of this fish. His broad back is spotted over with leopard-like marks; the belly is of a yellowish white; but to describe minutely so frightful a monster would be a difficult and ungracious task. Fancy a bloated toad, elongated to the extent of six or seven feet, and weighing some twenty stone; then cut off his legs, and you have a flattering likeness of the wobegong—two of which we killed this day. A heavy, sluggish fish, he lies in wait for his prey at the edge of some reef of rocks or bank of seaweed; swallows the bait indolently; appears but little sensible to the titillation of the barbed hook; and is lugged, hand over hand, to the slaughter without much trouble or resistance. Neither lance nor gaff will penetrate his tough hide, but a blow on the head with an axe proves instantly fatal.

The schnapper affords a long and strong pull at the line; and is considered by the colonists as one of their best table fish. We killed one today weighing twenty-one pounds. The flathead is half buried in the sand at the bottom, but bites freely; and is, in my mind, a much better fish than the former. Our fishing basket of this day comprised nine sharks, four schnappers and about forty flatheads.

Gold for Australia

In May 1851 a rather low-key announcement of the discovery of payable gold in Australia appeared in the *Sydney Morning Herald*. Within weeks the city was irrevocably changed. All thoughts of further convict transportation were banished, for thousands were soon paying for the pleasure of travelling to Australia under conditions little better than those endured by the felons.

Roger Therry reported that 'the immediate effect of the discovery...may be briefly described as creating a state of society in which there was the minimum of comfort combined with the maximum of expense'. Rents in Sydney rose enormously and the nature of goods offered in shops changed overnight; overpriced picks, shovels, pans and packs filled their windows. As the rush progressed Therry wrote that 'Sydney looked like a deserted village'. Some diggers at least returned as wealthy men, and the wealth they won from the earth would remodel the town, making it rival the great cities of the northern hemisphere in buildings and style.

Therry awarded the palm of merit for the discovery of gold in Australia to Count Strzelecki, but in fact a German geologist found scientific deposits in the 1830s. Thus, from a very early date, the authorities realised that gold existed in Australia, and they knew—and feared— the discovery of payable deposits would change the colony forever.

Sydney Morning Herald, 2 May 1851—It is no longer any secret that gold has been found in the earth in several places in the western country. The fact was first established on the 12th February, 1851, by Mr E. H. Hargraves, a resident of Brisbane Water, who returned from California a few months since.

While in California, Mr Hargraves felt persuaded that, from the similarity of the geological formation, there must be gold in several districts of this colony, and when he returned here his expectations were realised. What the value of the discovery may be it is impossible to say.

Three men, who worked for three days with very imperfect machinery, realised £2 4s. 8d. each per diem; whether they will continue to do so remains to be seen. The subject was brought under the consideration of the government, who admitted Mr Hargraves' claim for some consideration for the discovery, but of course could make no definite promise until the value of the goldfield was ascertained...

At present all that is known is that there is gold over a considerable district; whether it is in sufficient quantities to pay for the trouble of obtaining it remains to be ascertained. Should it be found in large quantities, a strict system of licensing diggers will be immediately necessary.

EBENEZER BERIAH KELLY

Chinese Whispers

An American, Ebenezer Beriah Kelly ran away from his employer at the age of thirteen and became a cabin boy on ships that sailed along the American coast and as far as the West Indies. In early 1798 he sailed to London and while there signed on to the convict ship *Hillsborough* bound for Botany Bay. Kelly arrived in Sydney in July 1799 and stayed until December before sailing to China.

In 1856, more than half a century later, Kelly penned his memoirs in which he told this shaggy dog story which seems to confuse the murder of Samuel Clode in 1799 with the disastrous attempt to hang Joseph Samuels four years later, and a few other macabre touches thrown in for good measure. Like any old salt, Kelly knew how to embroider a good yarn, especially if it was set in the hellhole of early Sydney. One wonders what the Americans made of the place after reading such hair-raising tales of lingual amputation and drawing and quartering.

There were two farmers—once convicts, but then reformed, and considered good men—who borrowed fifty dollars off a clergyman, promising to pay the same in a few weeks. A day or two after, they requested him to call at their house and receive his money. As he entered the gate, one of the farmers stood there with an axe in his hand, but did not molest him, though evidently stationed there with that intention.

When he entered the house, however, the other stabbed him with a carving-knife, and his wife cut out his tongue. They threw the body into a sawpit, half-filled with underbrush, where a gypsy kept his hoe, pickaxe and other tools. When the gypsy came for his pickaxe he pulled up with it a man's leg, and the farmers, who were watching, immediately seized him and carried him to the authorities, accusing him of murder.

He was tried, and though innocent, condemned to be executed instantly. When first swung off, the rope broke. The sheriff ordered it to be doubled, but this time the noose slipped over his head, and he fell to the ground. Greatly astonished, the sheriff carried him back to the prison and informed the governor of the event.

A few days later, while several little boys were playing near the barracks, one cried out, 'Cut his tongue out, as mother did the parson's!' The soldiers, overhearing this, questioned the boy, who told the whole story, and caused the arrest of the true murderers. The farmers were tried, condemned, and hung, and the farmer's wife hung and quartered.

The Wreck of the *Dunbar*

The shipwreck of the passenger vessel *Dunbar* on the night of 20 August 1857 was one of the worst maritime disasters ever to befall the city. Although it occurred within ten kilometres of Sydney Cove it was days before the extent of the damage would be known.

In this series of reports from the *Sydney Morning Herald*, the full scale of the tragedy gradually reveals itself. The eventual death toll was 122, with just a single survivor. The true cause of the vessel going aground below The Gap, rather than passing through the Heads a kilometre or so to the north, is still debated.

Sydney Morning Herald, Saturday 22 August 1857—Sydney was, yesterday, thrown into a state of great anxiety and alarm by the report that, during the previous night, a large ship, with a considerable number of passengers, had been wrecked outside the South Reef at the Heads. The first information was communicated by Captain Wiseman of the steamship *Grafton*. He stated that on rounding the North Head, and entering between the Heads, he was surrounded by pieces of timber, bales of goods, bedding and sundry things which made it evident that somewhere near a ship had gone ashore or been cast away. Various idle rumours and speculations continued during the day, as to its being an emigrant ship, a merchant vessel, and a Manila sugar ship, and also that seventy bodies had been washed ashore.

We have endeavoured to possess ourselves of all the facts which can, up to the time of going to press, be ascertained.

It appears that Mr Pilot Hyde first discovered the wreck about half-past seven yesterday morning. He immediately called Mr Pilot Robson and, together, they searched along the coast to the southward until they saw the remains of a vessel, halfway between The Gap and the lighthouse. They thought her a ship of 1000 tons, very heavily timbered, masts and bowsprits hooped; figure, a gilt scroll; had the appearance of an American-built ship, with copper fastenings, and her internal fittings consisted of a large quantity of unpainted light wood, such as is used in immigrant ships. A large quantity of soft goods have been washed ashore, consisting of calicos, prints, clothing, silks, carpeting, bagging, felt hats, shirts, candles, and children's toys. A pianoforte and sofa were also observed floating near the wreck. The pilots and their crews searched along the rocks and descended the cliffs, but could see nothing branded.

Captain Mollison is of opinion that the ship was of North American build, whilst Captain Forbes thinks she was a British-built vessel.

On proceeding to The Gap in the afternoon, we found the residents of that locality watching with great horror the dead and mutilated bodies as they were thrown upon the rocks, the succeeding waves washing off again the naked remains. There were men, women and children—their number was variously estimated at from twenty to fifty. But it was difficult to ascertain the number, as the bodies were thrown up on the ledge of the rocks and again taken off by the violence of the surf. Several hundred persons proceeded to the Heads during the afternoon in omnibuses, cabs and other vehicles, whilst numbers walked to the scene of this dreadful disaster.

The following facts were brought to us in the course of the evening: the portmaster Captain Pockley reports twelve bodies ashore in Middle Harbour, one, evidently an officer, with gilt buttons on the coat marked W. B. W. and a crest; mail bag, No. 2, marked per *Dunbar*, Plymouth, May 29; a cask of tripe, marked *Dunbar*. A large portion of the wreck had floated into Middle Harbour, and part of the handrails have the carving of a lion upon them. Mr Isaac Moore reports picking up, near the Sand Spit, Middle Harbour, two or three beer cask-heads with Tooth's brand; and the bodies of two respectably dressed men and of a woman, with a ring on her finger.

On George's Beach, as reported by a special messenger from this office, the body of a little boy, quite naked, and apparently about four years of age, with black hair, was picked up; also a cow, red with white spots, and short horns, was seen floating near this spot, surrounded by sharks, who were eagerly devouring the animal. The top of a case, marked J. C., was picked up; and a quantity of pork and boxes of candles. Amongst the articles were several boys' cricket bats, which correspond with an invoice of goods on board the *Dunbar* belonging to Messrs Thompson, Symonds, and Co...

It is somewhat surprising that guns were heard in Sydney and blue lights observed, but the pilots appear not to have been aware of that circumstance.

From a Visitor to the Heads—Having arrived at the scene of this melancholy disaster—the South Head—about a quarter to eleven this morning, I, like most of the spectators, mingled in the general excitement then prevalent, which may be far more easily imagined than described; and, after walking about for some time, listening to fears here and hopes there, hopes that some one or more might yet be found living to clear up the awful mystery that must ever hang over such a disaster, uncleared by such testimony, when, behold, the joy of everybody was expressed by a shout of 'A man on the rocks! A live man on the rocks. There he is! There he is!' And sure enough there he was. This was about eleven o'clock...

Of course the authorities there were soon on the spot, with ropes and a boy to lower to him, and after much anxiety and various attempts to bring it within his reach, they at last succeeded, and soon brought him on *terra firma*. He was then brought, supported by Robert Hutchinson, one of Captain Hawkes' pilot men, of Boat No. 4, and Mr James Smith, of No. 1, Share's Lane, Cumberland Street, city police pensioner, and who, with others, hauled him up to the Marine Hotel, where he was immediately attended to by Dr West.

The following were some of the particulars elicited from him, whose name is James Johnson, a seaman, in reference to the sad disaster. They were coming in under close reef topsail about midway between the two Heads, at a few minutes before twelve o'clock, on Thursday night, when the captain ordered the foresail to be hauled up which, being done, she lost headway so fast that they drove over, and struck a rock, and almost immediately broke up.

In answer to inquiries, he said, *There were no cannons fired, but blue lights were burnt. I believe all the others are lost. I have seen no others alive, only their dead bodies. I had a little sleep on the rocks.*

Dr West now thought it best to retire and let him have sleep, which we did. I may state that the doctor pronounced him to be perfectly sane, and he looked better far than might naturally have been expected. He is about thirty years of age, and a strong, tall, powerfully built Irishman...

Sydney Morning Herald, Monday 24 August—*Johnson's narrative*: They were off Botany at half past eight o'clock p.m.,

Thursday. The captain then stood off shore, on the starboard tack, ship with double-reefed fore and main topsails, a very dirty, dark and rainy night. Two men were placed at the wheel. Captain Green instructed them to keep their luff; he (Captain Green) had not been off the deck for two hours since they first made the land, some days previously.

At about half-past eleven p.m. the captain gave orders to square away, which was done. The ship then ran under close-reefed fore and main topsails, and foresail. As they neared the 'light', the captain ordered the foresail to be clewed up, sent the second mate to the forecastle to keep a lookout; then very dark; told him to 'keep a good lookout for the North Head'. The captain asked if he could see the Head. The mate replied no, it was solid darkness.

The second mate suddenly called out, 'Breakers ahead.'

The captain ordered the helm to be put hard to starboard to bring the ship round; then blowing strong; ship on a dead lee shore. Having such small sail upon her, the ship would not come round (this was about 12 o'clock) and, the sea lifting her in, she almost immediately struck.

The passengers, who had all been in bed, rushed up on deck in their nightdresses. Their shrieks were dreadful—Johnson describes the scene at this time the most terrible part of the whole. The ladies asked the captain, and entreated the seamen to know if there was any hope. The ship was still holding together, and the men thought and said that there was hope.

Almost immediately after, as if in angry denial of that expression, the decks burst up from the pressure of the water, the ship was rent into a thousand pieces, and all on board (except him) were hurried into the foaming and terrific sea. Johnson, with the old boatswain, and two Dutch seamen, were about the last who were washed from the wreck, they four holding on to a piece of plank from which the two Dutchmen were soon after washed.

A huge sea then threw Johnson and the boatswain on shore amongst some pieces of timber, from which Johnson scrambled to a higher shelving rock, to avoid the next sea, which he did, but the poor old boatswain, less active, was carried away, and perished. Johnson then climbed to a still higher position, and, being much exhausted, laid down and slept.

The next day he saw a steamer (the *Grafton*) go into the Heads. He made signals to her, but was not seen. During the day he saw another steamer (the *Washington*?) pass, and tried to attract their attention, as, also, that of a schooner running in. Friday night was passed in this state. On Saturday morning he endeavoured to get along the rocks. He could see people on the cliffs above but could not make himself seen, until a brave lad, Antonio Wollier, an Icelander, who had gone down 'Jacob's Ladder' and along the rocks, noticed Johnson waving a handkerchief.

Relief came, and he was soon after hauled up to the top of the cliffs, which are there about 200 feet high. The noble fellow (Wollier) was then hauled up, and received the hearty manifestations of the thousands there assembled. I opened a subscription, which was suggested by Captain Loring, of HM ship *Iris*, and in a few minutes about £10 was collected and handed over to this courageous boy who, in answer to my compliment when handing him the money, said, in broken English, *he did not go down for the money, but for the feelings of his heart.*

Johnson says that a blue light was burned when the ship struck, but it was very dim and could scarcely be seen. Captain Green must have taken the bluff north-end of The Gap for the North Head, for in ordering the helm to starboard he must have supposed that to be his position, and North Head a lee shore; for had the helm been put to port the ship would have cleared, and run for the entrance to the Heads.

Afterwards at The Gap, another brave fellow, whose name I have not yet learned, volunteered to go down to send up some of the mangled corpses, now and then lodging upon the rocks beneath us. Now a trunk of a female from the waist upwards, then the legs of a male, the body of an infant, the right arm, shoulder, and head of a female, the bleached arm and extended hand with the wash of the receding water, almost as 'twere in life, beckoning for help!

Then a leg, a thigh, a human head would be hurled along, the sea dashing most furiously, as if in angry derision of our efforts to rescue its prey. One figure, a female, tightly clasping an infant to the breast, both locked in firm embrace in death, was for a moment seen, then the legs of some trunkless body would leap from the foaming cataract caused by the receding sea, leaping wildly, with feet seen plainly upward in the air, to the abyss below, to be again and again tossed up to the gaze of the sorrowing throng above, and in this manner several portions of the mutilated remains were hauled up to the top of the cliff, until a huge sea suddenly came, and nearly smothered those on the cliff, wetting them all to the skin.

WILLIAM JEVONS

Life below the Privy

William Jevons was a man of many talents. He arrived in Australia in 1854 aged nineteen to work as assayer in the Sydney Mint. In Sydney he compiled Australia's first weather reports and studied a startling array of subjects, including astronomy, sociology and economics. While working as a journalist for the *Sydney Morning Herald* in the 1850s he took the first Australian news photograph (of wreckage from the *Dunbar*) as well as compiling this account of The Rocks. Later he would go on to become one of Britain's greatest economists.

Jevons detested the slovenly way that parts of Sydney had developed, writing in the 1850s that 'standing in many parts of Sydney, noting the bright sky above, the clear blue waters below, the varied form and slope of the land, the solid dry base of sandstone, the wide country which lies open before us for the free use of all, one is compelled to acknowledge how much Nature has done for us; how little we have done for ourselves'.

7 October 1858—The 'Rocks' are occupied by several so-called streets, running longitudinally like terraces, the names of the more remarkable of which are Harrington, Cambridge and Gloucester streets. There are also several cross lanes or passages, the ascent of which is sometimes facilitated by steps: these are named on the map Essex Street, Essex Lane, Brown Bear Lane, Globe Street, Cribb Lane, but the more significant name of Gallows Hill yet cleaves, I believe, to one of those. But in reality these streets are at least not roads, being scarcely traversable by vehicles, and destitute of all signs of forming, metalling, guttering, sewering.

The houses which line them are small and comparatively ancient stone cottages, so unevenly and irregularly built that the doorstep of one residence sometimes approximates to the eaves of another. Where the erections are of wood their dilapidated, filthy appearance is all the more striking. The interior of these abodes usually consists of two dirty bare rusty-coloured chambers, of small size, and yet too large for the scanty articles which constitute their furniture. Of the inhabitants I will not say much; in some cases misfortune may have led and may keep them there; but in others the unhappy, debauched, wicked face, the slovenly, dirtily clothed person, tell too plain a tale.

A young intoxicated woman with a black eye and bruised forehead, and a shrivelled old dame with a face of yellow-brown colour, sitting in a poverty-stricken room, enchained my attention—

they were striking pictures of the first and last ages of vice.

But what chiefly requires remedy in this ill-favored locality is the utter absence of all means of drainage or of removing filthy matter, which consequently lies where it is and poisons the ground beneath and the air above. It is a positive fact that in many cases the foul drainage of one cottage trickles down the hill till it encounters, as the case may be, the back or front wall of the house next below; here it accumulates, soaking down into the foundations, or sometimes actually running in at the door.

In other houses the occupants have prevented this accumulation by constructing a drain close beneath the floor, and running quite through the house. Certainly, a flowing stream of filth is to be preferred to a stagnant pool. The various *rejectamenta* of more solid nature which lie about the yards and streets where they chance to fall, of course add to the foul appearance and smell. Again, in many cases, the front or back of a house, or in some places of a whole row of houses, stand close to a wall of rock, upon the summit of which are erected the privies of the next higher row of houses, while various channels and shoots discharge incessant streams of drainage. What can be conceived more unwholesome than these moist surfaces of filth exposed to the sun's rays by day, and at night filling the whole surrounding still atmosphere with malaria.

I will also draw attention to a great (for the most part) wooden building, which stands in this neighbourhood, between Charlotte Place and Essex Street, and which is now occupied as a dwelling, although it is only fit to be burned. It was once my fate to enter this place, but I know not how to describe to others the filthy appearance of the whole—the wooden partitions covered by rotten, torn canvas, the uneven blackened floor, not free from human exuviae, the dark miserable rooms let out to different occupants. One small room was the only abode of a family, including several children.

The father, I think, was lying in bed. This building was originally a vinegar works, and was, I suppose, converted into a dwelling-place when manufacture became unprofitable and population at the same time numerous. The front part forms shops of decent appearance, in Lower George Street, nearly opposite the old *Herald* office. The objectionable part is entered from the back. The rents of such a place are indeed filthy lucre.

And, now I will venture to put a few plain questions with a view to remedy this state of things, disgraceful as it is to the community, but especially to the authorities, and to the landlords. If Dr Aaron is really a city officer of health at all, why do 'The Rocks' and the 'Vinegar Works' find no mention in his reports? Why does he not urge upon the council to abate these social and sanitary nuisances? What is the city engineer doing that he paves, drains, and forms streets above, below, and all round this region, while within the very centre of the evil appear no signs of his supposed ability? What are we to think of the aldermen, especially those representing Gipps' Ward, who meet opposite the Supreme Court to talk, vote other people's money away, and sometimes to quarrel, yet always to neglect the social plague spots and cesspools of the city? Where is the fulfilment of their election vows?

BLANCHE MITCHELL

Dreadful Was the Agony

In the late 1850s Blanche Mitchell, daughter of the famous explorer Sir Thomas, kept a childhood diary of her life in Sydney. In it she records that one day, aged fifteen and studying for her Confirmation, her mother took her to a phrenologist to have her head examined: 'He felt it up and he felt it down and said I had a very good head indeed. That I had very strong affections but that they required to be very much drawn out before they could be shown. That I required much sympathy and was very sensitive.' Next stop was the dentist, where poor Blanche's sensitivity and need for sympathy were to be made only too evident.

Monday 30 May 1859—I was made to sit down in the big chair and Mamma not having courage to remain in the room I was left alone to the tender cares of Dr Belisario and Dr Cox. The handkerchief was presented to my nose. I felt no fear whatever. It appeared to me as only fun, my eyes were closed and soon a wonderful sensation worked itself up in my brain. My senses left me, it seemed but for a minute, but curiously enough I still retained sense of what was going on without the feeling. I was not surprised when a gleam of consciousness shot over me to find that my teeth were out, although I had not felt them.

I stood up but found I could not stand. I tried to open my eyes, but found they were glued together, to move my tongue, but it was immoveable. My lips were closed and could not be opened. The only sense I retained was hearing and that was but slight—all I heard was the doctor say, 'Do not let the mother see her'—and 'Do you think she will ever recover?' sounded in my ears like a knell.

I soon fell into violent hysterics and then I believe I was carried to a cab and from there carried upstairs and laid in my bed and it was not till six or seven at night that I recovered fully all my powers.

Awoke to violent pain, started at first at seeing my pillow saturated with crimson blood, which poured from my mouth in large quantities. Oh, dreadful was the agony I suffered! My gums were torn to pieces from having five teeth rudely torn from their sockets. My lips and cheeks were all cut and my loose hair was glued to my face and streams of blood pouring all round.

Dreadful indeed must I have looked when Alice, coming in and seeing me suddenly, dropped on the floor and fainted right off. All that night my mouth poured blood. Dr Alloway was sent for. He was in a great rage and stuffed my gums with wadding which being instantly saturated he wet with turpentine, which however was but of little use.

Next morning it was the same. Blood all day. Sheets, handkerchiefs, pillowcases wet through. Towards night it gradually ceased, but all this week saliva in quantities has run from my mouth coloured only with blood. Oh, the pain has been dreadful! My mouth is still greatly swollen but the features of my face can be distinguished. Up all day and very tired and weak.

Tuesday 31 May—In bed till one. When up, feeling intolerable pain, worked hard to finish Confirmation questions. Dr Belisario has been here. He says my gums are improving...

Wednesday 1 June—Up, but obliged to lie down again. My gums in great pain, pieces of tooth perpetually coming out. Doctor ordered me to wash my mouth with boiled poppy heads. Went to the Confirmation meeting, when Mr Coxton expressed himself glad at my recovery and did not give us any very great scolding as he usually does with great severity.

FRANK FOWLER

Thirty Persons Dropped Dead

Sydney's six and eight-legged tribes terrified new chum Frank Fowler, who in 1859 also provided this legendary account of the city's fiery winds. Fowler sought refuge from the various discomforts Sydney presented in

picnics around the harbour, even though various denizens
of the bush interrupted these excursions. He records one
such foray: 'I was picnicking with some friends...and was
busy carving, or attempting to carve, an antiquated fowl,
when one of the party, a Dr P—, said, "Bring it to me,
I understand its anatomy, and can manage it better than
you." I stood up to carry the dish, when I was rather
surprised to see I had been squatting on a large snake. In
my astonishment I threw both fowl and dish at it, upon
which it put out its tongue and wormed off.'

Flies—black, blue, bumble and blow—mosquitoes, cock-
roaches, spiders, tarantulas, and even centipedes, annoy and
terrify the new arrival. The mosquito is a beast. It comes buzzing
against your cheek, with a drowsy singsong whirr, fixes its suckers
into the flesh, and bounds off with another song—a kind of
carmen triumphale—leaving a large red mark behind it, which is
far more irritating than a healing blister...

They use in the colony what are called mosquito curtains; but
so far from these keeping away the insects, I never found them of
any other use than in imprisoning the little fiends who had
sneaked in during the process of bed-making. Some nights they
have driven me almost mad, forced me out of bed, and compelled
me to dress myself, even to the putting on of gloves, in order to
protect my skin. They have a great relish—being epicures in their
way—for the round, fat, mottled part of the hand ridging the off-
side of the palm. In about two seconds one will sow it with
bumps and blisters from the wrist to the little finger.

Strange as it may read, I used to let my beard grow in order
that I might rub this part of my hand against my serried chin,
and thus allay the irritation. If I slept in gloves, they punished
my legs; if I slept in stockings, they riddled my hands; if I tried
both, they punctured the edges of my ears. The walls of my

bedroom were stencilled with their corpses; for whenever I was driven from the sheets, I used to go round with a slipper and—with intense satisfaction—settle hundreds of them as they stood stropping their stings upon the wall. They, too, especially hate and harass the new chum...

The evenings in Australia are singularly beautiful. I have often read a newspaper by the light of the moon. The stars are very white and large, and seem to drop pendulous from the blue, like silver lamps from a dome of calaite. I used to visit a house a long way out of Sydney, for the pleasure of being lighted home by the stars. Generally, I did not admire the Australian climate—its sudden changes, occasionally of thirty or forty degrees in two or three hours, its clouds of dust, its awful storms, and its hot winds; but an Australian evening—especially in winter—in its serene loveliness, defies all attempts at description. I have looked from my little study window sometimes at midnight, and seen the harbour so brightly argent with the moon, that it seemed as though He had walked again upon the sea, and left the glory of His footsteps on the water.

Having mentioned, in passing, a hot wind, let me endeavour to convey some notion of what a hot wind really is. It is early morning, and as you look from your window, in the suburbs of Sydney, you see a thin white vapour rising from the far-off bush. The sheep out there in the distance are congregated beneath the trees, while the old cows are standing knee-deep in those clayey creeks of water that trickle from the headed-up rocks above. You have seen all this before, and know too well what it means. Before breakfast time, there will 'be' a hot wind.

It comes. The white earth cracks as it passes over it, as though it were a globe of crystal struck by some invisible and mighty hand. The air is hot and murky, as the breath from an oven; and you see trees wither—the fruit shrivel and drop from the vines—as though the Last Seal were opened, and the breath of the destroying angel had gone forth. The cicadas seem to shriek (their shrill note is always shrillest in hot weather), and the birds drop dead from the trees. The dogs in the street lie down and hide their dry protruding tongues in the dust. Higher and higher rises the mercury in the glass, until now, at noon, it stands at 147 degrees! You stop up every keyhole and crevice in your room to keep out the burning sirocco, and endeavour, perhaps, to read. In a minute stars dance before your eyes, and your temples throb like pulses of hot iron. You allow the book to fall from your hands, and strive to drop to sleep. It is not much relief if you succeed, for you are safe to dream of the inferno or Beckford's hall of Eblis. There is only one thing you can do that gives relief. Light your pipe, mix your sherry-cobbler, and smoke and drink until the change arrives.

The 'Southerly Buster', as this change is called, generally comes...early in the evening. A cloud of dust—they call it, in Sydney, a 'brickfielder'—thicker than any London fog, heralds its approach, and moves like a compact wall across the country. In a minute the temperature will sink fifty or sixty degrees, and so keenly does the sudden change affect the system, that hot toddy takes the place of the sherry-cobbler, and your greatcoat is buttoned tightly around you until a fire can be lighted. Now, if you look from your window in the direction where you saw that white vapour ascending in the morning, a spectacle terrible in its magnificence will meet your eye. For miles around—as far as the gaze can reach—bushfires are blazing. You see the trail of the flame extending into the interior until it grows faint and thin along the hilltops, as though a wounded deer had moved, bleeding, upon the road. Nearer, however, the sight is grand and awful, and hints of the final apocalypse when the stars shall fall like those charred branches that drop with a thunderous crash and scatter a cloud of glowing embers around them.

No matter where you live in Sydney, looking from your

window across the harbour into the surrounding bush, you can always see sights like this after a hot wind. The reflection upon the water itself is very fine. The emerald changes into ruby—the water into wine. The white sails of boats become of 'purple' and 'their prows of beaten gold'. Everything seems bathed in an atmosphere of romance, and, if the impression was not lowered by the idea, the sheets of flame in the distance might be taken for the crimson walls of Aladdin's palace gleaming through the woods.

Sometimes these hot winds last for two or three days, and then the effects are something lamentable. Scarcely a blade of vegetation is left in the ground—the sere leaves fall from the trees as in a blast of autumn. The same week that I landed in Sydney, a hot wind lasted for four days, on the last of which no less than thirty persons dropped dead in the streets.

Manns' New Boots

The execution of Henry Manns was surely one of the most gruesome ever witnessed in Sydney. One wonders whether the bungling 'ratter' of a hangman was ever chastised for his deeds.

Sydney Morning Herald, 27 March 1863—Another of those sad and terrible spectacles, a criminal execution, took place at the Darlinghurst gaol, yesterday morning, the dreadful sentence of the law having been carried into effect on the body of Henry Manns, convicted together with John Bow and Alexander Fordyce, of participation in the gold escort robbery on the 15th June last...

Since the period of his condemnation, the unhappy young man, who was only twenty-four years of age, had conducted himself in gaol with great propriety, and under the zealous and untiring efforts of the clergymen who attended him, devoted himself earnestly to preparation for the awful ordeal through which he was to pass; though it would seem he was not wholly without hope up to Wednesday evening that his life would be spared...

There were but very few persons present at the distressing scene, the spectators not execeeding thirty in number, and the execution was delayed for nearly twenty minutes beyond the usual hour, probably with the humane object of allowing any communication in the shape of a respite or reprieve to reach the gaol.

No such document, however, arrived, and at about twenty minutes past nine the prisoner was pinioned and brought forth... He walked firmly and erect, and though somewhat pallid in expression, he displayed no agitation or want of fortitude—still less anything approaching to bravado or recklessness. Arrived at the foot of the gallows, he remained in prayer for five or six minutes with the reverend attendants, and then ascended the ladder in company with the venerable archdeacon and the Rev. Mr Dwyer.

On arriving at the drop, he spoke briefly to the persons assembled, stating that he had nothing further to say beyond what he had already told; adding that he was thankful to his friends and the good people in Sydney who had exerted themselves to save his life, for which service he hoped God would bless them.

The clergymen then parted with him, praying as they descended from the platform, while the executioner proceeded to perform his terrible office...a lapse of nearly two minutes occurring ere he had concluded his preparations.

When at length these were completed and the bolt was drawn, there ensued one of the most appalling spectacles ever witnessed at an execution. The noose of the rope, instead of passing tightly round the neck, slipped completely away, the knot coming round in front of the face, while the whole weight of the criminal's body was sustained by the thick muscles of the poll. The rope, in short, went round the middle of the head, and the work of the hangman proved a most terrible bungle. The sufferings and struggles of the wretched being were heartrending to behold. His body swayed about, and writhed, evidently in the most intense agony.

The arms repeatedly rose and fell, and finally, with one of his hands the unfortunate man gripped the rope as if to tear the pressure from his head—a loud guttural noise the meanwhile proceeding from his throat and lungs, while blood gushed from his nostrils and stained the cap with which his face was covered. This awful scene lasted for more than ten minutes when stillness ensued, and it was hoped that death had terminated the culprit's sufferings.

Shocking to relate, however, the vital spark was not yet extinguished, and to the horror of all present the convulsive writhings were renewed—the tenacity to life being remarkable, and a repetition of the sickening scene was only at last terminated at the instance of Dr West, by the aid of four confines, who were made to hold the dying malefactor up in their arms while the executioner readjusted the rope, when the body was let fall with a jerk, and another minute sufficed to end the agonies of death.

The executioner expressed his sorrow to the gaoler and undersheriff for what had happened, assuring them that it was no fault or intention of his, but solely the result of accident.

The body was lowered into a shell shortly before ten o'clock, and it was with deep regret and indignation that some of the spectators saw the hangman attempt to remove a pair of new boots from the feet of the corpse.

Not a Leg to Stand On

Early Sydney was inured to barbaric punishments and its citizens seem to have been bent upon devising more hellish ones. Perhaps the author of this letter was driven to ingenuity by the bungled hanging of Manns some months before.

Sydney Morning Herald, 28 October 1863—As the present mode of punishing our convicts neither intimidates the beginners from advancing deeper in crime, nor affords us any certainty that those who are caught and convicted of bushranging and such like crimes will not, on the completion of their sentences or sooner by escaping from gaol, again run a career of violence and robbery, I would bring the following plan for effecting these ends under your notice, knowing, as I do, that if you deem it practicable you will fearlessly urge its adoption by our legislators, although it may be severe and opposed to the popular notions of the day.

My proposal is shortly that an Act should be passed, condemning everyone convicted of robbery under arms or such like crimes, to lose a leg by amputation, or by some other quicker and less dangerous operation, which would render one of their limbs powerless...

Such a mode of punishment as this might, however, be deemed too cruel, and especially so by our 'felon worshippers', whose perverted judgment and ill-balanced principles lead them, on all occasions, to become the advocates of the criminal, while they entirely overlook those unfortunates who, through the want of a little assistance and advice, are being dragged into the mire of crime. But, as it is absolutely necessary that robbery and violence be put down, those who commit these crimes must suffer for doing so, and it is submitted that, taking everything into consideration, the punishment here proposed is the best for the country and for the criminal.

Nor could it be said to be unusually cruel, for it is plain that the pain of the operation (especially if the patient were put under the influence of chloroform) would be a trifle compared with the suffering endured by those offenders, who are punished by flogging, and that mode of punishment, instead of becoming obsolete, has lately been resorted to in England in cases where, years ago, it would not have been thought of.

The editor replies—A decisive objection against this scheme of amputation is that it would convert into a badge of crime one of the most common accidents of battle. When the stores were sent out to the Crimean War, although they forgot medical necessities, they sent out a large assortment of wooden legs.

Fancy the heroic Marquis of Anglesea meeting some liberated convict, and saluting his wooden leg as a companion in misfortune. It must not be!

ANTHONY TROLLOPE

The Very Best Cabs
in the World

The visit of author Anthony Trollope to Sydney in 1871 marks a turning point in the reportage of the city. Clearly enchanted with the place, he does not write of it as quaint, or criminal-ridden, or antipodean. Instead we see a city to rival—even exceed—those of Europe. In the eyes of the reading populace, Sydney had come of age and from now on its principal visitors would not be scientists or officials, but tourists.

I know that the task would be hopeless were I to attempt to make others understand the nature of the beauty of Sydney Harbour. I can say that it is lovely, but I cannot paint its loveliness. The sea runs up in various bays or coves, indenting the land all round the city so as to give a thousand different aspects of the water—and not of water, broad, unbroken and unrelieved—but of water always with jutting corners of land beyond it, and then again of water and then again of land. And you, the resident—even though you be a lady not over strong, though you be a lady, if possible, not over young—will find, unless you choose your residence most unfortunately, that you have walks within your reach as deliciously beautiful as though you had packed up all your things and travelled days and spent pounds to find them.

One Mrs Macquarie, the wife, I believe, of Governor Macquarie, made a road, or planned a road, or at any rate gave her name to a road, which abuts on the public domain, and is all but in the town. A mile and a half from the top of Hunter Street carries the pedestrian all round it. Two shillings does as much for him or her who prefers a hansom cab—and the Sydney hansoms are the very best cabs in the world. At the end of it is Mrs Macquarie's chair—with a most ill-written inscription—but with a view that affords compensation even for that. The public gardens, not half a mile from the top of Hunter Street, beat all the public gardens I ever saw—because they possess one little nook of sea of their own. I do not love public gardens generally, because I am called on to listen to the names of shrubs conveyed in three Latin words, and am supposed to interest myself in the locality from which they have been brought. I envy those who have the knowledge which I want; but I put my back up against attempts made to convey it to me, knowing that it is too late. But it was impossible not to love the public gardens at Sydney—because one could sit under the trees and look out upon the sea.

There is a walk from the bottom of Macquarie Street—not Mrs Macquarie's Road, but the old governor's own street— leading round by the fort under the governor's house, to the public gardens. The whole distance round may be a mile and a half from the top of Hunter Street, which opens on to Macquarie Street. It runs close along the sea, with grassy slopes on which you may lie and see the moon glimmer on the water as it only glimmers on landlocked coves of the ocean. You may lie there prostrate on the grass, with the ripple close at your feet within a quarter of an hour of your club. Your after-dinner cigar will last you there and back if you will walk fairly and smoke slowly. Nobody is ever there at that hour, the young men of Sydney preferring to smoke their cigars in their armchairs. Then there is the little trip by steam ferry over to the north shore, where lives that prince of professors and greatest of Grecians, Doctor Badham, of the university. I should like to be the ferryman over that ferry to Lavender Bay on condition that the doctor met me with some refreshment on each journey. Sydney is one of those places which, when a man leaves it knowing that he will never return, he cannot leave without a pang and a tear. Such is its loveliness.

The town itself, as a town, independently of its sea and its suburbs, was, to me, pleasant and interesting. In the first place, though it is the capital of an Australian colony, and therefore not yet a hundred years old, it has none of those worst signs of novelty which make the cities of the New World unpicturesque and distasteful. It is not parallelogrammic and rectangular. One may walk about it and lose the direction in which one is going. Streets running side by side occasionally converge—and they bend and go in and out, and wind themselves about, and are intricate. Philadelphia, which has not a want in the world, and is supplied with every luxury which institutions can confer upon human nature, is of all towns the most unattractive because it is so managed that every house in it has its proper place, which can be found out at once, so long as the mind of the seeker be given to ordinary arithmetic. No arithmetic will set the wanderer right in Sydney; and this, I think, is a great advantage. I lived at 213½ in a certain street, and the interesting number chosen seemed to have no reference to any smaller numbers. There was no 1, or 5, or 20 in that street. If you live at 213 in Philadelphia, you know that you are three doors from Two Hundred and Ten Street on one side, and seven from Two Hundred and Twenty Street on the other. Information conveyed in that manner is always to me useless. I forget the numbers which I should remember, and have no aid to memory in the peculiarity either of the position or of the name.

The public gardens at Sydney deserve more than the passing mention just made of them. The people of Australia personally are laudably addicted to public gardens—as they are to other public institutions with which they are enabled to inaugurate the foundation of their towns, by the experience taught to them by our deficiencies. Parks for the people were not among the requirements of humanity when our cities were first built; and the grounds necessary for such purposes had become so valuable when the necessity was recognised, that it has been only with great difficulty, and occasionally by the munificence of individuals, that we have been able to create these artificial lungs for our artisans. In many of our large towns we have not created them at all.

The Australian cities have had the advantage of our deficiencies. The land has been public property, and space for recreation has been taken without the payment of any cost price. In this way a taste for gardens, and, indeed, to some extent, a knowledge of flowers and shrubs, has been generated, and a humanising influence in that direction has been produced. There are, in all the large towns—either in the very centre of them or adjacent to them—gardens rather than parks, which are used and apparently never abused. Those at Melbourne in Victoria are the most pretentious, and, in a scientific point of view, no doubt the most valuable. I am told that in the rarity and multiplicity of the plants collected there, they are hardly surpassed by any in Europe. But for loveliness, and that beauty which can be appreciated by the ignorant as well as by the learned, the Sydney gardens are unrivalled by any that I have seen. The nature of the land, with its green slopes down to its bright little sea bay, has done much for them, and art and taste combined has made them perfect.

It may be said that of all drawbacks to public parks distance is the greatest. We know that in London, Hyde Park is but of little service to those who live at Mile End. The great park at New York, though it is connected by omnibuses with the whole city, requires an expedition to reach it. The gardens of the Crystal Palace at Sydenham are so far off from the multitude that the distance rather than the cost of entrance deters the crowd which might take delight in them. Even the Bois de Boulogne are too remote for daily purposes. But the gardens of Sydney are within easy reach of every street of the combined towns of Sydney and Woolloomooloo.

A little beyond the gardens, almost equally near to the town, are the sea baths—not small, dark, sequestered spots in which, for want of a better place, men and women may wash themselves, but open sea spaces, guarded by palisades from the sharks which make bathing in the harbour impracticable, large enough for swimming, and fitted up with all the requisites. It is a great thing for a city to be so provided; and it is a luxury which, as far as I am aware, no other city possesses to the same degree. There is no place for bathing in England like it, or at all equal to it.

Living Memory

'I first saw the light of day in my father's cottage in Pitt Row,' wrote Obed West in the 1880s when he was one of the city's oldest residents. Born in 1807 he was a farmer and gardener who spent most of his life at his property Barcom Glen in Paddington. West also dabbled in real estate and was reputed to have a keen eye for deceased estates, not surprising given his intricate knowledge of the city.

In these reminiscences, recorded between 1882 and 1884, West recalls the city of his boyhood and the stories he heard about the earliest European contact. 'I have often conversed with Cruwee,' he wrote, 'who was an intelligent fellow, and was told by him that he was at Kurnell when Captain Cook sailed into Botany Bay. It was very amusing to hear him describe the first impression the blacks had of the vessels, and although very fearful, they were curious and would, with fear and trembling, get behind some tree and peep out at the monsters which had invaded their shores. He said they thought the vessels were floating islands.'

West's account reminds us just how much change can occur in one human lifetime, as he describes the racecourse around Hyde Park, the fate of the city's suicides, the gathering places of Aborigines ('the original owners of the soil'), and Sydney's eastern beachside suburbs. Obed West died in 1891.

A barbarous practice of the old days, and one which has happily been abolished, might be mentioned in connection with Pitt Row. The executions took place in public on the site of the old burying ground in Elizabeth Street, and the criminals, when on their way to suffer the extreme penalty of the law, were sometimes brought along Pitt Row for the public to gaze upon. I have seen men taken along this street with a cart in front of them on which their coffins were carried and exposed to view. Sometimes the criminals were made to ride in the cart, sitting on the top of the coffin which an hour or so afterwards would contain their lifeless bodies.

Pitt Row at that time virtually terminated at Bathurst Street, ending in what is termed a 'dead road'. Beyond this point was what might be said to be the country, for there were only a few dwellings dotting the slope down to the Haymarket. These houses, generally built with thatched roofs, stood in large blocks of ground, and were surrounded with vegetable and fruit gardens. The Haymarket was taken up by the government brickyards, and the place beyond was quite out in the country. It is astonishing to think what rapid strides the city has made in the lifetime of a single individual. Such a transformation has been made in the streets that it is like a dream, or a fanciful creation to picture old Pitt Row and compare it with the Pitt Street of today...

Proceeding along George Street, we come to the site of the markets. The ground was enclosed by a substantial four-railed fence, having entrance gates about the middle of George and York streets. Inside the fence, and near the George Street entrance, was a two-storey weatherboard house, kept as an inn, while along the York Street frontage were a series of sheds in which all manner of wares were exhibited and sold...At the south end of the market was a large wooden pillory made to accommodate two persons at a time, and subsequently in the market place were four stocks, one fronting George Street, another York Street, and two about the middle of the square. In order to better exhibit the smiling beauties who were honoured with a place in them, the stocks were placed on a frame raised about eight feet above the surrounding space. The one at the south-eastern corner of George Street had a frame which could be put on it for use as a pillory, and several persons were pilloried on it. In addition, the market place was where prisoners were publicly whipped, the culprits being brought in and then tied to a cart tail to receive their punishment...

Chapel Row...commenced from Hunter Street and on the north side of that street stood a weatherboard public house, and next to it on the corner of Bligh Street, a small watchhouse. On the south-west corner there was another weatherboard public house, 'The Kings Arms', in a large allotment of land with some very fine peach trees growing in front. Between there and King Street there were not more than nine dwelling houses, the 'St Patrick' public house, and on the corner another public house bearing the name of 'The Cherry Tree'. One of the inhabitants of this block was a person named Payne who kept a small dairy.

Mr Payne was of rather eccentric habits and was well known by the name of 'The Miser'. His appearance and manner were in every respect typical of a person of that ilk. His wardrobe was not very extensive for the principal part of this costume consisted of a patched coat and a pair of unmentionables which, like Joseph's coat was very variegated. They were patched with all the colours and descriptions of cloth then known in the colony, and he wore them so long and patched them so much that there was not a bit of the original garment to be seen. His better half, too, must have imbibed the spirit of her husband, for her habiliments were patched and variegated in just the same fashion. They were truly a funny couple. The old man was reputed to have amassed a considerable amount of money by his parsimonious habits, and left with his wife—indeed he could go nowhere without her— for England to enjoy in their own way what they had made in that terrible Botany Bay...

Turning from Chapel Row, or as I should call it, Castlereagh Street, into Elizabeth Street, the property was very little built upon and it is unnecessary that I should particularise it. However, it may be of interest to the reader if I furnish a short report on the old Sydney racecourse, now called Hyde Park, which was inaugurated by Governor Macquarie.

The course commenced from a point opposite Market Street, went round St James Road, passed the front of the Prince Consort's statue; thence along College Street to about Stanley Street where it took a semi-circular turn towards Liverpool Street, and continued the turn until it reached the 'Obelisk'. There it began (in racing parlance) the straight running. At about the corner of Park Street—which at that time had not yet been cut through—stood the 'distance stand', and from there to the judges' box at the corner of Market Street was the struggling ground. This ground was roped off from the excited spectators, just as the saddling paddock, with the weighing scales adjoining the judges' box, which in fact was a semi-circular brick structure, about ten yards from Elizabeth Street, was roped in. On the other side of the judges' box was the wooden grandstand which, when packed to its utmost limit, was capable of accommodating fifty or sixty people...

The carnival, as it was called, used to be held once a year, generally in August and lasting for a week. No charge was made for admittance and the good-conduct prisoners were always allowed some recreation at this festival time to attend the races. The town was very busy, parties were held late into the night, and the military band played at the races.

The settlers used to come in from all parts of 'the interior' which in those days meant the Hawkesbury and as far south as Campbelltown. The great interior was then practically a *terra incognita* about which the people had the most absurd and erroneous ideas, numbers of them thinking that if only they were able to get over the mountain ridges they could walk to China.

To furnish sufficient sport for the races, the contests were generally three miles in length, and in nearly every case they were run in heats, the course being one mile round. The horses were not exactly high bred, and it was not uncommon to see regular cart horses engaged in the contest; indeed they were often taken out of the carts on the ground, saddled up there and then, and started off in a race, creating 'rare ould fun'...

At the time the races were held the park was all unfenced and across it were cart tracks in all directions. The only outlet eastwards was by the South Head Road (Oxford Street); William, Park and the other streets being unformed. Subsequently the ground was enclosed with a three-rail fence of sawn timber and planted with a single row of ornamental trees. Intersecting walks were laid out and a proclamation issued at the same time prohibiting wood carts from crossing over it. It was where these old cart tracks crossed each other that they used to bury suicides, and I could point out spots now where some of those who did away with their lives were buried, and, in accordance with the custom of the times, had a stake driven through their bodies...

Woolloomooloo was long a gathering place for the blacks. I can recollect on their festive occasions seeing 200 or 300 of the original owners of the soil camped about the bay. The sight—a strange contrast to the present day—was a happy one, for then the civilisation of the white men had not thinned the ranks of our sable brethren. In their merry chatter one would often hear some such word as 'Wallamullah', the name they had for this locality. The present name is, therefore, a perversion of the original one; but how it came to be called so, I am unable to say.

So far as the contour of the shores is concerned, Elizabeth Bay does not materially differ now from what it was some sixty-five years ago. Looking at the dense masses of foliage in which Mr Macleay's house nestles, an observer can partly imagine the appearance of the bay many years ago. The place was known among the Aboriginals as 'Currah Gin'—a cranky female...The subsequent history of the bay shows the kindly and humane interest that Governor Lachlan Macquarie took in the welfare of the original owners of our land, for about the year 1815 he had 'Currah Gin' reserved for a camping place for the Aboriginals; bark huts were erected about the bay for their use, and two assigned men appointed to look after the settlement. A carriage drive, branching off from the Old South Head Road near the Darlinghurst courthouse, and for a long time one of the principal places of interest out of Sydney, being particularly used on Sundays when numbers of the townspeople went to visit the camp, which was known as 'Blacktown'.

The blacks, however, did not improve by this thoughtful act on the part of Macquarie; they had, ere this, acquired a taste for the firewater of the whites and this, with their natural indolence, did not form a combination that would help them to better their condition. Numbers of them died, and I could today point out the spot where lie the remains of at least two score of the unfortunate blacks. In connection with their love of ardent spirits, I may mention an incident which occurred in this locality. One day some of the blacks, in walking over the south-east corner of the estate, discovered a plant of spirits which it is supposed had been manufactured in an illicit still in Middle Harbour. A day's wild dissipation followed, and while they were in a state of intoxication a fire occurred, by which a number were burnt to death and others severely injured.

The blacks managed to provide in a measure for their wants by fishing, and the scene in and about the bay was rendered peculiar by seeing the blacks in their frail canoes as they floated about, engaged in this work. Among the best known of the Aboriginals was Major White, who must have been seventy years of age and well remembered the arrival of the first ships and white men in Port Jackson. And then there were Marroot, Crangarang, Cullabar, Tommera, Blueit, Dulnuke and Boolmema (all spelled phonetically). But they, with all their descendants, have long since passed away and left the territory to pioneer colonists.

Adjoining Elizabeth is the well-known Rushcutters Bay. The name itself is suggestive of its origin and it is hardly necessary to state that the bay received its title on account of a number of men at one time coming here to cut the rushes, which grew in great abundance, and were used for thatching the houses at that time.

The Aboriginal name for it was 'Kogarah', a name also applied to a place near Georges River. The ground running down to the bay (Barcom Glen) was also a great camping place for the blacks, particularly the slope on the Darlinghurst side, and even to a very recent period the blacks had a lingering fondness for the old camping ground. In former days I have watched them in their canoes in the bay, the gins fishing with the line while their sable lords used their spears to get the fish that swam beneath them. It was not always, however, such peaceful sights were seen. On one occasion, just after the country was colonised, on a party of rush-cutters coming into the bay they were met and fiercely attacked by a body of blacks, the results being that either two or three of the white men lost their lives.

Running from the shores of the bay is Barcom Glen and flowing through it is a stream now dirty and miserable looking, but which was at one time a beautiful running creek of pure clear water. The creek is the boundary of the city, so that Barcom Glen lies partly within the city and partly within the municipality of Paddington. The estate was granted to my father by Governor Lachlan Macquarie for the erection of a water-mill thereon, the first one established in Australia. As soon as the grant was noti-fied, preparations were made for the erection of the mill, the timber required being obtained on the ground, the land about being thickly timbered with splendid specimens of the mahogany, blackbutt, the blood tree and the red gum. The mill was completed in 1812—just seventy years ago—and its completion

was considered to be an event of great importance in the settlement. Governor Macquarie himself attended and started the
working of the mill, and, with some ceremony, christened the
place Barcom Glen. The old mill was a single-motion one, having
one pair of stones and an overshot wheel about twenty-four feet
in diameter. It stood a few yards back from the present residence
at Barcom Glen. Nearby the creek was a large dam in which was
stored the water required for the working.

At that time, the place had the appearance of a dark and dense
forest, immense mahogany trees, blackbutt and other of the eucalyptus species growing in great profusion, while in the glen
leading up to the house a number of large cabbage-trees used to
grow, and for many years the stems of these palms, quite two feet
in diameter at the base, were to be standing. About 200 yards
from the mill a large swamp commenced and ran down to where
Bentley's Bridge stands, and then across by the present Glenmore
Road to the head of the gully where the Glenmore Distillery was
afterwards built. The swamp was a regular Slough of Despond
and could not be crossed. It swarmed with aquatic birds of every
description—red bills, water hens, bitterns, quail, frequently all
kinds of ducks, and when in season, snipe, landrails, and at all
times bronze-winged pigeons could be had in abundance. Brush
wallabies were also very numerous in the vicinity, and many
scores of them I have shot. It may seem strange to hear that,
within the memory of any person living, the head of the swamp
was a great resort for dingoes. I have killed numbers of them
where the Bus Company's stables stand; and often in daylight,
when the day was dull, I have seen them come up, up to my very
door and take the poultry...

At Bondi there was a Mr Roberts who at one time kept the old
'Kings Arms' at the corner of King and Castlereagh streets, and
who had a grant of land which he cultivated as a farm. It is pleasing to note that the Aboriginal name, although pronounced by

them as Bondi, has been retained. It is a matter of regret to me that the significant and euphonious titles which the blacks gave to the places in the colony, and about Sydney in particular, have been discarded while personal and harsh English words have been substituted in their places.

At one time Sydney was the centre of an extensive whale fishery, but the increasing traffic along the coast, together with the continued pursuit has long since driven them away. Whales in the early days of the colony were numerous enough, and I have on three occasions seen whales driven up high and dry on the beach at Bondi and also on Coogee beach. The next bay, known as Nelson's, was known to the blacks as 'Cramaramma', and it was a great fishing ground for them.[†] Following this is a small bay which is really Nelson's, but I do not know the Aboriginal name for it; indeed I never recollect seeing them about it. The bay in front of Mr Thomson's residence was known to the blacks as 'Coogee', but this name has been transferred to the bay further south, where the two hotels are, which was called by them as 'Bobroi'.

All along the coast the sea swarmed with fish of all descriptions from the great whale to the little bream. Standing one day, about sixty years ago, on the headland overlooking Bobroi, I witnessed a scene which even now comes vividly to my memory. The sea from the beach to the little rocky island, was one living mass of fish of all kinds, which were jumping from the water in all directions, their scaly sides glittering in the sunlight. The sight was indeed a grand one, which I suppose will never be seen again; but what the reason was for such a congregation of fish at one place, I am unable to say.

Leaving Bobroi, and after passing a few rocky indentations, Maroubra Bay is reached, and I am glad it still retains the

[†] Now Tamarama.

Aboriginal name. I saw, many years ago, a peculiar sight in this bay. A large number of fish had been driven in towards the beach by a school of porpoises, which formed a sort of outer line and kept guard like sentries. The sight was a pretty one, the smaller fish darting hither and thither near the white sands of the beach, while, as each wave rose and fell, the porpoises could be seen some little distance back, like a line of soldiers.

Adjacent to Maroubra is Long Bay and then Little Bay. The command of language and ingeniousness in naming some of our places is wonderful indeed. The blacks called Long Bay 'Boora', and it was long before white men came to this country; and for long afterwards, the principal camping place for the Aboriginals between Sydney. Several well-beaten paths led down to the bay, the ground around which was a great deal more open than at the present day. It is a peculiar coincidence that the native hospital for blacks who were afflicted with smallpox was in the immediate vicinity of the site selected for the present government for a sanatorium for our own people.

From conversations I have had with old blacks, some of whom were strongly pockmarked, I gathered that they contracted the disease from the men of La Perouse's ships. On the south side of the bay, about 200 yards back from the beach, there is a large overhanging rock, forming a cave. This was shown to me by the blacks as the place where all who had the disease went. The blacks had a great horror of the disease and were afraid to go near any who were suffering. The patients were made to go into the cave, and then at intervals supplies of food, principally fish, were laid on the ground some little distance from the cave. Those of the sufferers, who were able, would crawl to the spot for the food and go back again.

In the circumstances, it can be easily imagined that a great number of the blacks died, and when passing the cave in question—which was afterwards known as the Blacks' Hospital—I have seen numbers of skulls and bones scattered about, the remains of those I was given to understand who had perished during the prevalence of the plague.

EDMOND MARIN LA MESLÉE

Queen of the South

The Frenchman Edmond Marin la Meslée arrived in Melbourne in 1876. There he obtained a position as private secretary to the French consul-general, Monsieur le Compte de Castelnau, and travelled extensively in company with the consul, his Brazilian mistress and her twelve-year-old son. While in Sydney he fell in love with Clara Louise Cooper, and they married there in 1880. He was then twenty-eight and she twenty-three. After Trollope, Sydney began to get a much better press. La Meslée's 1883 account, including his perceptive comparisons with Melbourne, is a homage to an environment that had fully shrugged off its scabrous beginnings.

There is quite a difference between Melbourne and Sydney. The first is a city built wholly in the one style, as though created at a stroke by the wand of a magician: the second, already nearly a hundred years in age, retains some old-fashioned houses and streets. At Melbourne man found a flat, monotonous plain devoid of vegetation and replaced it with city streets a mile long and a hundred feet wide, surrounded by suburbs bowered in greenery of his own creation. At Sydney he found a magnificent site on a uniquely beautiful harbour, and he has been content, like the birds, to nest in the bosom of this marvellous natural phenomenon. These are the essential differences between these two rival cities which dispute the honour of being the capital of Australia...

The two colonies and their inhabitants also exhibit their own characteristics. In the capital of Victoria the twenty years of gold fever have been succeeded by a mania for speculation, and commercial life is plagued by a perpetual series of booms and slumps...In Sydney, by contrast, there are generally more old established fortunes than in Melbourne: credit plays a less important role and the people are much less given to gambling on the stock exchange. For many years their Victorian neighbours have bestowed upon Sydney the rather ungracious nickname of 'Sleepy Hollow'. It hardly merits the title today, for in the past five or six years it has gone ahead enormously. Its population now is almost equal to that of its rival, which for many years held the first place among all Australian cities. Within ten years Sydney will have passed Melbourne...By the time of the next census in 1891, it will have regained its old position of leadership among Australian cities. This position was really pre-ordained by its situation on the most wonderful natural harbour in the world, where whole navies could anchor in perfect safety...

It would take at least several days to see Sydney and all its suburbs, for these latter are scattered about on both sides of the harbour right up to the entrance of the Parramatta River. Although containing only 230,000 inhabitants, Sydney covers a much greater area than Paris. People generally do not live in the city itself; they go there each day to work and return to their suburban homes in the evening. Contrary to the French practice of accommodating several families in a single multi-storey building, the Australian, like the Englishman, lives in his own house in some suburb a little way out of the city. Even working people adopt this style of living and they quite often own their own homes...

Of all the middle-class suburbs the North Shore is now, perhaps, the most exclusive. The heights of St Leonards and

Willoughby enjoy uniquely beautiful views and summer temperatures cooled by the sea breeze. But to see Sydney at its best, to
admire at leisure the wonderful panorama of the harbour, one
should take the road along its southern shore to the 'Heads' of
Port Jackson. Dear reader, if ever chance places you on Australian
shores and you would like to spend a day or two in the capital of
New South Wales, do as we did and go to South Head.

No matter which way you turn, you are confronted with the
most glorious views. Before you the great blue ocean rollers break
into a seething mass of white foam at the foot of the cliffs. Farther
off North and South Head stand like two advance-posts, guarding
the entrance to that incomparable harbour whose waters are
bounded by a labyrinth of verdant headlands, on which human
beings have built their nests. Over there the water seems to be cut
off by a great bluff, but it is merely diverted to twist around for
many miles inland between banks of sandstone covered in ever-
greens. That is Middle Harbour and to its right, at the head of
another deeply indented cove, stands Manly, the future *Trouville*
of Sydney. Manly is built between two beaches, one in North
Harbour on the edge of the bay and the other, vastly more extensive, facing the ocean.

In the distance can be seen the sinuous northern shores of the
harbour and, first of all, George's Head which juts out almost
between North and South Heads.[†] Two batteries were built there
recently, one at the top of the bluff and one at water level, recessed
into the rock itself. In addition to these batteries defending the
harbour mouth, there are forts armed with cannon of heavier
calibre on the end of the cliffs which enclose it on the south.

In the background of this picture stands the city of Sydney
and the North Shore suburbs and, still further away, the waters of
the harbour begin to mingle with those of the Parramatta River.

---

† George's Head is now known as Middle Head.

The observatory, silhouetted against the skyline in the midst of a park, dominates the town and the tower of the Holtermann villa crowns the North Shore. Nothing could surpass the beauty of the whole panorama: the water seems to pink the shoreline like lacework. There are nothing but capes, peninsulas, cliffs and islets, surrounded by a dancing sheet of water, as placid as a lake, on which scurry a fleet of white-winged yachts, and some fast steamers plying constantly between the two sides of the harbour. Sydney is indeed *the Queen of the South*, the Australian city beautiful, destined to future greatness…

MARK TWAIN

There Are Liars Everywhere

Samuel Leghorn Clemens, alias Mark Twain, visited Sydney in 1895, accompanied by his wife Olivia and daughter Clara. The sixty-year-old author of *The Adventures of Tom Sawyer* and *The Adventures of Huckleberry Finn* was in parlous financial straits after a disastrous series of speculations and had embarked on a world lecture tour. Twain, by his own account, had a marvellous time in Australia. He had no sooner arrived in Sydney than he was asked his impressions. 'I don't know,' Twain replied. 'I'm ready to adopt any that seem handy.' He also announced that he intended to begin writing a book about Australia at once. 'You know so much more of a country when you haven't seen it,' he declared.

Wherever Twain spoke, shuffling about on stage in his black claw-hammer evening suit wearing 'a pince nez for style and spectacles to see through', the lecture hall was crammed to overflowing. Henry Lawson heard him

in Sydney, and kicked the planking of the stage so
enthusiastically in appreciation of his performance that
Twain's shock of white hair reputedly vibrated. And it
was in Sydney that Twain was to hear the grandaddy of
fishing stories, starring a young man improbably named
Cecil Rhodes, a story which suggested that the world
would in future find its way to the city faster than
hitherto imagined.

15 September 1895—We entered and cast anchor, and in the
morning went oh-ing and ah-ing in admiration up through the
crooks and turns of the spacious and beautiful harbour—a
harbour which is the darling of Sydney and the wonder of the
world. It is not surprising that the people are proud of it, nor
that they put their enthusiasm into eloquent words. A returning
citizen asked me what I thought of it, and I testified with a
cordiality which I judged would be up to the market rate. I said it
was beautiful—superbly beautiful. Then by a natural impulse I
gave God the praise. The citizen did not seem altogether satisfied.
He said:
   'It *is* beautiful, of course it's beautiful—the harbour; but that
isn't all of it, it's only half of it; Sydney's the other half, and it
takes both of them together to ring the supremacy-bell. God
made the harbour and that's all right; but Satan made Sydney.'
   Of course I made an apology; and asked him to convey it to
his friend. He was right about Sydney being half of it. It would be
beautiful without Sydney, but not above half as beautiful as it is
now, with Sydney added. It is shaped somewhat like an oak-leaf—
a roomy sheet of lovely blue water, with narrow offshoots of
water running up into the country on both sides between long
fingers of land, high wooden ridges with sides sloped like graves.
Handsome villas are perched here and there on these ridges, snug-
gling amongst the foliage, and one catches alluring glimpses of

them as the ship swims by toward the city. The city clothes a cluster of hills and a ruffle of neighbouring ridges with its undulating masses of masonry, and out of these masses spring towers and spires and other architectural dignities and grandeurs that break the flowing lines and give picturesqueness to the general effect.

The narrow inlets which I have mentioned go wandering out into the land everywhere and hiding themselves in it, and pleasure-launches are always exploring them with picnic parties on board. It is said by trustworthy people that if you explore them all you will find that you have covered 700 miles of water passage. But there are liars everywhere this year, and they will double that when their works are in good going order...

Sydney has a population of 400,000. When a stranger from America steps ashore there, the first thing that strikes him is that the place is eight or nine times as large as he was expecting it to be; and the next thing that strikes him is that it is an English city with American trimmings...The Australians did not seem to me to differ noticeably from Americans, either in dress, carriage, ways, pronunciation, inflections, or general appearance. There were fleeting and subtle suggestions of their English origin, but these were not pronounced enough, as a rule, to catch one's attention. The people have easy and cordial manners from the beginning—from the moment that the introduction is completed. This is American. To put it in another way, it is English friendliness with the English shyness and self-consciousness left out.

Now and then—but this is rare—one hears such words as *piper* for paper, *lydy* for lady, and *tyble* for table fall from lips whence one would not expect such pronunciations to come. There is a superstition prevalent in Sydney that this pronunciation is an Australianism, but people who have been Home—as the native reverently and lovingly calls England—know better. It is 'coster-monger'. All over Australasia this pronunciation is nearly as common among servants as it is in London among the uneducated and the partially educated of all sorts and conditions of people. That mislaid *y* is rather striking when a person gets enough of it into a short sentence to enable it to show up.

In the hotel in Sydney the chambermaid said, one morning, 'The tyble is set, and here is the piper; and if the lydy is ready I'll tell the wyter to bring up the breakfast.'

I have made passing mention, a moment ago, of the native Australasian's custom of speaking of England as Home. It was always pretty to hear it, and often it was said in an unconsciously caressing way that made it touching; in a way which transmuted a sentiment into an embodiment, and made one seem to see Australasia as a young girl stroking mother England's old grey head.

In the Australasian home the table-talk is vivacious and unembarrassed; it is without stiffness or restraint. This does not remind one of England so much as it does of America. But Australasia is strictly democratic, and reserves and restraints are things that are bred by differences of rank...

Sydney Harbour is populous with the finest breeds of man-eating sharks in the world...The shark is the swiftest fish that swims. The speed of the fastest steamer afloat is poor compared to his. And he is a great gadabout, and roams far and wide in the oceans, and visits the shores of all of them, ultimately, in the course of his restless excursions. I have a tale to tell now, which has not as yet been in print. In 1870 a young stranger arrived in Sydney, and set about finding something to do; but he knew no-one, and brought no recommendations, and the result was that he got no employment. He had aimed high, at first, but as time and his money wasted away he grew less and less exacting, until at last he was willing to serve in the humblest capacities if so he might get bread and shelter. But luck was still against him; he could find no opening of any sort. Finally his money was all gone. He walked the streets all day, thinking; he walked them all night, thinking, thinking, and growing hungrier and hungrier. At dawn he found himself well away from the town and drifting aimlessly along the harbour shore.

As he was passing by a nodding shark-fisher the man looked up and said, 'Say, young fellow, take my line a spell, and change my luck for me.'

'How do you know I won't make it worse?'

'Because you can't. It has been at its worst all night. If you can't change it, no harm's done; if you do change it, it's for the better, of course. Come.'

'All right, what will you give?'

'I'll give you the shark, if you catch one.'

'And I will eat it, bones and all. Give me the line.'

'Here you are. I will get away, now, for awhile, so that my luck won't spoil yours; for many and many a time I've noticed that if—there, pull in, pull in, man, you've got a bite!—I knew how it would be. Why, I knew you for a born son of luck the minute I saw you. All right—he's landed.'

It was an unusually large shark—'a full nineteen-footer,' the fisherman said, as he laid the creature open with his knife.

'Now you rob him, young man, while I step to my hamper for a fresh bait. There's generally something in them worth going for. You've changed my luck, you see. But my goodness, I hope you haven't changed your own.'

'Oh, it wouldn't matter; don't worry about that. Get your bait. I'll rob him.'

When the fisherman got back the young man had just finished washing his hands in the bay, and was starting away. 'What, you are not going?'

'Yes. Good-bye.'

'But what about your shark?'

'The shark? Why, what use is he to me?'

'What *use* is he? I like that. Don't you know that we can go and report him to government, and you'll get a clean solid eighty shillings bounty? Hard cash, you know. What do you think about it *now*?'

'Oh, well, you can collect it.'

'And keep it? Is that what you mean?'

'Yes.'

'Well, this is odd. You're one of those sort they call eccentrics, I judge. The saying is, you mustn't judge a man by his clothes, and I'm believing it now. Why yours are looking just ratty, don't you know; and yet you must be rich.'

'I am.'

The young man walked slowly back to the town, deeply musing as he went. He halted a moment in front of the best restaurant, then glanced at his clothes and passed on, and got his breakfast at a 'stand-up'. There was a good deal of it, and it cost five shillings. He tendered a sovereign, got his change, glanced at his silver, muttered to himself, 'There isn't enough to buy clothes with,' and went his way.

At half-past nine the richest wool-broker in Sydney was sitting in his morning-room at home, settling his breakfast with the morning paper. A servant put his head in and said, 'There's a sundowner at the door wants to see you, sir.'

'What do you bring that kind of a message here for? Send him about his business.'

'He won't go, sir. I've tried.'

'He won't go? That's—why, that's unusual. He's one of two things, then: he's a remarkable person, or he's crazy. Is he crazy?'

'No, sir. He don't look it.'

'Then he's remarkable. What does he say he wants?'

'He won't tell, sir; only says it's very important.'

'And won't go. Does he say he won't go?'

'Says he'll stand there till he sees you, sir, if it's all day.'

'And yet isn't crazy. Show him up.'

The sundowner was shown in. The broker said to himself, *No, he's not crazy; that is easy to see; so he must be the other thing.* Then aloud, 'Well, my good fellow, be quick about it; don't waste any words; what is it you want?'

'I want to borrow a hundred thousand pounds.'

'Scott!' (*It's a mistake; he is crazy...No—he can't be—not with that eye.*) 'Why, you take my breath away. Come, who *are* you?'

'Nobody that you know.'

'What is your name?'

'Cecil Rhodes.'

'No, I don't remember hearing the name before. Now then— just for curiosity's sake—what has sent you to me on this extraordinary errand?'

'The intention to make a hundred thousand pounds for you and as much for myself within the next sixty days.'

'Well, well, well. It is the most extraordinary idea that I—sit *down*—you interest me. And somehow you—well, you fascinate me; I think that that is about the word. And it isn't your proposition—no, that doesn't fascinate me. It's something else, I don't quite know what; something that's—born in you and oozes out of you, I suppose. Now then—just for curiosity's sake again, nothing more: as I understand it, it is your desire to bor—'

'I said *intention.*'

'Pardon, so you did. I thought it was an unheedful use of the word—an unheedful valuing of its strength, you know.'

'I knew its strength.'

'Well, I must say—but look here, let me walk the floor a little, my mind is getting into a sort of whirl, though *you* don't seem disturbed any.' (*Plainly this young fellow isn't crazy; but as to his being remarkable—well, really he amounts to that, and something over.*) 'Now then, I believe I am beyond the reach of further astonishment. Strike, and spare not. What is your scheme?'

'To buy the wool crop—deliverable in sixty days.'

'What, the *whole* of it?'

'The whole of it.'

'No, I was not quite out of the reach of surprises, after all. Why, how you talk! Do you know what our crop is going to foot up?'

'Two and a half million sterling—maybe a little more.'

'Well, you've got your statistics right, anyway. Now, then, do you know what the margins would foot up, to buy it at sixty days?'

'The hundred thousand pounds I came here to get.'

'Right, once more. Well, dear me, just to see what would happen, I wish you had the money. And if you had it, what would you do with it?'

'I shall make two hundred thousand pounds out of it in sixty days.'

'You mean, of course, that you *might* make it if—'

'I said "shall".'

'Yes, by George, you *did* say "shall". You are the most definite devil I ever saw, in the matter of language. Dear, dear, dear, look here! Definite speech means clarity of mind. Upon my word I believe you've got what you believe to be a rational *reason* for venturing into this house, an entire stranger, on this wild scheme of buying the wool crop of an entire colony on speculation. Bring it out—I am prepared—acclimatised, if I may use the word. *Why* would you buy the crop, and *why* would you make that sum out of it? That is to say, what makes you think you—'

'I don't think—I know.'

'Definite again. How do you know?'

'Because France has declared war against Germany, and wool has gone up fourteen per cent in London and is still rising.'

'Oh, in-deed? *Now* then, I've *got* you! Such a thunderbolt as you have just let fly ought to have made me jump out of my chair, but it didn't stir me the least little bit, you see. And for a very simple reason: I have read the morning paper. You can look at it if you want to. The fastest ship in the service arrived at eleven o'clock last night, fifty days out from London. All her news is printed here. There are no war-clouds anywhere; and as for wool, why, it is the low spiritedest commodity in the English market. It is your turn to jump, now...Well, why don't you jump? Why do you sit there in that placid fashion, when—'

'Because I have later news.'

'Later news? Oh, come—later news than fifty days, brought steaming hot from London by the—'

'My news is only ten days old.'

'Oh, Mun-*chausen*, hear the maniac talk! Where did you get it?'

'Got it out of a shark.'

'Oh, oh, oh, this is *too* much! Front! call the police—bring the gun—raise the town! All the asylums in Christendom have broken loose in the single person of—'

'Sit down! And collect yourself. Where is the use in getting excited? Am I excited? There is nothing to get excited *about*. When I make a statement which I cannot prove, it will be time enough for you to begin to offer hospitality to damaging fancies about me and my sanity.'

'Oh, a thousand, thousand pardons! I ought to be ashamed of myself, and I *am* ashamed of myself for thinking that a little bit of a circumstance like sending a shark to England to fetch back a market report—'

'What does your middle initial stand for, sir?'

'Andrew. What are you writing?'

'Wait a moment. Proof about the shark—and another matter. Only ten lines. There—now it is done. Sign it.'

'Many thanks—many. Let me see; it says—it says—oh, come, this is *interesting*! Why—why—look here! Prove what you say

here, and I'll put up the money, and double as much, if necessary, and divide the winnings with you, half and half. There,
now—I've signed; make your promise good if you can. Show me
a copy of the *London Times* only ten days old.'

'Here it is—and with it these buttons and a memorandum
book that belonged to the man the shark swallowed. Swallowed
him in the Thames, without a doubt; for you will notice that the
last entry in the book is dated "London", and is of the same date
as *The Times*, and says, "Per consequenz der Kriegeserklärung,
reise ich heute nach Deutschland ab, auf daß ich mein Leben auf
den Altar meines Landes legen mag"—as clean native German as
anybody can put upon paper, and means that in consequence of
the declaration of war, this loyal soul is leaving for home *today,* to
fight. And he did leave, too, but the shark had him before the
day was done, poor fellow.'

'And a pity, too. But there are times for mourning, and we
will attend to this case further on; other matters are pressing,
now. I will go down and set the machinery in motion in a quiet
way and buy the crop. It will cheer the drooping spirits of the
boys, in a transitory way. Everything is transitory in this world.
Sixty days hence, when they are called to deliver the goods, they
will think they've been struck by lightning. But there is a time for
mourning, and we will attend to that case along with the other
one. Come along, I'll take you to my tailor. What did you say
your name is?'

'Cecil Rhodes.'

'It is hard to remember. However, I think you will make it
easier by and by, if you live. There are three kinds of people—
Commonplace men, Remarkable men, and Lunatics. I'll classify
you with the Remarkables, and take the chances.'

The deal went through, and secured to the young stranger the
first fortune he ever pocketed...In time the shark culture will be
one of the most successful things in the colony.

NAT GOULD

Eaters of Raw Meat

As early as 1852 Godfrey Mundy was bemoaning the larrikin element in Sydney society—'the cabbage-tree mob' he called them, for their dress of 'fustian or colonial tweed, and the emblem of their order, the low-crowned cabbage-tree hat'. The life work of these idlers, Mundy divined, was to assault respectable wearers of black beavers by tipping their hats over their eyes.

By the 1890s, the larrikins had discarded their cabbage hats for the slouch variety and found more sinister employment, for the city's various 'pushes' were in full swing. Nat Gould, a sportswriter and successful tipster, was appalled by these louts in bell-bottoms, and by the loafers who loved nothing more than to buttonhole a man in a bar. His discussion of Sydney's Chinese community in the same breath as the European undesirables is symptomatic of the racism of the day, although he redeems himself somewhat with a tribute to the great Quong Tart, the first Chinese Australian to wear a kilt and dance a fling.

Gould's 1896 account also makes it clear that for more than a century Sydney has been the city in which to welcome the new year.

The Australian larrikin is different from any other type of low character I have ever seen. The English rough cannot be compared with him, although brutality and cowardice are prominent in each. Larrikinism is rampant in most Australian cities. A typical larrikin is easily distinguishable from an ordinary ne'er-do-well. He has a language, manners, and dress peculiarly his own. How and where these larrikins are bred it is impossible to tell, for many of them seem at some remote period to have been born to better things. These idle, dissolute youths—they are mostly young—consort together for the purpose of waging war upon society. They band together in 'pushes', and are known by the names of the localities in which they reside—such as the 'Rocks Push', the 'Gipp Street Push', or the 'Woolloomooloo Push', as the case may be.

A larrikin alone is harmless, for the simple reason he is too cowardly to attack anyone unless supported by members of his push. It takes at least half a dozen larrikins to tackle one fair-sized man, and he has a good chance of defeating them, provided he can use his fists before he is stunned by a brick or a stone. Peaceable men have been done to death in the streets of Sydney and Melbourne by these brutes. I recollect one unfortunate man being killed in Lower George Street, Sydney, and left lying in the road until he was discovered by a passer-by. Sailors have been murderously assaulted by these pushes when under the influence of liquor. Men have been robbed by them and brutally ill-treated, and policemen have been severely mauled by them. The larrikin is no respecter of sex. He takes a fiendish delight in frightening girls and women until they are half dead with terror, and occasionally they suffer disgusting indignities at the hands of these fiends. Even children of tender years are attacked by them, and often rendered nervous for the remainder of their lives.

On holidays the larrikins hold high festival. They select a favourite resort, and make for it in the hope of destroying the pleasure of respectable people. At Chowder Bay, on the shores of the harbour, a push of larrikins made a descent one holiday. They collected all the old bottles and other missiles they could find, and when a crowd of people were enjoying themselves, dancing and holding sports, they descended upon them and bombarded them with the ammunition they had collected.

Most of them are hideous-looking fellows, whose features bear traces of unmistakable indulgence in every loathsome vice. There is no redeeming feature about the larrikin. He does not possess one good point. He is not even faithful to the members of his own push. He is utterly selfish and brutal, and lives to indulge in every vice he knows. There is no reclaiming him—the task is beyond human power. He laughs and scoffs at everything wholesome. It is not in his nature to understand how any man can be honest.

I have seen the larrikin on many occasions and in divers places, and he is an unhealthy sight to look upon. His touch is contamination, his name synonymous with everything that is bad. He is a sneak, a thief of the lowest type, and in the depths of degradation to which he can sink goes lower than the vilest Asiatic.

The man who invents a method of stamping out larrikinism will deserve well of the country. At present there is no remedy for the disease, but it is held in check as much as possible. Most larrikins are born such, but there are a few exceptions. The cheapness of meat has, I think, a good deal to do with the nourishing of the larrikin element.

These larrikins gorge themselves with meat in an almost raw state. Their orgies are disgusting, and no respectable wild beast in the zoo would behave with half their beastliness over a meal. If they possessed the means, they would drink themselves to death. They have been known to raid a public-house and ransack it of everything on the premises. Smashing windows is a favourite pastime with them. When they dare not smash windows, they perform upon the faces and bodies of their female acquaintances, familiarly called 'donahs'. It is strange, but true, that there are many unfortunate women and girls who are infatuated with these brutes who ill-treat them.

Many a wretched woman hands over the wages of sin to these fellows, and the coin is received with curses and blows because it is not enough to satisfy them. I know a case in which one human devil—he can be called by no other name—lived on the proceeds of the infamy of his sister and his own wife, both of whom he had terrified into the life they led...

A larrikin, when in full dress, presents an extraordinary spectacle. He has a slouch hat, stuck on the back of his head in order to fully expose the greased fringe or curls that cover his low forehead. His face is of the lowest cast, and he generally has a grin on it. All larrikin grins are formed on the same fashion—a cross between the snarl of a hyena and a dingo. He wears no collar, but a bright-coloured handkerchief round his neck. His coat hangs loosely on him, and he has no waistcoat. His trousers are fastened tightly round his waist by a strap at the back, and his shirtfront bulges out and hangs slightly over in front.

His nether garments he pays particular attention to. They are the hallmark of genuine larrikinism. They fit tightly all the way down, and then are bell-shaped at the bottom—the wider the better, in order to show very little of his boots. The larrikin, if he takes a pride in anything, does so in his feet. He cramps and pinches them, and has high, cut-under heels on his boots, which give him a stilted, jerky walk. He seldom carries a cane, as it would interfere with his exercise in the bottle and brick-throwing department. Think of the most villainous-looking creature you have ever seen, and dress him in this fashion, and you will have some faint idea of the real larrikin...

There are many Chinese dens in Sydney and Melbourne. Lower George Street, Sydney, is a Chinese quarter. A dozen years ago it was far worse than at the present time. There are many respectable Chinese merchants in Sydney, and they do all in their power to stamp out the vices of the lower classes of their race.

One of the most respected and popular citizens of Sydney is Mr Quong Tart. He has the manners of an educated European and the habits of a gentleman. He is a good employer, and a man of unbounded generosity. His wife is an Englishwoman, and Mr Quong Tart sometimes poses as a Scotchman. It is an unaccustomed sight to see a Chinaman in kilts, and to hear him sing a Scotch song.

Mr Quong Tart is partial to the Scotch—the men, not the whisky—and puts on the kilt, sings a Scotch song, and dances the Highland fling with great gusto. He is a liberal patron of all manly sports, and his name may generally be found on a subscription list. When stump orators rant in Sydney Domain, and say 'the Chinese must go', they forget there are Quong Tarts and other members of that race like him.

An opium den, with which is generally combined a fantan and lottery shop, is not a pleasant place to enter. The noxious fumes seem to pervade the whole building. There is always a peculiar smell about a Chinese shop. It is an indescribable smell. It is not altogether offensive, and yet it is offensive. It is a sickly odour which clings to everything—the sort of odour a man seems to feel, and wants to wipe off his clothes when he gets into the fresh air.

Chinamen of the lower orders always look sleek, fat, and greasy. They are great eaters and delight in fatty food. I have seen them eating poultry literally swimming in fat, and ducks and geese are one mass of oily substances when served up to their taste.

Opium dens are, I suppose, very much alike the world over. I have been in them for purposes of investigation in Sydney, Melbourne, and Brisbane. I will endeavour to describe one of these dens in Sydney.

The front of the shop has once been respectable-looking, but has become ashamed of the foulness within, and lost all pride and cleanliness. The window is dirty, and papers with Chinese hieroglyphics on are stuck on the glass. Inside the window, bare boards with more Chinese papers and perhaps a few empty quarter-chests of tea, a pair of Chinese slippers, an odd fan or two, and a screen. Flies pay particular attention to these windows, and seem to know they are free from molestation.

The entrance door is plain wood. There is a curtain at one side, and a small counter. Behind the counter sits a sleek-faced China-man and a lean, skinny, shrivelled, parchment-faced countryman, whose hands are like a skeleton's covered with dried skin. The sleek man has a dull, yellowish complexion; the other man is as dead-looking as a mummy. One takes his opium, if he takes it at all, moderately; the other cannot live without it.

Pass inside and see the men playing fantan, and gambling their last coin and their valuables away. There are Europeans here as well as Chinamen. Most Chinamen are gamblers. Many of them work in order to gamble and smoke opium. They are all too intent upon the game to take notice of strangers.

In a small room at the back of the building are men and women in various stages of stupefaction with opium. Some are lying on the floor, apparently dead. Others are half dazed, and gaze about with lacklustre eyes. There is no attempt at decency on the part of either men or women. Sex is forgotten in this den of infamy.

It is by means of opium that girls are lured to destruction by these yellow fiends. There are women and girls so degraded that life with a vile, low-bred Chinaman becomes possible. Can anything more horrible be conceived? The sight of a low opium den is too fearful to describe. Suffice it to say the most morbid-minded individual could not overdraw the picture.

The Chinese are excellent gardeners, and many of them good cooks. Many people have a decided objection to eat vegetables grown by Chinamen. Australian cities would, however, be badly off for vegetables if there were no Chinese gardeners. The bulk of the white men who sell vegetables purchase them from Chinamen, and retail them at a considerably higher figure than the yellow men charge. Chinese gardeners quickly turn a most unpromis-ing plot of ground into a first-rate garden...

Numerous people I have met on this side of the world labour under the erroneous impression that there is no poverty or actual starvation in the colonies. I have seen many terrible cases of genuine distress in Australian cities.

The loafer, the genuine article, is seldom in dire distress. He manages things better than that. In the first place, the real loafer detests work of any kind. He scorns to labour for his daily bread. He possesses an amount of cheek beyond imagination. He seems to occupy his time in concocting schemes of 'how to live without work'. There are hundreds of loafers in every Australian city. They can be divided into several classes.

The loafer who has seen better days, and who is constantly reminding people of the fact that he is a gentleman-born, is, I think, the most contemptible of the lot. There is a shabby gentility about him that appeals to anyone innocent of his real character. He is always expecting a remittance from Home by the next mail, and wishes to negotiate a loan on account. In a lordly sort of way he requests the loan of a 'fiver' for a week or two. If the 'fiver' is not forthcoming, he is very glad to accept a shilling, or even the price of a drink.

Nothing pleases this class of loafer more than to buttonhole a man in a bar and give him his history. To hear this loafer talk, one would imagine him to be the most ill-used man in the world.

The parks and the Domain are the haunts of loafers. They occupy the best seats, and take good care not to move for anyone. When tired of sitting, they pick out a shady spot, and proceed to indulge in a prolonged sleep. Scores of men can be seen yawning and idling at almost any time in Hyde Park or the Domain...

On New Year's Eve the rougher element is let loose. Bands of youths, with more impudence than brains, parade the streets and make night hideous with unearthly sounds. Occasionally one of these 'pushes' takes possession of an arcade, and then law-abiding and peaceful citizens give them a wide berth in that particular quarter. The streets of Sydney on New Year's Eve are not pleasant places; half-drunken mobs of larrikins rush from place to place, clearing all before them, and smashing windows and lamps. This sort of thing is continued in the suburbs until an early hour on New Year's Day.

At midnight there is a great ringing of bells, the whistles of steamers in the harbour are turned on at full steam; tin trays are belaboured with rolling-pins, or any other weapon that comes handy; dinner-bells are violently rung in private houses; doors are flung wide open to let the old year depart and the new year come in; house-to-house visitations take place, and the callers are generally invited inside to toast the new year. I have heard many discordant rows in my time but, for a veritable pandemonium of hideous sounds, give me Sydney on New Year's Eve.

Notes on Sources

Jacques Arago (1786–1855)
Jacques Arago was a botanic artist who accompanied Louis de Freycinet's expedition to the Pacific which set out in the *Uranie* from Toulon on 17 September 1817. This extract is from *Narrative of a Voyage round the World*, Treuttel and Wurtz, Treuttel Jnr and Richter, London, 1823, the first English translation of Arago's *Promenade Autour du Monde*, Leblanc, Paris, 1823. A facsimile edition was published in 1971 by N. Israel, Amsterdam, and De Capo Press, New York.

Bennelong (1764?–1813)
Bennelong was captured by William Bradley, on Governor Phillip's instructions, in 1789, and lived in Sydney. In 1792 he travelled to England with Phillip, returning home in 1795. A copy of his letter to Mr Phillips is in the National Library of Australia. It is reproduced in *Bennelong: First Notable Aboriginal, A Report from Original Sources*, arranged by John Kenny and published by the Royal Australian Historical Society in association with the Bank of New South Wales, Sydney, 1973.

George Bennett (1804–93)
Doctor and naturalist, George Bennett first visited Australia in 1829. Returning in 1832 he travelled inland and made significant contributions to zoology, notably in his studies of the platypus. Bennett's account of William Wall's whale is in George Bennett, *Gatherings of a Naturalist in Australasia*, John van Voorst, London, 1860. A facsimile edition was published in 1982 by The Currawong Press, Sydney.

Hyacinthe de Bougainville (1781–1846)
In 1821 Hyacinthe de Bougainville was selected to command an expedition of exploration around the world in the frigate *Thétis* and the corvette *Espérance*. He arrived in Sydney in July 1825, a quarter of a century after his first visit. M. de la Touanne illustrated the atlas that accompanies de Bougainville's account, entitled *Journal de la Navigation Autour du Globe de la Frégate la Thétis et de la Corvette l'Espérance Pendant les Années 1824–1826*, Arthus Bertrand, Paris, 1837. This extract was translated by Penny Hueston.

William Bradley (1757–1833)
A naval officer, Bradley assisted with the surveying of Port Jackson, Broken Bay and Norfolk Island. Bradley's journal is in the State Library of New South Wales. It was reproduced in facsimile as *A Voyage to New South Wales: The Journal of Lieutenant William Bradley RN of HMS* Sirius *1786–1792*, The Trustees of the Public Library of New South Wales in association with Ure Smith Pty Ltd, Sydney, 1969.

J. C. BYRNE

Byrne, like many of his contemporaries, was concerned that of the many emigrants who had made for the colonies, 'the greater portion...have done so without being in the least acquainted with the real condition and prospects of the land which they have chosen for their future home'. Byrne's attempt to enlighten settlers was published as J. C. Byrne, *Twelve Years' Wanderings in the British Colonies from 1835 to 1847*, Richard Bentley, London, 1848.

GEORGE CALEY (1770–1829)

A naturalist and explorer, Caley arrived in Australia in 1800. The 1803 and 1808 letters from Caley to Banks are among the Banks Papers in the *Historical Records of New South Wales*, 1892. A facsimile of the *Historical Records* was published by Lansdown Slattery & Co. in 1978.

RALPH CLARK (1755–94)

Lieutenant Ralph Clark sailed on HMS *Friendship* in the First Fleet. His diary and letters were published as *The Journal and Letters of Lt. Ralph Clark 1787–1792*, Paul G. Fidlon & R. J. Ryan (eds), Australian Documents Library, in association with the Library of Australian History, Sydney, 1981. The original manuscript is in the Mitchell Library, Sydney [Z 1/27]. His letters to his wife Alicia form a large and enthralling part of this written record.

DAVID COLLINS (1756–1810)

Deputy judge-advocate and secretary at Port Jackson, then first lieutenant-governor of Tasmania, David Collins was responsible for all legal matters in the early years of the colony. These passages were published in his *An Account of the English Colony in New South Wales*, T. Cadell & W. Davies, London, 1798.

JAMES COOK (1728–79)

James Cook, arguably the greatest maritime explorer ever, undertook three voyages of discovery between 1768 and 1779. This extract is from the original journal of Captain James Cook on the voyage of HMS *Endeavour*, 6 May 1770 and is held in the National Library of Australia, Canberra, [MS 1].

PETER CUNNINGHAM (1789–1864)

As surgeon-superintendent in convict matters, Peter Cunningham made five trips from England to New South Wales between 1819 and 1828. This extract is from *Two Years in New South Wales*, vol. 1, Henry Colburn, London, 1827. The Libraries Board of South Australia published a facsimile edition in 1966.

CHARLES DARWIN (1809–82)

When Charles Darwin published *The Origin of Species* in 1859, he changed the way we perceive the world. Inspiration for this work came from his globetrotting voyage of two decades earlier. This extract is from *Narrative of the Surveying Voyages of His Majesty's Ships,* Adventure *and* Beagle, *between the Years 1826 & 1836, Describing their Examination of the Southern Shores of South America, and the* Beagle's *Circumnavigation of the Globe,* 2 vols, Henry Colburn, London, 1839. This work has been republished many times, sometimes with abridgments. A recent edition of the journal was published by Penguin Books, Harmondsworth, in 1989 as *The Voyage of the* Beagle.

WILLIAM DAWES (1762–1836)
During his short stay at Port Jackson from 1788 to 1791 Lieutenant William Dawes distinguished himself as an amateur astronomer and ethnologist, compiling the first grammar of the Eora language. His unpublished notebooks are in the William Marsden collection [M686] in the library of the School of Oriental and African Studies, Thornhaugh Street, Russell Square, London. The extract is reproduced with the library's kind permission. A copy of the notebooks is in the Mitchell Library.

FRANK FOWLER (1833–63)
This extract is from Fowler's *Southern Lights and Shadows: Being Brief Notes of Three Years' Experience of Social, Literary, and Political Life in Australia,* Sampson Low, London, 1859. A facsimile edition was published by Sydney University Press in 1975.

A FEMALE CONVICT
This letter from an anonymous female convict is reproduced from the British Museum papers in the *Historical Records of New South Wales,* 1892.

ROSE MARIE DE FREYCINET (D. 1832)
The wife of cartographer and naturalist Louis-Claude de Saulles de Freycinet, Rose de Freycinet secreted herself on board her husband's ship. After spending Christmas 1819 in Port Jackson, the *Uranie* was wrecked in the Falkland Islands in 1820. Rose and her husband survived, but much of the expedition's botanical work was destroyed. Her journal was first published in 1927 as *Journal de Madame Rose de Saulles de Freycinet, d'Après le Manuscript Original, Accompagné des Notes,* Société d'Editions Géographiques, Maritimes et Coloniales, 1927. The extract here is from *A Woman of Courage: The Journal of Rose de Freycinet on Her Voyage around the World 1817–1820,* Marc Serge Rivière (ed. & trans.), National Library of Australia, Canberra, 1996 and is reproduced with the permission of Marc Serge Rivière.

NAT GOULD (1857–1919)
Nathaniel Gould was born in Manchester. After working as a journalist on provincial and London newspapers he went to Australia in 1884 and became racing editor of the Sydney *Referee.* His serialised work *The Double Event* (1891) was made into a highly successful melodrama. After his return to England in 1895 he wrote more than 130 novels, mainly thrillers with sport-related plots. The extract here is from his second biographical work, *Town*

and Bush, George Routledge & Sons, London, 1896. A facsimile edition was published by Penguin Books in 1974.

FRANCIS GROSE (1758–1814)
An English army officer and administrator, Grose was the first commander of the New South Wales Corps, and served as acting governor of New South Wales from 1792 to 1794. Grose's letter to Under Secretary Nepean was published in the *Historical Records of New South Wales.*

JOHN HARRIS
Transported to Sydney with the First Fleet, Harris was emancipated after excelling as a principal of the nightwatch on Norfolk Island. His letter to Lord Hobart is found in the *Historical Records of New South Wales.*

ROBERT HOBART (1760–1816)
Politician and soldier, Robert Hobart, the fourth Earl of Buckinghamshire, was from 1801 to 1804 secretary of state for war and the colonies. His letter believed to be to Governor King is reproduced from the *Historical Records of New South Wales.*

JOSEPH HOLT (1756–1826)
Joseph Holt was an Irish Protestant transported to Port Jackson in 1799. The material here is from *The Memoirs of Joseph Holt, General of the Irish Rebels in 1798*, T. C. Croker (ed.), Henry Colburn, London, 1838. The extract was also published in Joseph Holt, *A Rum Story: The Adventures of Joseph Holt Thirteen Years in New South Wales (1800–12)*, Peter O'Shaughnessy (ed.), Kangaroo Press, Kenthurst, 1988.

CHARLES VON HÜGEL (1795–1870)
An Austrian diplomat, army officer and courtier, Baron von Hügel was, in the nineteenth century, celebrated across Europe for his magnificent gardens of exotic plants. He spent most of 1834 in the Australian colonies. After the March 1848 revolution in Vienna he fled with Metternich's entourage to England until 1849, when he returned to Vienna, rejoining the Austrian army and serving as *charge d'affaires* at the court of Tuscany in Florence. From 1860 to 1867 he was Austrian ambassador in Brussels. The baron's *New Holland Journal*, Dymphna Clark (ed. & trans.), was published by Melbourne University Press in 1994. This extract is reproduced with the permission of Melbourne University Press.

JOHN HUNTER (1737–1821)
John Hunter was second governor of New South Wales. He arrived in the colony aboard the First Fleet, serving under Phillip as commander of the *Sirius*. These extracts are from the *Historical Records of New South Wales.*

STEPHEN HUTCHINSON
It is likely Hutchinson arrived in Sydney in 1798 on the *Britannia* with its

cargo of ninety-four female convicts. The extract is from a copy, in the State Library of New South Wales [A2022] and in the handwriting of Sir Joseph Banks, of a letter describing the conditions at Port Jackson for the female convicts. The letter was reproduced in *My Dear, Dear Betsey: A Treasury of Australian Letters*, compiled by Warwick Hirst, Hale & Iremonger, Sydney, 1993.

WILLIAM JEVONS (1835–82)

Jevons came to Australia in June 1854 to work in the new Sydney branch of the Royal Mint. A respected early colonial journalist with the *Sydney Morning Herald*, he went on to become one of the greatest English economists.

RICHARD JOHNSON (1753–1827)

Richard Johnson, the first clergyman in Australia, was chaplain at Port Jackson from 1788 to 1800. The letter from Reverend Johnson to Mr Thornton is found in the *Historical Records of New South Wales*. A footnote to the letter in the *Records* reads 'Although not official, it [the description of the condition of the convicts of the Second Fleet] has been considered worthy of a place in the records. The statements contained in it are confirmed by the despatches of Governor Phillip and the reports of the naval and military officers.' The letter is undated but was written about July 1790. The letter to Governor Phillip is also in the *Historical Records of New South Wales*, as is Johnson's letter to Henry Dundas. The account of the murder of Mr Clode, set out in a letter from Johnson to Joseph Hardcastle, treasurer of the Missionary Society, was published in George Bond, *Brief Account of the Colony of Port Jackson, in New South Wales, its Native Inhabitants &c. &c., with an Interesting Account of the Murder of Mr Clode*, R. Wilkes, London, 1809.

GEORGE JOHNSTON (1764–1823)

Born in Scotland, Johnston was reputedly the first man ashore at Port Jackson in 1788. Soldier and pioneer landowner, he led the troops that arrested Governor Bligh in 1808. Johnston's letter to Lieutenant-Colonel Paterson is published in the *Historical Records of New South Wales*.

EBENEZER BERIAH KELLY

Ebenezer Kelly was born in Connecticut. A sailor, he first went to sea at thirteen. He visited Sydney in 1799. This extract is taken from his work *Ebenezer Beriah Kelly: An Autobiography*, Norwich, 1856, written when he was in his dotage.

PHILIP GIDLEY KING (1758–1808)

King was second lieutenant of the *Sirius* in the First Fleet, and served as governor of New South Wales from 1800 to 1806. The journal of his experiences was published as an appendix to Hunter's *An Historical Journal of the Transactions at Port Jackson and Norfolk Island*, John Stockdale, London, 1793. The material reproduced here was drawn from King's journal as published in the *Historical Records of New South Wales*.

EDMOND LA MESLÉE (1852–93)
La Meslée's account of Australia in the early 1880s was published as
l'Australie Nouvelle, E. Plon, Paris, 1883. This extract is from *The New
Australia: Edmond Marin La Meslée 1883*, introduced by Russel Ward (trans.
& ed.), Heinemann Educational, London, 1973 and is reproduced with the
permission of Reed Educational and Professional Publishing Australia.

ELIZABETH MACARTHUR (1766–1850)
Pioneer pastoralist Elizabeth Macarthur arrived in Sydney in 1790 with her
husband John. In 1793 he received a grant of land at Parramatta. He named
it Elizabeth Farm and built a house there which Elizabeth occupied for over
forty years. The letter dated 1791 is in the Macarthur Papers in the
Historical Records of New South Wales. The letter of 1795 from Elizabeth
Macarthur to Bridget Kingdon survives as a copy only, made from the orig-
inal by her son Edward, and is found in the State Library of New South
Wales [SLNSW A2908]. The contents suggest it probably should have been
dated 1798. This letter is also reproduced in *My Dear, Dear Betsy: A
Treasury of Australian Letters*, compiled by Warwick Hirst, Hale &
Iremonger, Sydney, 1993.

LACHLAN MACQUARIE (1762–1824)
Macquarie's governorship of New South Wales from 1810 to 1821 was
notable for his encouragement of public works programs, further inland
exploration and humanitarian policies towards convicts. These extracts were
drawn from various issues of the *Sydney Gazette*, between 16 February and
6 October 1810.

ALEXANDRO MALASPINA (1754–1809)
Alexandro Malaspina di Mulazzo's report on the Port Jackson settlement was
first published in *The Secret History of the Convict Colony: Alexandro
Malaspina's Report on the British Settlement of New South Wales*, Robert J.
King (ed.), Allen & Unwin, Sydney, 1990. The extract is reproduced by
permission of Robert J. King.

LOUISA ANN MEREDITH (1812–95)
Louisa Meredith née Twamley emigrated to Australia in 1839 and settled on
the east coast of Tasmania. The extract is from Mrs Charles Meredith, *Notes
and Sketches of New South Wales during a Residence in That Colony from
1839 to 1844*, John Murray, London, 1844. A facsimile edition was published
by Penguin Books in 1973.

BLANCHE MITCHELL (1843–69)
The youngest of Sir Thomas and Lady Mitchell's eleven children, Blanche
Mitchell enjoyed a prosperous youth living at Darling Point. The early
death of her father in 1855 placed the family in much reduced circumstances. Blanche's diary covers the years 1858 to 1861—her fourteenth to
eighteenth year—by which time she lived in comparative poverty in

a small terrace house. She died of consumption in 1869 aged twenty-six. Her diary is in the Mitchell Library, and was published as *Blanche: An Australian Diary 1858–1861: The Diary of Blanche Mitchell*, notes by Edna Hickson, Jill Francis (illus.), John Ferguson, Sydney, 1980.

JAMES MUDIE (1779–1852)

After a failed book publishing venture, Mudie and his four daughters arrived in Sydney in 1822. He established one of the colony's most successful farms, Castle Forbes, and was in 1830 made a justice of the peace. His service was characterised by harsh treatment of convicts. After a mutiny by convict servants at Castle Forbes, an inquiry into the affair criticised Mudie's treatment of his servants. Returning to England in disgust he attacked his opponents in *The Felonry of New South Wales*, self-published, London, 1837.

GODFREY CHARLES MUNDY (1804–60)

In 1846 Lieutenant Mundy, a well-travelled and perceptive man, was appointed deputy adjutant-general of the military forces in Australia. The extract here is from *Our Antipodes: or, Residence and Rambles in the Australasian Colonies, with a Glimpse of the Gold Fields*, Richard Bentley, London, 1852. The material was published in facsimile in Godfrey Charles Mundy, *Sydney Town 1846–1851*, arranged and presented by Bill Hornadge, Review Publications Pty Ltd, Dubbo, 1971.

JAMES F. O'CONNELL (1808–54)

This material is from *A Residence of Eleven Years in New Holland and the Caroline Islands*, B. B. Mussey, Boston, 1836, a copy of which is in the Mitchell Library. An edition edited by Saul H. Riesenberg was published by Australian National University Press, Canberra, 1972.

AN OFFICER AT PORT JACKSON

This anonymous letter appeared in the *Oracle* of 25 April 1791 and is reproduced in the *Historical Records of New South Wales*.

THOMAS PALMER (1747–1802)

One of the 'Scottish Martyrs', transported for promoting political unrest, clergyman Palmer was sentenced to seven years' transportation for sedition in 1793. His letter to Reverend Joyce is published in the *Historical Records of New South Wales*.

FRANÇOIS PÉRON (1775–1810)

The eminent naturalist Péron sailed with Nicholas Baudin from 1800 to 1804. The extract here is from the first English publication of Péron's journal, *A Voyage of Discovery to the Southern Hemisphere*, Richard Phillips, London 1809. A reprint was published in 1975 by Marsh Walsh Publishing, Melbourne.

ARTHUR PHILLIP (1738–1814)
Captain general of the First Fleet and governor of New South Wales 1788–92, Phillip left his stamp on every aspect of the young settlement. The 1788 extract is from *The Voyage of Governor Phillip to Botany Bay; with an Account of the Establishment of the Colonies of Port Jackson and Norfolk Island*, John Stockdale, London, 1789. The extract recording the first land grant is from the deed of grant which is reproduced in the *Historical Records of New South Wales*.

ROBERT ROSS (1740–94)
Commander of the marines and first lieutenant-governor of New South Wales from 1786 to 1790, Ross clashed with almost everyone in the colony. This private letter to Under Secretary Nepean is reproduced from the *Historical Records of New South Wales*.

ALEKSEY ROSSIYSKY
Rossiysky's journal of 1813–16 was published as 'Zhurnal shturmana Alekseya Rossiyskogo, puteshestvuyushchego na korable "Suvorov"' ['The Journal of Navigator Aleksey Rossiysky, who sailed the ship "Suvorov"'], in the St Petersburg periodical *Sorevnovatel prosveshcheniya I blagodeyaniya* [*The Emulator of Enlightenment and Beneficence*], 1820, nos 11 and 12. The extract here was translated by Glynn Barratt and was published in his *The Russians at Port Jackson 1814–1822*, Australian Institute of Aboriginal Studies, Canberra, 1981. Barratt's translation rests on *Russkiye flotovodsty: M. P. Lazarev*, A. A. Samarov (ed.), Moscow, 1951, and is reproduced with the permission of Dr Barratt.

JOSEPH SMITH
This material is from Samuel Sidney, *The Three Colonies of Australia*, Ingram, Cooke & Co., London, 1852. Sidney drew the material from Caroline Chisholm's collection of 'voluntary statements' from the people of New South Wales, which formed the basis for her *Prospectus of a Work to Be Entitled 'Voluntary Information from the People of New South Wales'*, W. A. Duncan, Sydney, 1845, *Emigration and Transportation Relatively Considered, in a Letter Dedicated by Permission to Earl Grey by Mrs Chisholm with Voluntary Statements*, John Olliver, London, 1847, and *Comfort for the Poor! Meat Three Times a Day!!! Voluntary Information from the People of New South Wales Collected in That Colony in 1845–6*, self-published, London, 1847.

ARTHUR BOWES SMYTH (1750–90)
As surgeon on the *Lady Penrhyn*, the First Fleet ship carrying female convicts, these women were a great cause of consternation for Arthur Bowes Smyth. His journal, also available on microfilm, was published as *The Journal of Arthur Bowes Smyth: Surgeon, Lady Penrhyn, 1787–1789*, Paul Fidlon and R. J. Ryan (eds), Australian Documents Library, Sydney, 1979. The original manuscript is in the National Library of Australia.

DANIEL SOUTHWELL (1764?–1797)

Southwell was a mate on the *Sirius* and arrived in Port Jackson as part of the First Fleet in his twenties. In February 1790 he was ordered to take charge of the lookout station at South Head where he stayed until ordered home in 1791. The extract is from the Southwell Papers in the *Historical Records of New South Wales*. The original journal and letters are preserved in the British Museum.

GEORGE SUTTOR (1774–1859)

Settler and pioneer orchardist, George Suttor brought a consignment of trees and shrubs (sent by Sir Joseph Banks) to New South Wales in return for free passage for him and his family. His letter to Joseph Banks is published in the *Historical Records of New South Wales*.

SYDNEY GAZETTE

The *Sydney Gazette* was first published in May 1803 under the direction of Governor King. As a publication condoned by the government it was carefully censored. Its first editor was West Indian George 'Happy' Howe, who served from 1803 till his death in 1821. He was succeeded by his son Robert, until he drowned off Fort Macquarie in 1829. The last issue of the *Gazette* appeared in 1842. A short history of the paper, *The Sydney Gazette: Australia's First Newspaper*, by Renée Erdos, was published in Sydney in 1961 by Longmans.

SYDNEY MORNING HERALD

The *Sydney Herald* was first published in 1831 as a weekly newspaper. In 1840 it became a daily and the following year John Fairfax and Charles Kemp purchased it and changed its name to the *Sydney Morning Herald*. It has been published continuously since then. An account of the early years of the paper is in Gavin Souter's *Company of Heralds: A Century and a Half of Australian Publishing by John Fairfax Limited and Its Predecessors 1831–1981*, Melbourne University Press, Carlton, 1981.

WATKIN TENCH (1758–1833)

Watkin Tench sailed to Botany Bay aboard the First Fleet as a lieutenant in the marines. A well-educated man, Tench's account is the most readable of those that describe the foundation of settled Australia. The extract is from Tench's *A Complete Account of the Settlement at Port Jackson*, G. Nicol & J. Sewell, London, 1793, republished in *1788*, Tim Flannery (ed. & intro.), Text Publishing, Melbourne, 1996.

ROGER THERRY (1800–74)

Appointed commissioner of the small debts court of New South Wales, Roger Therry arrived in the colony with his family in 1829. An ardent campaigner for the rights of Catholics, he retired to England in 1859 to write his controversial *Reminiscences of Thirty Years' Residence in New South Wales and Victoria*, Sampson Low, London, 1863.

ANTHONY TROLLOPE (1815–82)
Trollope was among the most famous English authors of the nineteenth
century. This extract was first published in his *Australia and New Zealand*,
Chapman and Hall, London, 1873. It was reprinted in Anthony Trollope,
Australia, P. D. Edwards and R. B. Joyce (eds), University of Queensland
Press, St Lucia, 1967.

JOHN TURNBULL
Turnbull left England in July 1800 for Port Jackson. He spent six months in
the colony before embarking on a tour of the Pacific islands. After he was
shipwrecked and stranded for three months in Tahiti, he returned to Sydney
and arrived back in England in 1804. This piece is taken from Turnbull's
work, *A Voyage around the World in the Years 1800–1804*, A. Maxwell,
London, 1813.

MARK TWAIN (1835–1910)
The piece reproduced here was first published in Twain's *Following the
Equator*, American Publishing Company, New York, 1897. It also appears
in Mark Twain, *Mark Twain in Australia and New Zealand*, Penguin Books,
Ringwood, 1973.

FRANCISCO XAVIER DE VIANA (1764–1820)
Xavier de Viana was an ensign on the *Descubierta* in Malaspina's expedition.
He probably emigrated to Uruguay before 1820. His account of the expedi-
tion, *Diario del Viage Explorador de las Corbetas Espanolas* Descubierta *y*
Atrevida, *en los Anos de 1789 a 1794*, Cerrito de la Victoria, 1849, was
published by de Viana's eponymous son at a military press in Montevideo.
A copy of this work is in the National Library of Australia. The extract here
is from a translation by Virginia Day of de Viana's account of Port Jackson,
which was published in Malaspina and de Viana's *The Spanish at Port
Jackson, 1793*, Australian Documentary Facsimile Society, Sydney, 1967.

THOMAS WATLING (B. 1762)
Thomas Watling was an orphan and was raised by his aunt, Marion
Kirkpatrick. Transported to Port Jackson in 1791 for forgery, he remained in
the colony until his pardon in 1797. Watling's long-distance correspondence
with his aunt was first published in Scotland as *Letters from an Exile at Botany-
Bay, to His Aunt in Dumfries; Giving a Particular Account of the Settlement
of New South Wales, with the Customs and Manners of the Inhabitants*, Ann
Bell, Penrith, 1794. The letter reproduced here was also published in George
Mackaness's *Australian Historical Monographs*, v. XII, 1945.

OBED WEST (1807–91)
This material, first published in the *Sydney Morning Herald* in 1882, and
subsequently as a series of pamphlets issued by Edward Hordern & Sons,
was reproduced in *The Memoirs of Obed West: A Portrait of Early Sydney*,
Edward West Marriott, Barcom Press, Bowral, 1988.

JOHN WHITE (1756?–1832)

John White was surgeon-general to the First Fleet and the settlement at Port Jackson. His *Journal of a Voyage to New South Wales* was first published in 1790 in London by J. Debrett. An edition introduced by Rex Rienits, Alec H. Chisholm (ed.), was published by Angus & Robertson, in association with the Royal Australian Historical Society, Sydney, 1962. The letter to Mr Skill of April 1790 is found in the *Historical Records of New South Wales* and was published in the *Public Advertiser* of London, 31 December 1790. Mr Skill was there identified as 'dealer in hams, tongues, salt salmon, &c., in the Strand'.

Notes on Illustrations

William Bradley, *Position of the encampment & Buildings, Sydney Cove, Port Jackson, as they stood 1 March 1788*, from *A Voyage to New South Wales: The Journal of Lieutenant William Bradley RN of HMS* Sirius *1786–1792*. Ink and watercolour. Courtesy of the Image Library, State Library of New South Wales.

Port Jackson Painter, *Native Name Ben-nel-long*, 1788. Ink and watercolour. From the Watling Collection [41], courtesy of the Natural History Museum, London.

Francis Wheatley, *Governor Phillip*, 1786. Oil painting. Courtesy of the Image Library, State Library of New South Wales.

William Bradley, *First Interview with Native Women at Port Jackson in New South Wales 1788*. Watercolour. Courtesy of the State Library of New South Wales.

Port Jackson Painter, *A New South Wales native Stricking fish while his wife is employed fishing with hooks & lines in her Canoe*, 1788. Watercolour. The inscribed title of this picture is believed to be in John White's hand. From the Watling Collection [29], courtesy of the Natural History Musem, London.

Thomas Watling (?), *View of Sydney*, c. 1795. Watercolour. Courtesy of the Image Library, State Library of New South Wales.

Unknown artist, *Castle Hill Riot*, 1804. This work bears the title 'Major Johnston with Quarter Master Laycock, one sergeant and twenty-five privates of ye N.S.W. Corps defeats two hundred and sixty-six armed rebels, 5th March, 1804'. Watercolour. Courtesy of the Rex Nan Kivell Collection, National Library of Australia.

John William Lancashire, *View of Sydney, Port Jackson, New South Wales, Taken from ye rocks on the Western Side of the Cove*, c. 1804. Watercolour. Courtesy of the Image Library, State Library of New South Wales.

Robert Havell (engraver) and James Taylor (artist), *The Town of Sydney in NSW*, 1823. This picture is the second part of a panoramic triptych painted by James Taylor in 1821. It was later engraved and published by Robert Havell and Colnaght in London in 1823. The third section, *Part of the Harbour of Port Jackson, and the country between Sydney and the Blue Mountains*, is the cover image of this book. Hand-coloured acquatint. Courtesy of the National Library of Australia.

Henry Curzon Allport, *George Street—Looking South from Martin Place*, 1842. Watercolour. Courtesy of the Image Library, State Library of New South Wales.

George Peacock, *Sydney from Wooloomooloo*, 1849. Oil painting. Courtesy of the Image Library, State Library of New South Wales.

Unknown artist, *Picnic at Mrs Macquarie's Chair*, c. 1855. Oil painting. Courtesy of the Image Library, State Library of New South Wales.

William Stanley Jevons, *Dawes Battery. Milson's Point, Green's yard and Remains of the* Dunbar, 1857. Black and white photograph. Reproduced courtesy of the director and university librarian, John Rylands University Library of Manchester, England.

Alexander Brodie, *View of Sydney from St James Church*, c. 1872. Black and white photograph. Reproduced courtesy of the Historic Photographic Collection, Macleay Museum, University of Sydney.

Unknown photographer, *Sydney General Post Office*, c. 1900, from *The City's Centrepiece: The History of the Sydney GPO*, Hale & Iremonger, Sydney, 1988. Black and white photograph. Reproduced courtesy of Australia Post.